Empower and Ignite Your
Financial Destiny

CINERGY FINANCIAL

PRAISE FOR
THE RISE OF WOMEN AND WEALTH

"Cindy Couyoumjian has done a superb job of explaining the history of women in society. She gives women the confidence to learn about investing and take charge of their finances."

—**MAUREEN MALOOF,** founder, Uniforms for Hope

"This book represents a paradigm shift of opportunity as a tidal wave of positive change coming our way! Cindy is a guiding light forging a global pathway of awareness for women toward their financial wealth and freedom."

—**JODI ANN LOVULLO,** sales, Super Color Digital

"*The Rise of Women and Wealth* is an impassioned, insightful, and plausible rendering of both the past and current situation women and men find themselves in. Cindy Couyoumjian lays out a balanced approach to this situation that respects both our rational and intuitive capacities. And she speaks to and invites our higher spiritual nature to engage in a cooperative effort to create a preferred future for the benefit of all."

—**DONNA MARIE SCHEIFLER, M.A.,**
mentor for women in transition in midlife and beyond,
www.yourtimetoblossom.com

THE
RI$E
OF
WOMEN
AND
WEALTH

OUR FIGHT *for* FREEDOM, EQUALITY,
and CONTROL *of* OUR FINANCIAL FUTURE

CINDY COUYOUMJIAN

with R. F. GEORGY

GREENLEAF
BOOK GROUP PRESS

Published by Greenleaf Book Group Press
Austin, Texas
www.gbgpress.com

Distributed by Greenleaf Book Group

For ordering information or special discounts for bulk purchases, please contact Greenleaf Book Group at PO Box 91869, Austin, TX 78709, 512.891.6100.

Design and composition by Greenleaf Book Group
Cover design by Greenleaf Book Group with Vince Giuseffi

Publisher's Cataloging-in-Publication data is available.

Print ISBN: 978-1-62634-943-8

eBook ISBN: 978-1-62634-944-5

Audiobook ISBN: 978-1-62634-945-2

Part of the Tree Neutral® program, which offsets the number of trees consumed in the production and printing of this book by taking proactive steps, such as planting trees in direct proportion to the number of trees used: www.treeneutral.com

Printed in the United States of America on acid-free paper

22 23 24 25 26 27 28 29   10 9 8 7 6 5 4 3 2 1

First Edition

This book is dedicated to all women of every race and color, past and present, who fought against the tyranny of patriarchy. It is the indominable spirit of women who dared greatly by transforming their vulnerabilities into the enduring spiritual affirmation of sisterhood.

Whatever contribution I make, however modest, to the ideals of gender equality, justice, compassion, and the shared responsibility of uplifting our humanity is due to the fact that I stand today on the shoulders of the giants who came before me.

CONTENTS

PREFACE

"One is not born, but rather becomes a woman."

—SIMONE DE BEAUVOIR

In April of 1910, President Theodore Roosevelt went hunting in Central Africa and toured Northern Africa and Europe, where he gave speeches in Cairo, Berlin, Naples, and Oxford. On April 23, he traveled to Paris, where he gave a speech called "Citizenship in a Republic," which would later be remembered as "The Man in the Arena." There were more than 2,000 people in attendance that day. He closed his speech with an inspirational message that is worth quoting in full.

> It is not the critic who counts; not the man who points out how the strong man stumbles, or where the doer of deeds could have done them better. The credit belongs to the man who is actually in the arena, whose face is marred by dust and sweat and blood; who strives valiantly; who errs, who comes short again and again, because there is no effort without error and shortcoming; but who does actually strive to do the deeds;

who knows great enthusiasm, the great devotions; who spends himself in a worthy cause; who at the best knows in the end the triumph of high achievement, and who at the worst, if he fails, at least fails while daring greatly, so that his place shall never be with those cold and timid souls who neither know victory nor defeat."[1]

Roosevelt's powerful words can only be understood in the context of the era in which they were spoken. To reveal the power and sense of urgency of what it means to strive valiantly for all of humanity, we need to transpose the gender.

Imagine for a moment if we refashion Roosevelt's rallying cry on behalf of women: We must celebrate the women whose faces are marred by struggle, doubt, sweat, humiliation, and the indignities of transmitted trauma. We must give credit to the women who strived valiantly, who erred, who came up short again and again, who engaged, who turned their vulnerabilities into punctuated moments of historical change. We must look in awe at the women who actually strive to do the deeds; who embrace passion and devotion; who embrace the triumphs of hard-fought achievements, where failure is accepted as part of that inexorable movement to dare greatly. It is this idea of daring greatly—of being immersed in the moment—that will define how women shape and define their own financial destiny.

Women today are standing on the precipice of unprecedented financial change. Currently, "women control more than $10 trillion, or about a third, of total U.S. household financial assets, and that could jump to $30 trillion by the end of the decade."[2] This unprecedented transfer of wealth approaches the annual gross domestic product of the United States. A new report published by McKinsey & Company discussed "a survey of more than 10,000 affluent investors, nearly 3,000 of whom were female—and it indicates that compared to 5 years ago, 30% more married women are making financial and investment decisions and that 'more women than ever' are the family breadwinner. Another figure shows that 44% of companies have three or more women in their C-suites (top-level executive positions such as CEO), an increase of 29% from 2015."[3] It seems that women are on the verge of economic breakthroughs, but the map that will guide us toward financial freedom has yet to be written.

Despite these promising numbers, problems remain. Men still dominate the financial planning sector. Women who work in the industry, as well as those who seek financial help, "believe their gender is a key factor in the disrespect and condescension they have often experienced and the poor financial advice they have received."[4] What we have today is a disconnect between a promising future where women will be the financial decision makers and the skewed reality of women being intimidated by a male-dominated financial world. To reconcile this glaring contradiction, we need to be reminded of Roosevelt's "Man in the Arena" speech. Today, it is the woman who is in the arena, fighting valiantly and daring greatly to challenge, and overcome, the male-dominated world of finance.

We have all heard the truism that knowledge is power. This, of course, is especially true when it comes to the socially constructed idea that men are more suited to the complex world of high finance. As the French philosopher Michel Foucault argued, "'Power is everywhere' and 'comes from everywhere,' so in this sense it is neither an agency nor a structure. Instead, it is a kind of 'metapower' or 'regime of truth' that pervades society, and which is in constant flux and negotiation."[5] In other words, power for Foucault is created by "accepted forms of knowledge, scientific understanding and 'truth.'"[6] In order to better understand the dense language of Foucault, consider that financial knowledge was once the exclusive province of men. It was men who framed economic theory, lectured the rest of us on financial matters, and derived power and influence from such knowledge. What I hope to do in this book is to inspire women, first to understand this power dynamic, and second to assert their own unique power by increasing their historical, political, economic, and financial knowledge.

Despite the lack of financial knowledge, women today have amassed more wealth than at any other time in history. It is this density of wealth that must be managed and leveraged in order to produce generational wealth for women. Once you create generational wealth, future generations of women can collectively gain the financial literacy to match, or exceed, the knowledge and power of men. The profound irony here, as Suze Orman notes, is that regardless of the level of professional success women were beginning to enjoy in recent years, "they weren't in control; they were in denial. Incredibly smart and strong women felt powerless about money. They had kids, but no life insurance. A good salary, but no sizable emergency savings account in the bank. A retirement account, but no clue whether they were on track or not."[7] The fact that women are beginning to amass wealth is a step in the right direction, but women will not become equal players until they are proportionally represented in the very structure of financial decision making.

Part of the problem behind financial literacy for women includes the idea of a self-fulfilling prophecy. That is to say, "some women hinder themselves with excuses such as 'I don't understand money,' or 'my husband takes care of our money, so I don't bother/don't need to know.' These women are building a 'Chinese Wall' between themselves and their 'relationship' with money."[8] What this suggests is that women, after centuries of being marginalized, have internalized their economic status as secondary to men.

That does not mean this will be true in the future. I wrote this book to tell all women, regardless of status or background, that they are on the threshold of powerful change. Change, however, is not something that will be given to us on a silver platter. Change must be shaped, directed, written, forced into existence, and embraced by those who are willing to stand on the shoulders of those who sacrificed, suffered, forged ahead, and delivered to us possibilities both real and imagined. I wrote this book to tell you that our vulnerabilities and setbacks are the source of our strength.

It is setbacks, of course, that define us. It was Thomas Carlyle, the British philosopher, historian, and essayist, who said, "Permanence, perseverance and persistence in spite of all obstacles, discouragements, and impossibilities: It is this, that in all things distinguishes the strong soul from the weak."[9]

I'm sure many of you remember the stock market crash of 2002. The crash was in response to the tech bubble that had been forming since the late 1990s. At the time I had a few clients who trusted me with their money. By 2003 many of my clients had lost a significant amount of money due to the crash. My investment strategy at the time was the 60/40 portfolio (60 percent equities, 40 percent bonds). Although my clients understood that market crashes may occur, I was emotionally devastated by their situation. Despite the fact the stock market crash was the result of forces beyond my control, I internalized the losses as if it was my fault. I felt responsible and became despondent.

In order to help you better understand and appreciate my setback, I need to offer some brief biographical comments. I have spent most of my adult life in the financial sector. I spent eight grueling years studying and preparing for several exams administered by the Financial Industry Regulatory Authority (FINRA). The Series 7 registration is a comprehensive exam that one takes to become a registered representative. Also administered by FINRA, this registration enables a financial representative to sell many types of investment products. A Series 7 financial professional may sell stocks, bonds, options, and mutual funds.[10] The 7 exams meant that I passed 7 securities exams, which include the 6, 7, 22, 24, 26, 63, and 65 exams. I thought I was ready and prepared to take on clients. I saw my fiduciary obligations as a sacred trust, and I have applied the knowledge and experience that I acquired with honesty and integrity.

The stock market crash of 2002 forced me to question everything I learned—including the financial industry and my place in it. I experienced doubt and uncertainty. Let me tell you something about doubt. It is a crippling feeling that freezes you into inaction. Once doubt finds its way into your soul, you become burdened by something I call existential density, which is the experience of incessantly questioning everything, including your identity. I was so distraught that I was ready to leave the financial industry.

That's when I went to see my pastor for guidance. I told him what happened and how I was feeling. The wisdom he imparted was invaluable. First, he asked me a few simple questions. He asked if I was a truthful person. I immediately answered him: Yes, of course I am. He then proceeded to ask me other questions in a rapid-fire fashion. Do I have integrity? Do I care about my clients? Do I have passion for what I do? I answered yes to all of his questions. He looked me in the eye and told me that I had a moral obligation not to leave my clients. In fact, he told me I have a moral obligation not to leave my clients of tomorrow, as they will need guidance. His final words to me were powerful in their capacity to jolt me out of my all-consuming doubt. He told me to move forward by embracing the divine spark of ethical engagement in order to help others.

Setbacks are defining moments that present us with opportunities. It is how we respond to these opportunities that will determine our existential value in the world. The choice we make in the face of setbacks is binary; we can either allow the setback to define us, or we can take charge of our own destiny by transforming ourselves into something that transcends our preconceived limitations. Shortly after the 2002 stock market crash, and after a great deal of soul-searching and reflection, I chose to not only continue to help my client, but also fundamentally change my investment strategy. Once I recognized the fundamental flaws in the 60/40 investment portfolio, I set out to find an innovative investment strategy that was flexible and adaptable to our complex and globally interconnected world. I spent endless days and sleepless nights doing research to find a strategy that could potentially withstand unexpected market forces.

All of my hard work and relentless resolve would result in the creation of my *Retail Endowment Allocation Like Model (REALM)*. Developing a new investment strategy was not enough for me, however. I started to offer monthly lectures to both men and women on such wide-ranging topics as financial literacy and multi-asset investment strategies. I went on to write my first book, *Redefining Financial Literacy*, which explored such themes as the poor state of financial literacy, the retirement crisis in America, why the 60/40 investment portfolio is potentially broken, and the potential benefits of my REALM strategy. I did all this because I see myself not only as a financial planner but also as an educator. I wrote this book so that women can begin to embrace the truth that has been in front of them all along. Women are powerful agents of change if only they recognize their boundless potential. It is time for women to stop being spectators and enter the arena of hope and change. It is time for women to stand up and assert their inalienable right to financial self-determination.

My purpose in this book, though, is to emphasize these topics as they impact women. To do that, it is also important to understand the past—how patriarchy prevented women from realizing their financial dreams. Only then can women embrace a future filled with endless possibilities and the affirmation "Yes, I can."

COURAGE, TRUTH, AND RECLAIMING OUR LIBERTY

I named this book *The Rise of Women and Wealth*, but although powerful change is underway, women still need the courage to confront the past in order to reclaim the power and liberty that was taken away from them. Women are more than the sum of their past experiences. This is an important concept to understand. Regardless of our shared collective trauma, women are resilient enough, and courageous enough, to shape and define their future direction. At the heart of our courage is the belief that women are on the precipice of dramatic change. This change encompasses the three waves of feminism that cover some 170 years of struggle. Women fought for the right to vote, be educated, have careers outside the home, and be treated with dignity and respect.

On a superficial level, dignity is "the quality or state of being worthy, honored, or esteemed."[11] From a moral perspective dignity can represent "the special potentiality associated with rational humanity, or the basic entitlements of each individual."[12] What I want you to take away from this fancy definition is that we are all—men and women— entitled to dignity. Let me also add that we all have an inalienable right to dignity, which means that our dignity cannot be transferred or denied to us by patriarchy or any other set of beliefs. The good news is that women for the first time in recorded history are beginning to be treated with dignity. Of course, more needs to be done, which is why I decided to contribute something to the ongoing conversation of what it means to be a woman in a post-patriarchal world.

Let's take a moment now to review a brief history of the concepts of courage and liberty. For Plato, courage was a moral virtue that "allow[ed] reason to rule, both in the individual and society."[13] For Aristotle, courage was the middle ground between fear and confidence. During the medieval period, courage was looked upon as one of the cardinal, or primary, virtues, along with wisdom, prudence, temperance, and justice. In modern philosophy (existentialism, for example) courage is "connected to the notion of authenticity in which an individual takes responsibility for the meaning and direction of one's life."[14] My own definition is this: Courage is the rational capacity to confront injustice for the purpose of reclaiming liberty. All of the freedom that women enjoy today came about as a result of the courage of those who came before.

Courage is the force within all of us, both men and women, that pushes us to fight for what is rightfully ours. Courage is what drives us, moves us, and gives us hope that our cause is noble and just. Courage is a rational action in the world. It represents our resolve to both identify and change the injustice around us. For women, courage is the ongoing affirmation that our liberty matters. You need to understand that courage and liberty are intertwined, always moving forward in history so that future generations can continue the struggle for equality. On a practical level, courage guides our demand for equal pay, equal opportunity, financial freedom, and a life free from harassment and assault. Courage is hope in the face of seemingly insurmountable odds. Courage is the belief that the collective voice of women will lead us toward a better tomorrow and a world where men and women can share in the responsibility of creating liberty and justice for all.

Just as courage and liberty are intertwined, so too are courage and truth. Women cannot move forward without confronting the truth of the past, of how we've been treated in a patriarchal society. As I was writing this book, I agonized over whether or not I should keep certain material. After all, I set out to write an inspirational book. The more I studied the history of women, the more I realized one cannot sugarcoat this material. The truth of our collective suffering must be confronted with courage. That's why truth and courage are also intertwined. It takes courage to confront our past so that we might find a way forward. If we as a society ignore the past, we do so at our own peril. In order to find the light of hope, we must first be willing to confront the pain and suffering of our past. It is only by confronting the past that we can find the courage, strength, and inspiration to move forward. Although we will touch on some dark themes, the overarching message in this book is very much a hopeful one, filled with intuitive truths about a brighter tomorrow.

ACKNOWLEDGMENTS

This book was a labor of love and a cathartic experience. The act of writing, particularly about a subject that is as emotionally triggering as patriarchy, can be therapeutic. This book would not have come into existence without the love and support of all those I hold dear to me. I want to take this opportunity to thank my office staff, beginning with Connie Hernandez, Prisma Oseguera, Thess Williams, Danny Martinez, and Michelle Lopez. Collectively, these individuals have been with me over 15 years. Without their unwavering dedication and support, my journey would not be complete. I must also thank the not-forgotten angels, Peggy Olsen and Jean Burns, who inspired me from the beginning to realize my potential and become an impactful agent of change. I also want to thank my new team members, David Lustig, Charlene Ogami, and McKenzie Frank, who are instrumental in helping me realize the Cinergy vision.

I must also offer a special thank you to Leticia Hewko, who has been my partner, friend, confidant, and support for over ten years now. Leticia's tireless dedication, unwavering support, and relentless dedication to Cinergy Financial has been a singular source of comfort to me. Leticia spent more hours than I can even count keeping my practice going while I was busy writing this book. Leticia stands as a towering symbol of hope and courage to all women who aspire for something greater.

I would be remiss if I didn't thank my family, beginning with my parents, John and Clara Koczkodan. My mother, Clara, is a powerful figure who instilled in me, and my four sisters, an enduring work ethic. It was my mother who set me on a path to financial independence. In many ways, my mother was ahead of her time. My mother raised all five girls with a sense of purpose; in particular the necessity of liberating ourselves from the patriarchy that is all around us. I also want to thank my four sisters—Laura Galvin, Pam Wilks, Cheri Schultz, and Debbie Buza—for epitomizing what it means to succeed in a world filled with unnecessary obstacles. Both Laura Galvin and Pam Wilks hold degrees in engineering, as well as MBAs. Cheri Schulz holds multiple degrees in computer science and is thriving as a self-employed woman. Debbi Buza supported her husband's neurology practice. In addition, Debbie is a professional chef. It is the biographical traces of my life, all of the hope and encouragement from my parents and sisters, that have made this book possible.

Lastly, I must thank my immediate family, beginning with my husband, Harry Couyoumjian. Harry has always encouraged me to not only realize my financial dream, but also pick up the mantle of responsibility by helping other women achieve greatness. I must also thank my two wonderful children, Claire and Kobe Couyoumjian, for achieving excellence in everything they do. Claire is currently studying mathematics and physics at the University of California, Berkeley, while Kobe is following in his mother's footsteps by studying to become a financial advisor. Kobe has already passed the Series 7 and Series 63 license exams, which makes me so proud.

INTRODUCTION

WOMEN AND THE FINANCIAL REVOLUTION

"The best protection any woman can have is courage."

—ELIZABETH CADY STANTON

Today there are two financial forces that are converging toward each other to produce a kind of unsettling reality for women. The first force is that men control "the vast majority of US household wealth."[1] The second force, which is intertwined with the first, is that many women are financially dependent upon men. Money, of course, has long been an issue in relationships and marriages. To illustrate this point, a study of "2,000 married and cohabitating women discovered that two-thirds of respondents whose partners are the primary providers feel 'trapped.' In all, 70% of those surveyed said they feel societal pressure to be subservient to their husbands and take their last name."[2] This concept of feeling economically subservient to men is at the heart of the wage gap, and it is the reason why women reach a glass ceiling and can't seem to go higher.

Despite the academic and economic gains that women have made over the past several decades, women's financial knowledge is alarmingly low when compared to their male counterparts. One of the more disturbing ironies of women's larger contribution to household income is the absence of financial literacy. According to a recent study published by U.S. Trust, "the majority of women defer financial and investment decisions to men. Sixty-four percent of baby boomer men are the dominant investment decision makers in their home while 27 percent claim equal partnership with their wives."[3] Similarly, according to new research by the Financial Industry Regulatory Authority Investor Freedom Foundation (FINRA Foundation), "female investors lag behind their male counterparts when it comes to investment knowledge and confidence."[4] This is why improved financial literacy for women is critical.

In my book, *Redefining Financial Literacy*, I argued that both men and women need to improve their knowledge of not only basic financial and investment concepts but also the hidden forces that shape and define our financial future. Some of these hidden forces, particularly for women, involve the psychological fear of entering what has long been considered a man's world. This fear freezes women into financial inaction regardless of their employment status or academic achievement. Consider this sobering fact: Twice as many women as men have no money in the stock market. Furthermore, according to a survey by S&P Global, only 26 percent of American women have money in the stock market and 65 percent have a large percentage of their assets in cash, compared to 51 percent of men. Also, 41 percent of women have no plans to invest that cash, compared to 31 percent of men.[5]

Let's acknowledge some fundamental truths. Women are on

the verge of historic change when it comes to financial awareness. According to the Forté Foundation, which is a non-profit that supports women in business through education, 41 percent of MBA students are female—2 percent higher than in 2020.[6] In addition, while men currently control the majority of wealth, women nevertheless control a substantial amount: $22 trillion in personal wealth in 2020. Women are also "benefiting from dramatic demographic, economic, and technological changes, bolstering their financial independence as well as their authority over the family balance sheet."[7] The digital age is creating an entirely new category of female entrepreneurship and corporate advancement, which will further contribute to wealth acquisition.

Although change is not happening fast enough, particularly at the highest level of corporate America, the push for change is already occurring. Given the number of MBA students who are women, their academic near parity with men will undoubtedly be reflected in the corporate positions of tomorrow. Currently, the number of women running Fortune 500 companies is at an all-time record of 37. While this represents only 7.4 percent of the Fortune 500–ranked businesses, it is a significant jump from 2018, when there were only 24 women CEOs.

The list of companies led by women includes some of the largest corporations in the world: General Motors, UPS, Best Buy, Oracle Corporation, Northrop Grumman, Rite Aid, Kohl's, Synchrony Financial, Ross Stores, JCPenney, Hertz Global Holdings, and dozens of others. It is not simply that more women are becoming CEOs; they are also becoming successful leaders. According to an S&P Global Market Intelligence study, "companies with female

CEOs or CFOs often were more profitable and had better stock price performance."[8]

Although women are making significant improvement, it is important to note that there is a lack of racial diversity. Of the 37 women who lead Fortune 500 companies, only three are women of color. This is unacceptable and must change.

There is a fancy word—intersectionality, which means the ideas of gender, race, and economic opportunity must, and will, intersect to create equality for all women. Women today represent more than half of the US workforce. What is more meaningful is that "about half of women say they out-earn or make the same amount as their husbands, according to a new survey from TD Ameritrade. That marks a rapid change within a few generations, given that only 3.8% earned more than their husbands in 1960."[9] This represents a powerful cultural shift in attitude toward women's economic viability.

We also know that women will continue to dominate the work-force, "given that more women are enrolled in college now than men."[10] And better education will lead to better-paying jobs for women. There is also a generational shift in terms of how women embrace financial independence. According to Dana Marineau, vice president and financial advocate at Credit Karma, millennials "value their independence more than other generations, specifically as it relates to their finances."[11] It is now becoming normal for women to keep a separate bank account from their partner. Despite these powerful changes in terms of the economic status of women, there persists a financial literacy gap between men and women. We need to erase this gap if we are to truly have a financial revolution for women.

I will discuss the ramifications of these statistics—the connections between women, money, and power—in more detail in chapter

8. To better understand these intersections, it is important to delve into the way women's vulnerabilities are actually their strengths, the societal obstacles that have historically been put in their way, and the successive waves of progress that have propelled women over the last century and a half.

It is important to understand that with each successive wave of feminist change, women found themselves closer to realizing their full potential. The first wave gave us a public voice with the vote. The second wave shattered the illusion that women were happy and fulfilled by domestic work. The third wave exposed the ugly side of patriarchy, which lived in the shadows until women brought global attention to the toxic side of certain men in power. The fourth wave, which I'm calling the financial revolution, will empower women to fulfill their financial destiny.

Financial literacy will help women demand wage equity, plan and invest for their retirement, and stop depending on men for their financial well-being. The financial revolution that I'm calling for is critical for women to stand on their own two feet. Women will soon become the architects of their own future. Financial knowledge will give women the power to overcome any and all obstacles that stand in their way. Our vulnerabilities will become our greatest ally to help us embrace a future with limitless possibilities.

PART I:

WOMEN'S VULNERABILITIES AND STRENGTHS

1

WOMEN AND THE INTUITIVE MIND

"The primary wisdom is intuition."

—RALPH WALDO EMERSON

Think of all the decisions you've made in your life. Were all your decisions based on reason or did you utilize intuition? For centuries, women's intuition has been dismissed as a uniquely feminine weakness. Women have been looked upon as irrational and incapable of controlling their emotions. This idea of having a "gut feeling" that guides our decisions is no longer considered nonsense; rather, recent scientific research is proving that feminine intuition not only is real but also adds serious value to how we navigate complex decisions. According to Professor Gerard Hodgkinson of the Centre for Organizational Strategy, Learning and Change at Leeds University Business School, "intuition is the result of the way our brains store, process and retrieve information on a subconscious level and so is a real psychological phenomenon which needs further study to help us harness its potential."[1] The research from the University of Leeds recorded numerous instances where intuition either prevented catastrophes or was responsible for remarkable recoveries of patients when doctors used their gut feelings.

Although the scientific community has dismissed intuition as pseudoscience, recent research is proving that intuition is a valid form of knowledge. A 2008 study in the *British Journal of Psychology* defined intuition as "what happens when the brain draws on past experiences and external cues to make a decision—but it happens so fast that the reaction is at an unconscious level."[2] Our intuition, or sixth sense if you prefer, has a biochemical component that responds to external stimuli. In her book *Guide to Intuitive Healing: Five Steps to Physical, Emotional, and Sexual Wellness*, Judy Orloff, who is a clinical professor of psychiatry at UCLA, has proposed that "just like the brain, there are neurotransmitters in the gut that can respond to stimuli and emotions in the now—it's not just about past experiences."[3] In this respect, the "gut instinct" that many of us have felt might in fact be signals being sent to the brain.

While it is true that we all have this intuitive sense, men have been socialized to ignore their intuitive power. According to Orloff, "men can be powerfully intuitive—they have the same capabilities as women, but in our culture, we view intuition as something that's warm and fuzzy, or not masculine, so men have often lost touch with those feelings."[4] From a masculine perspective, intuition has been rejected, ignored, ridiculed, dismissed as superstition, and generally defined in relation to the weakness of women. Think of this basic logical argument that men have used to discredit feminine intuition. The argument goes something like this:

Premise 1: If women use intuition, then they do not possess logic and reason in order to understand the world.

Premise 2: Women indeed use intuition.

Conclusion: Women do not possess logic and reason and cannot understand the world.

The above argument is valid, of course, *if* we accept the premises. The first premise is false, however, because it conflates the use of intuition with the absence of logic and reason. Women do possess logic and reason, but they also have a very powerful intuitive sense that further shapes their understanding of the world.

It is important to note that if we use logic and reason as the measure of gender superiority, then women might in fact win that contest. A woman, Marilyn vos Savant, had an independently confirmed IQ of 190 in 1985. Although measuring IQ is an inexact science, and the *Guinness Book of World Records* has eliminated the highest IQ category, vos Savant's score is a remarkable achievement.[5] Similarly, one cannot discuss female intellectual superiority without mentioning Marie Curie, the Polish-born physicist and chemist. In addition to having an IQ score in the range of 180–200, Marie Curie was the first woman in history to win the Nobel Prize twice and only one of four individuals to ever do it.[6] My point is that women possess extraordinary intellectual gifts and, in addition, are endowed with profound intuitive insights about the nature of reality.

Perhaps one of the most powerful definitions of intuition comes from Judy Orloff:

I'm defining intuition as a potent form of inner wisdom not mediated by the rational mind. Accessible to us all, it's a still, small voice inside—an unflinching truth-teller committed to our well-being. You may experience intuition as a gut feeling, a hunch, a physical sensation, a snapshot flash, or a dream. Always a friend, it keeps a vigilant eye on our bodies, letting us know if something is out of sync.[7]

If intuition is a potent form of wisdom, then it should come as no surprise that women have tapped into this calmness of spirit to become more empathetic and caring for others. While logic and reason serve as powerful ways of knowing and understanding the world, intuition seems to shape this understanding by opening us up to empathize with others. In *Men Are from Mars, Women Are from Venus*, John Gray argued that men are problem solvers and women want to talk about their problems. It is the complex interaction between the intuitive and the logical functions that characterize brain activity in women. In fact, according to a 2019 study published in the *SAGE Journals* by Grant Soosalu, Suzanne Henwood, and Arun Deo, "there is a growing body of literature that supports the idea that decision making involves not only cognition, but also emotion and intuition."[8] This complex set of interactions offers us critical insights into how women's brains work.

Recent research shows that women's brains are far more active than men's brains in several areas, according to a study in the August 2017 *Journal of Alzheimer's Disease*. Researchers at the Amen Clinics used sophisticated imaging technology to monitor blood flow and activity patterns in the brain. The study involved 25,000 men and women, which included healthy individuals, as well as those with various psychiatric conditions, such as bipolar disorders, mood disorders, brain trauma, and attention-deficit hyperactivity disorders. A total of 128 brain regions were analyzed during rest and when participants were focused on a 15-minute task. What the researchers found was quite extraordinary. The results showed that women had enhanced activity in the prefrontal cortex and "more blood flow in the limbic or emotional areas, which involve mood, anxiety and depression. The hippocampus, or the memory center, was also more active in the women's brains."[9] The research also suggests that "the female brain is wired for leadership," as evidenced by increased activity in the insular cortex, which is the area of the brain that involves empathy.[10]

While this research does not fully explain why women possess a greater level of empathy and intuitiveness, it does point to one possible explanation as to why women have a heightened empathic sense. It is undoubtedly the case that both the environment and socialization play critical roles in how men and women develop empathy and intuition, but the neurochemical research does point to the fact that women are more empathetic. Long before science investigated intuition as a valid form of knowing, philosophers, religious leaders, writers, and poets had contributed something to its meaning. The word "intuition" is derived from the Latin *tuere*, which means "to look at, watch over." According to Oxford psychiatrist Neel Burton, intuition "is a disposition to believe evolved without hard evidence or conscious deliberation."[11] Think of intuition as having an awareness that is not necessarily provable by reason. Reason and logic help us "know" something about the world; intuition, however, is an awareness that transcends reason itself.

The history of Western civilization is filled with references to intuition. Socrates, who is often looked upon as a philosopher who engaged his students in rational discourse, claimed that he didn't possess much knowledge. All he had, Socrates said, "was a *daimonion* or 'divine something,' an inner voice or sense that prevented him from making grave mistakes such as getting involved in politics or Athens after his trial and conviction: 'This is the voice which I seem to hear murmuring in my ears, like the sound of the flute in the ears of the mystic.'"[12] Intuition for Socrates is an inner voice that helps us navigate where reason and logic may no longer be of help.

For Plato, intuitive knowledge resides in the soul for eternity. Even Aristotle, who developed logic and formalized our scientific understanding of the world, had to account for intuition. In his major work, the *Nicomachean Ethics*, Aristotle identifies five ways of knowing. The first is scientific knowledge, which offers us eternal truths about the world. The second form of knowledge comes from art, which represents the world. The third is practical wisdom, which involves securing the good life and includes political knowledge. The fourth is intuition, which offers us insights and awareness that science is incapable of penetrating. Finally, the fifth way of knowing is wisdom, which is the combination of science and reason with intuition.

These two broadly defined ways of knowing—reason and intuition—would exist in a kind of tension, always competing for dominance. The 17th-century French mathematician Blaise Pascal articulated the paradox between these two ways of knowing by stating, "The heart has its reasons that are unknown to reason."[13] Although modern philosophy has elevated reason as the more dominant form of knowing, intuition continued to exert its influence as a valid form of knowledge.

German philosophers such as Immanuel Kant, Georg Wilhelm Friedrich Hegel, Arthur Schopenhauer, and Friedrich Nietzsche stressed that intuition is our primary access to reality. During the 19th century, the American philosopher Ralph Waldo Emerson elevated intuition as a fundamental way of perceiving the world. Emerson, who was influenced by German philosophy and the British historian and essayist Thomas Carlyle, embraced intuition as a sacred way of understanding the world.

In his 1831 essay, "Characteristics," Carlyle tries to "describe just what is meant by the 'intuitive' as opposed to the 'logical' and the 'argumentative.' Doubt and inquiry are both necessary but are only to be understood as an intermediate phase in human thought."[14] Emerson classified the two types of knowing as tuition and intuition. Tuition is the knowledge we have of the material world, which includes reason and rationality. Intuition, on the other hand, is our capacity to have access to a universal reality. Tuition allows us to analyze, deduce, measure, quantify, and observe the world. Intuition "does not bother with words, ideas or reasoning, but seizes reality directly."[15] In his essay "Nature," Emerson defends the intuitive approach by arguing that one must acquire knowledge from intuitive insights rather than books and the academic tradition. It was Emerson who started the Transcendentalist movement, which was based on the belief that "people, men and women equally, have knowledge about themselves and the world around them that 'transcends' or goes beyond what we can see, hear, taste, touch or feel. This knowledge comes through intuition and imagination not logic or the senses."[16] It was this idea of intuition and imagination that inspired early feminist writers such as Margaret Fuller, Susan B. Anthony, and many others.

2

THE MYSTERY OF INTUITION

"You must train your intuition—you must trust the small voice inside
you which tells you exactly what to say, what to decide."

—INGRID BERGMAN

For millennia women have been taught to ignore their feminine energy,
or intuitive insights. Women were looked upon as irrational, overly
emotional, and lacking any sense of logic or reason. From Aristotle
to Sigmund Freud, women have been reduced to a kind of abhor-
rent anomaly that contribute nothing of value to the world. Aristotle
viewed women as "deformed men with fewer teeth."[1] In his 1925 paper
"The Psychical Consequences of the Anatomic Distinction between
the Sexes," Freud wrote, "Women oppose change, receive passively, and
add nothing of their own."[2] After countless generations, women have
been made to feel second to men, so much so that many of us believe it
today. But we have all been programmed to believe a spectacular lie. In

fact, as Dr. Cynthia Miller points out, "a neural program enmeshed in our DNA passed down for ages doesn't make it true or right. Women being second rate is a lie. It's all made up by patriarchy."[3]

In chapter 1, I explored how writers and philosophers viewed intuition as a powerful mode of perceiving the world. These philosophers were, of course, men, which leads us to a seeming contradiction. How is it possible that the majority of these men elevated intuition as a powerful mode of understanding the world while simultaneously reducing women to an existential footnote to history? The simple answer, in my opinion, is that all of the writers and philosophers who wrote about the power of intuition were influenced by the patriarchy of their time. Some, like Plato and Emerson, were able to go beyond the cultural norms of their time. Others, however, were incapable of connecting intuition to women or acknowledging that women have been guided by an intuitive force.

The intuition that has guided women like a beacon of hope has too long been dismissed as useless knowledge. It turns out that we've been sold a lie, about not only the weakness of our gender but also our intuitive insights. We have been chained down by untruths, falsehoods, pseudoscience, philosophers, religious figures, and a host of other men in positions of authority who exerted power over us. The message I want you to understand is that feminine intuition is both powerful and the source of our strength. What is ironic, of course, is that the very thing that made us vulnerable is today our salvation.

Part of the process of transforming the world around you is to trust your intuition. It is absolutely imperative that women let go of the metaphorical chains that bind them to the past. Women need to abandon the ideas and beliefs embedded into their subconscious by embracing their vulnerabilities as strengths. Intuition helps us perceive the world by clearing all the clutter and noise of facts and figures, numbers, logical arguments, and so on. I'm not suggesting that intuition is irrational, meaning it is not logical or reasonable; rather what I am suggesting is that intuition is nonrational. In other words, intuition transcends the boundaries of the rational and logical by having direct access to the world. Intuition is primal in the sense that it helps us, particularly women, access the world at a fundamentally holistic level.

Let me introduce a philosophical term whose meaning is easy to grasp. Epistemology is a branch of philosophy that explores different sources of knowledge. Think of the statement "twice two is four." The source of knowledge here is mathematical. There are other sources of knowledge that we rely upon for our understanding of the world; these include scientific, literary, poetic, historical, religious, and artistic, among others. All of these areas of knowledge have their own set of logic and governing rules. Science, for example, has the scientific method and uses inductive logic to arrive at certain truths. Religious knowledge relies upon deductive logic to interpret religious texts. Intuitive knowledge is perhaps the most important, and least understood, source of knowledge. Unlike other sources of knowledge, intuition is not analytical or reducible to component parts.

Intuitive knowledge is "hard to quantify or define, but it is there."[4] Intuitive awareness helps us take leaps in terms of our understanding of the world. In one respect, intuition is an enveloping force; it's all around us if we pay attention to the signals it gives us. According to economist Robin M. Hogarth, "the essence of intuition or intuitive responses is that they are reached with little apparent effort, and typically without conscious awareness. They involve little or no conscious deliberation."[5] This is why intuition comes to us in the form of sudden insights or epiphanies. Professor Seymour Epstein, who taught psychology at the University of Massachusetts Amherst, argued, "'Intuition involves a sense of knowing without knowing how one knows' based on the unconscious processing of information."[6] In other words, the mystery of intuition is that we gain deep insights about the world without fully understanding the mechanism of how we arrived at such insights.

In his groundbreaking book, *Educating Intuition*, Hogarth explores the mystery of intuition that is so "fundamental to daily life by offering the first comprehensive overview of what the science of psychology can tell us about intuition—where it comes from, how it works, whether we can trust it."[7] Hogarth argues that intuition is our sixth sense, which is why we need to learn how it works and why we need to trust it. This sixth sense expresses itself after a period of intense intellectual activity. Think of a time you searched for a solution to a problem. It probably seemed to you that the harder you thought about the problem the more elusive the solution became. It was only when you rested your mind that an epiphany hit you like a bolt of lightning. According to W. I. B. Beveridge, author of *The Art of Scientific Investigation*, intuition comes to us when we are not trying so hard to search for answers or solutions to problems.

Beveridge suggests that perhaps intuition comes from "the subconscious activities of the mind which has continued to turn over the problem even though perhaps consciously the mind is no longer giving it attention."[8] If intuition does indeed occur at a subconscious level, then it has a natural rhythm. In fact, "the most characteristic circumstances of an intuition are a period of intense work on the problem accompanied by a desire for its solution, abandonment of the work perhaps with attention to something else, then the appearance of the idea with dramatic suddenness and often a sense of certainty."[9] The rhythm of intuition is a conscious focus on a problem or reflection on something, then a period of surrendering the problem or focusing on something else, and finally a dramatic burst of insights. That's the gift of intuition.

Another way of describing the rhythm of intuition is that the rational mind focuses on an idea, or set of ideas, and then when analysis and logic fail, the intuitive mind takes over, offering us sudden bursts of insights that guide the rational mind toward a solution. In this sense, intuition is primary and rationality is secondary. It was Einstein, of course, who described reason and rationality as subservient to intuition. Einstein needs no introduction; he epitomized our very understanding of genius. In addition to developing the special theory of relativity, as well as the general theory of relativity, he was also responsible for developing a new theory of gravity. According to astrophysicist Paul Sutter, "[Einstein's] seven-year journey to develop a new theory of gravity was filled with leap after startling intuitive leap—with pregnant pauses in between as he worked out the consequences of how gravity works."[10] Einstein called these intuitive leaps "thought experiments."

In 1687 Sir Isaac Newton published one of the most remarkable books ever written, *Principia Mathematica*, or mathematical principles. In this groundbreaking work, Newton introduced the three laws of motion, which formed the foundation of classical physics as we know it: electromagnetism, calculus, the universal law of gravity, as well as numerous other original ideas. Although Newton offered us a description of how gravity works, he didn't tell us what the nature of gravity is or why gravity behaves the way it does. Two hundred and twenty years later, Einstein would take on the seemingly impossible task of figuring out what gravity is. He spent years conducting thought experiments, which followed the rhythm of intuition. He would spend time creatively playing with ideas, pause for a while, and then experience intense epiphanies or intuitive insights.

Here's an example of one of Einstein's thought experiments. Suppose that you are soundly sleeping in your comfortable bed. Let's further suppose that your cozy bed, and your entire bedroom for that matter, was somehow transported to a rocket with you blissfully unaware of the change. The rocket is launched into space and moving at a constant 1 g acceleration.

Now, some of you might say, "Wait a minute, you lost me. What is 1 g acceleration?" Fair enough. The g stands for gravity, and 1 g acceleration is the force we experience on the surface of Earth. Back to the rocket. You are still asleep and oblivious to the fact you are moving in space at an acceleration of 1 g. You wake up after a good night's sleep and reach for a bottle of water on your nightstand, inadvertently dropping the bottle to the ground. It falls as it would if you were back on Earth.

So far you have no clue that you are hurtling through space. But let's say you decide to get out of bed and walk over to the window, which is covered with drapes. Behind the drapes is a circular window that reveals the environment outside—the cold vacuum of space. The only way you would realize that you are no longer on Earth is if you looked through the window.

What this thought experiment taught Einstein was that gravity is the same thing as acceleration. If a rocket ship could accelerate to a speed that would duplicate the gravity on Earth, then gravity is simply a form of acceleration. That was his intuitive insight. Of course, a great many complex mathematical equations were involved to prove this insight, but without that initial intuitive breakthrough, we would not have a clear understanding of gravity. What is important to understand is that intuition sparks our imagination and creative impulse to perceive reality at a fundamental level. Intuition does not involve a high level of complexity; rather it is simplicity in its natural form, unclouded by reason or logic.

The intuitive mind is a gateway to our imagination. Intuition existed long before the introduction of an alphabet-based language, and it favored women who were, and continue to be, right-brain dominant. As you will read in chapter 3, the introduction of an alphabet-based language system "reinforced the brain's linear, abstract, predominately masculine left hemisphere at the expense of the holistic, iconic feminine right one."[11] What I want to say to all of you, particularly the women reading this book, is that we are all endowed with an intuitive mind. Of course, we are not at Einstein's level. He was a uniquely gifted individual. But we all have the capacity for intuition if we open ourselves to its signals and messages. Below are five steps that can help you become more in tune with your intuitive side.

- Be present.
- Tune inward.
- Write it down.
- Trust it.
- Act on it.

The idea of being present, or in the moment, is a powerful method of pushing to the side all of the distractions that add to the density of our lives. To be present means that you "first slow down. Breathe deeply. Tune into your senses. Notice your surroundings—what do you see, hear, feel, smell?"[12] Being present means immersing yourself in the moment, free from distractions. Despite the many wonderful things the digital age has accomplished, it has given us endless distractions. Ask yourself how many times you interact with your smartphone and other smart devices in a single day. There are many ways you can be in the moment. You can meditate, read a book in quiet solitude, completely unplug from the digital world for a day, and take a daily leisurely walk.

The list of famous people who took leisurely walks is both extensive and revealing. These individuals contributed something profound and original to our understanding of the world: Aristotle, Charles Dickens, Henry David Thoreau, Ludwig van Beethoven, Charles Darwin, and Albert Einstein, to name a few. Each of these individuals and numerous others took long walks to help open the intuitive mind, thus increasing their creative and imaginative output. Immanuel Kant was known to take three-hour walks every day from noon to 3 p.m.; he emerged as one of the greatest philosophers of the Western intellectual tradition. Now, you may have noticed something revealing on my list. There are no women on it. I spent a great deal of time researching famous women who took leisurely walks. I could not find a single one. This does not mean famous women did not walk; rather it reveals that the biographical details of women have been ignored.

The purpose of being in the moment is to allow yourself the opportunity to turn off the rational mind and tune inward. Remember the rhythm of intuition? When we actively and rationally use our mind to think about something, intuition tends to be kept at a distance. It is when we turn off our rational mind that intuition comes to us. There are those who claim that when they experience epiphanies, which are intuitions, it feels like a wake-up call, as if sudden bursts of insights are coming in all at once. To encourage such epiphanies, you may want to sit in a quiet place, eyes closed, and let your imagination run free. If you are walking, avoid the unnecessary distractions of logically sequenced ideas. Remember, intuition is simplicity; the complex layers of rationality come only after an intuitive mystery is revealed to you.

Once you've experienced the creative beauty and intuitive harmony of your inner voice, you need to write it down. Think of the last time you experienced a sudden burst of awareness. What happened? If you didn't write it down, you would later remember it as a distant and fading memory, as if it was a dream. Then, after writing down these insights, you will need to learn to trust them; trust your intuition because it is yours.

We women have been taught to ignore our intuition. Over and over, we've been told that our intuitive insights are irrational, illogical, emotionally dense, and ultimately irrelevant. What I'm telling you is that you need to consciously ignore these voices of doubt. You need to incorporate your intuition with your rational mind and act on what you believe will best serve you. If you apply these steps, you will feel a liberating sense of empowerment. Think of intuition as your compass to the world. If you ignore it, you do so at a heavy cost. Einstein did not achieve his extraordinary breakthroughs because he solved mathematical equations or applied the scientific method; rather, he experienced powerful intuitions as a result of his thought experiments and only later was he proven correct.[13]

I want to close this chapter by describing how intuition has guided my professional life. When I started in the financial business in the 1980s, there weren't many women I could look to for guidance. The industry was dominated by men. Through my early career there were moments when I wanted to quit. Although my rational mind offered me compelling reasons to leave the industry, I pushed on. I experienced powerful epiphanies that my destiny was to help people, particularly women, to work toward their financial goals. It's difficult to put in words the intuitive awakening that I experienced. It was spiritual in nature in the sense that I felt a powerful intuitive wave envelop me.

After the 2002 stock market crash happened—when most of my clients lost money and my pastor convinced me to stay—I knew there had to be a better way to help people invest than the traditional 60/40 model. This strategy of investing 60 percent in stocks and 40 percent in bonds had enjoyed success in the past, but it was susceptible to wild market swings. On an intuitive level, I knew there must be another way.

When I asked my colleagues and other investment professionals about alternative investments, they looked at me with condescension, as if to tell me that if there was another way, they would be using it. I refused to accept this defeatist attitude. Instead, I immersed myself in rigorous study. I read books and articles on the modern portfolio theory, macroeconomics, the history of the stock market, and so on. Still, I did not find myself any closer to a solution. It was when I turned my rational mind off that I experienced profound intuitive breakthroughs.

I remember my intuitive insights as moments of calm and clarity. One of these moments helped me understand that I was not so much looking for an alternative strategy as I was trying to find a way to protect my clients. In fact, on a simpler level, I did not ever want to go through the emotional burden of having my clients lose their money again. I was so busy searching for a rationally governed, mathematically rigorous alternative investment approach that I had forgotten why I was searching for it in the first place. Following this moment of intuitive clarity, I experienced other powerful epiphanies. I realized that a two-asset class investment model (stocks and bonds) was not optimal in protecting my clients against risk. That's when it hit me. I knew that a multi-asset class strategy was needed to potentially reduce the risk. How exactly this new model would work would come later, but the intuitive breakthrough set me on a path to prove it.

For too long now, women have been made to believe that their intuition is a vulnerability. The simple truth of the matter is that intuition is our greatest strength. It is intuition that helps us become aware of the world at a much deeper level than rationality. It is intuition that can help us reclaim our dignity by liberating us from the psychological chains of our painful past. It will be our collective intuitive insights that will shape and direct our destiny to finally, once and for all, tear down the remaining walls of patriarchy. That destiny will help men and women embrace each other as equals set on a path of reconstituting the world in the image of respect, dignity, empathy, hope, partnership, and the kind of love that uplifts all those around us. This brings me to the intersection between knowledge, intuition, and wisdom.

According to Dictionary.com, knowledge is defined as the "acquaintance with facts, truths or principles, as from study or investigation; general erudition."[14] Knowledge can be derived from books or experience. Think of knowledge as the process of acquiring and interpreting information that largely comes to us from texts and our experience of the world. Wisdom, on the other hand, is "having the power of discernment and judging properly as to what is true or right."[15] Where does this power of distinguishing truth from falsehood come from? It is my contention that the point of intersection between knowledge and wisdom is intuition. Intuition is what mediates the tension between our knowledge of the world and our choices and actions. Knowledge alone is insufficient to help us navigate the difficult choices we must make in life.

Intuition is what connects us to the world at a much deeper level than knowledge alone. Intuition is what allows us to have insights about the human condition and our impulse toward others. It is this impulse, spiritual in nature and intimately connected to the welfare of others, that needs to be the driving force behind our actions. In other words, our choices and actions must be informed by something greater than ourselves.

When it comes to women's situation in the world, meaningful and enduring change can only come about when both men and women develop the intuitive insight to uplift each other, to develop the wisdom to reshape the world in the image of transparency and equality. I wrote this book not simply to point out the unequal status of women but also to explore cooperative pathways of working together in order to transmit to future generations a positive sense of equality and fairness.

Throughout this book you will notice that each chapter concludes with a positive message for women. I wrote this book to inspire women, and the men in their lives, to transcend the troublesome history that has transmitted trauma to all of us.

I want to emphasize that feminine intuition has long been a powerful source of knowledge. Sadly, in patriarchal societies, women have been ignored, condescended to, sidelined, rendered irrelevant, and dismissed as a result of their powerful intuition. This is no longer the case. Our vulnerabilities are now becoming our strengths.

This book is also about affirmations. To the men reading this book, you, too, have powerful intuitions. Some of the most brilliant men in history, from Ralph Waldo Emerson to Albert Einstein and Steve Jobs, just to name a few, have relied upon intuition to achieve greatness. And for all the women reading this book, remember that your intuitive insights are powerful and impactful. Trust your intuition, as it will guide you toward your dreams. Your vulnerabilities will be your greatest strengths.

3

THE POWER OF SISTERHOOD AND CONFRONTING PATRIARCHAL TRAUMA

"Each time a woman stands up for herself, without knowing it
possibly, without claiming it, she stands up for all women."

—MAYA ANGELOU

I believe that women today are on the verge of a revolution whose aim is to fundamentally change the prevailing balance of power. This revolution will not only empower women to take their rightful place as equals alongside men but also bring awareness to the historic and systematic silencing of women throughout history, which has been a catalogue of wars, conquests, inventions, innovations, scientific discoveries, philosophical reflection, literary insights, and economic power written by and for men. As Rosalind Miles states in her powerful book *Who Cooked the Last Supper*, "the ages rolled on with hardly a female in view. Among history's colorful pageant of wars, popes and kings, women surfaced only in default of men."[1] While I believe that situation is about to change, one cannot write about women without peeling away the layers of history that has transmitted to us the alienation, doubt, vulnerabilities, hesitation, beliefs, and cruelties that shape and define our collective identity.

THE POWER OF SISTERHOOD

The Italian philosopher Antonio Gramsci observed that we are all the product of an infinity of traces that impact our consciousness.[2] What Gramsci is saying is that our sense of identity, the self-image that we all have, is the result of intersecting and overlapping historical and biographical forces that influence how we think and act. These forces not only frame our understanding of women's history but also transmit the horrors of how women were treated. When Gramsci talks about an infinity of traces that frame our awareness of the world, he is talking about all the historical details, the thousand little pieces, that form our understanding, beliefs, psychological quirks, emotional baggage, and endless list of scars that we carry with us as women.

One effect is that women have a shared reality centered on the idea of collective suffering. And while this reality is general and diffuse, spread over time and space, the trauma of being female in a male-dominated world has created an identifiable sisterhood.

What I mean by sisterhood is not a defined group of social or political activists, as was the case during the second-wave feminism of the 1960s and '70s. Rather, I'm describing something more fundamental. What I mean by sisterhood is the shared experience of women—regardless of time and place, social class, race, or any other consideration. Of course, certain women, Black women especially, have suffered far more than others, but my point is that on a basic level, all women share the scars of patriarchy.

Sisterhood is not something that is fixed or that we can immediately point to, but it is there. Sisterhood is manifested in our fears and doubts, represented in our accomplishments, and defined by a shared legacy. Sisterhood is in the air we women breathe and the narrative we all share. Sisterhood is in the language we speak and the silence that acknowledges our collective suffering. I am in no way suggesting that women are a monolithic group. They are most assuredly not. Women are just as diverse as men, with different political views, economic statuses, levels of education, and so on. When it comes to gender, however, women have been inescapably affected by the patriarchy.

Part of the reason I wrote this book is to address women in the spirit of sisterhood. I want women everywhere to know that what binds us is not only the trauma of the past but also the hope for a future where sisterhood is celebrated for its extraordinary achievements. I want women to understand that powerful change is coming and that we will be able to write our own narrative. For too long, we've had to endure the humiliation of having men control our narrative and our existential value in the world.

The power of sisterhood will change all this. In the not-too-distant future, the financial power of women as a group will empower us to stand on our own two feet and realize our own dreams. As someone who spent decades in the financial industry, I can tell you from my personal experience that a financial revolution is coming. But women need to be empowered economically, which first requires knowledge. As I argued in *Redefining Financial Literacy*, both men and women need desperately to improve their financial awareness.

I remember starting out in the financial industry more than 30 years ago. I had few women colleagues then, and I felt alone in a field dominated by men. In fact, it's still dominated by men. I had to work twice as hard as my male colleagues to stand out. As a young woman out of college, I was plagued by doubts and uncertainty. I allowed my vulnerabilities to get the best of me. I was intimidated. I was reminded endlessly that I didn't belong. Despite these challenges, I pushed on. I believed in my self-worth and my potential contribution. I was not going to be denied my opportunity by the false doctrine of an outdated and absurd belief in male superiority. Over time, my vulnerabilities became my strengths, and my doubts were transformed into powerful resolve.

If there is one thing I want women, and men for that matter, to get out of this book, it is this: Don't ever internalize your shortcomings or failures in terms of gender. Don't ever let your vulnerabilities freeze you into inaction. Your vulnerabilities, those thousand little pieces that fracture us, that force us to doubt ourselves, will become your strengths. I'm telling you this not as a matter of academic research but from painful experience. There was a time when I was frozen in place, when I was weighed down by the density of despair. I pushed on because I refused to submit to the poisonous patriarchy that almost got the better of me. I pushed on in the belief that I could contribute something to the world—to both men and women. I pushed on because I developed the courage to believe in myself.

MENTORSHIP

The concept of sisterhood naturally lends itself to the idea of mentoring. Regardless of time and place, culture or politics, women have always had an implicit bond defined by a unique set of shared experiences. So, it's no surprise that throughout the history of feminism, women have played a mentoring role to inspire other women to take action and fight against the entrenched patriarchy of their time. Let me introduce two broad categories of mentorship.

The first is what I call contemporary mentorship, in which successful women in every conceivable field have a tangible impact on younger generations who will continue to build equity for women. Some of these women today include Angela Merkel, former chancellor of Germany; Kamala Harris, vice president of the United States; Melinda Gates, co-founder of the Bill and Melinda Gates Foundation; Mary Barra, CEO of General Motors; Janet Yellen, former chair of the Federal Reserve; Ginni Rometty, former CEO of IBM; Mary Callahan Erdoes, CEO of J.P. Morgan's Asset and Wealth Management; Oprah Winfrey, talk show host, television producer, actress, author, billionaire, and philanthropist; Viola Davis, award-winning actress and producer; Abigail Johnson, chairman and CEO of Fidelity Investments; and Suze Orman, CFP and author of dozens of books on finance. The list, of course, can go on for several more pages, but my point is that there are very successful women today in a broad range of enterprises who can, and do, act as change agents. Through their positions, status, actions, writings, and extraordinary success, they stand as contemporary mentors, towering figures who guide future generations of women who will embrace their self-worth and value in the world as equal to men in every conceivable area of human existence.

The second category is what I call historical mentorship. This includes the pioneers and visionaries who came before, the giants upon whose shoulders all women stand upon. Some of these women include Marie Curie; Mary Wollstonecraft, early feminist and author of *A Vindication of the Rights of Woman*; Elizabeth Cady Stanton, another early leader of the women's rights movement and author of the Declaration of Sentiments; Susan B. Anthony, also a women's rights activist; Betty Friedan, author of *The Feminine Mystique*; Harriet Tubman, political activist and abolitionist during the American Civil War; Mary Jackson, mathematician and aerospace engineer at NASA; Simone de Beauvoir, French philosopher, writer, activist, and feminist theorist; and Frances Perkins, US secretary of labor under President Franklin D. Roosevelt and the first woman to serve in a presidential cabinet. Again, the list could go on and on, but you get the point.

Now, how do these exceptional women, both past and present, mentor the women of tomorrow? Let me put this simply. The more girls see and read about powerful women, the more they will want to be like them. It isn't that difficult. And the message is clear: Educators need to highlight and celebrate the accomplishments of women. The film and television industry needs to increase the number of roles for women. That includes ending the way Hollywood has objectified women, portraying them as sexualized objects. In the financial industry more women need to be encouraged to enter the field. When women everywhere take up the mantle of mentorship, future generations will thrive as empowered women who can, and will, change the world.

In the meantime, however, women everywhere still have to deal with the long-term effects of generations of trauma.

TRAUMA AND THE BIOLOGY OF SUFFERING

Let's define trauma as a "psychologically upsetting experience that has lasting negative effects on a person's thoughts, or behaviors. Trauma can manifest itself on a communal, national, or societal scale as a response to catastrophic loss or rupture. It can also be historical, comprising an enduring communal reaction to events such as genocide, slavery, or colonization."[3]

The idea that trauma can be passed down from one generation to the next was recognized in the mid-1960s. Two decades later, in 1988, a study found that "the grandchildren of Holocaust survivors were overrepresented by about 300% in referrals to psychiatric care. Researchers theorized that the effects of trauma can be transferred from one generation to the next."[4] Think of generationally transmitted trauma as the historical suffering of one group passed down to future generations. Native Americans, African Americans, Jews, and other groups have all experienced trauma that was so powerful and widespread that it was transmitted to future generations.

A growing body of evidence suggests that trauma is also inherited at the genetic level. In other words, trauma is no longer viewed as an abstract psychological concept; rather it is embedded in our biology. Today there is powerful evidence that suggests that our biology can expose what happened to women throughout countless generations of patriarchy. This process is known as epigenetics, "where the readability or expression of genes is modified without changing the DNA code itself. Tiny chemical tags are added to, or removed from, our DNA in response to changes in the environment in which we are living."[5] The implications of these genetic markers for trauma are profound and far-reaching.

Think of epigenetics as a very powerful program that transmits and stores trauma on a biological level. In other words, women have been programmed to become aware of the deep-rooted traumas of past generations. This is perhaps why women immediately know when they are being treated in a condescending manner or looked upon as objects rather than human beings with agency.

What do I mean by that? Agency is having the power to choose how we want to live our lives. Agency is both liberating and empowering. While past trauma may be programmed into us, it is also the key to our freedom. How? The awareness that we have about our past will force us to confront our trauma, which in turn will help us move beyond the pain and hurt by pushing us to reclaim our power to shape the world. In this dynamic history is a powerful teaching tool that helps us confront the past in order to move forward.

If we take a sample of history over the past several thousand years, we will be immediately impressed by what I call punctuated moments that helped humanity take giant leaps forward. From the invention of the wheel in 3500 BCE to the invention of the iPhone in 2007, from the first written language in 3000 BCE to Google's quantum computers in 2019, sweeping change has opened up boundless vistas of human ingenuity. But history is also a mirror that reflects back to us the unimaginable abuses of women. Despite dramatic and far-reaching innovations that spanned hundreds of generations, the one constant that connects us to those who lived eons ago is patriarchy.

Think about this for a moment. Human beings created unimaginable progress, conquered the limitations of space and time, fought for freedom, composed sublime music, developed literature that captured the human condition, engaged in philosophy, and generally improved upon every form of human activity, and yet the cruel injustice of patriarchy remains.

PATRIARCHY AND PATRIARCHAL TRAUMA

I'll delve into the history and persistence of patriarchy in the next section of the book, but it's important here to understand what I mean by the term. Patriarchy is a male-centered worldview that affirms the superiority of one gender over another. It is the most elaborate, pervasive, and enduring system of human control ever devised. It is simultaneously everywhere and nowhere. Think of the air you breathe. Because air is everywhere, we don't think much about it. It is this duality of being everywhere and nowhere that makes patriarchy difficult to pin down.

To those who suggest loudly that women have made great strides in the last 50 years or so, I would simply remind them of the patriarchal legacy that defines us today. According to sociologist Allan G. Johnson, we are all, men and women, trapped inside a patriarchal legacy. It is this legacy that transmits to us thousands of years of trauma, a legacy that insists upon marginalizing women and maintaining the status quo. Johnson, in his book *The Gender Knot*, frames this legacy as follows:

> Patriarchy is male dominated in that positions of authority—political, economic, legal, religious, educational, domestic—are generally reserved for men. Heads of state, corporate CEOs and board members, religious leaders, school principals, members of legislatures at all levels of government,

senior law partners, tenured professors, generals and admirals, and even those identified as "head of households" all tend to be male under patriarchy. When a woman finds her way into such positions, people tend to be struck by the exception to the rule and wonder how she'll measure up against a man in the same position.[6]

It is this idea of being an exception that women had to live with for centuries. This is what Rosalind Miles meant when she said women only existed in default of men. The very prism by which we perceive the world is filtered by a male lens. This is why when women achieve the impossible, some men will always want to undermine the accomplishment.

Despite a century of demanding change, our patriarchal structure persists. Our society, "like every society in the world, remains a patriarchy; they are ruled by men. That is not just because every country (except Rwanda) has a majority-male national parliament, and it is despite the handful of countries with women heads of state. It is a systematic characteristic that combines dynamics at the level of the family, the economy, the culture and the political arena."[7]

Patriarchy is also vertical, meaning that the higher you move up in terms of the corporate ladder or political institutions, the more masculine the organizational structures become. Patriarchy is a culture with "the core value of control and domination in almost every area of human existence."[8] Patriarchy is the constant reminder that women exist in someone else's universe and must abide by the rules of masculinity, which are established by men.

So we have to ask, how has this affected countless generations of women? The historical trauma transmitted from one generation to the next needs to be addressed. Yet in doing research for this book, I was surprised by the lack of literature and psychological studies about trauma that women have endured as a result of their gender.

Let me introduce a new term here—"patriarchal trauma," which I define as the hidden historical forces that have marginalized women in every aspect of public life. These social, political, and economic forces have kept women down for countless generations, with each generation transmitting the trauma to the next. It is like an echo from the past, telling women they are incapable of thriving in a man's world.

Perhaps one reason patriarchal trauma has not been studied is because it's diffuse. Patriarchy has existed for so long and has become so widespread that it is difficult to study. Meera Atkinson, the author of *Traumata*, argues that the way society treats women is "inherently traumatic."[9] I'm not suggesting here that every woman today is traumatized as a result of gender; rather, women are collectively carrying the trauma of what came before—vulnerabilities, doubts, hopes and fears, struggles, setbacks, questioning, and thwarted dreams. And let's not forget that men are also carrying the collective guilt of the misdeeds of past generations, and that they have largely internalized the worst qualities of masculinity.

TOXIC MASCULINITY

We cannot fully understand and appreciate how generational trauma impacts women without understanding how the same patriarchy transmits psychological scars to men. According to sociologist Raewyn Connell, gender is defined "as the product of relations and behaviors, rather than as a fixed set of identities and attributes." This means that men must live up to impossible standards of masculinity such as "social respect, physical strength, and sexual potency."[10] "From birth, men are discouraged from showing emotion, which is seen as a feminine attribute—boys don't cry, right? Without a culturally approved outlet for their feelings, this stifling of emotion has led generations of men to turn to unhealthy coping mechanisms such as alcohol abuse, which men are more likely to experience than women."[11] Men are often viewed as "weak" when they demonstrate the feminine qualities of empathy and compassion. Thus, toxic masculinity leads men to overcompensate by acting out in the form of sexual aggression and assault against women.

Just as women have impossible standards to live up to in terms of feminine beauty and sexuality, men also have impossible standards to live up to in terms of masculinity. The concept of masculinity and femininity need to change so that both men and women can move forward together with a sense of respect, empathy, and an acknowledgment of their vulnerabilities.

PATRIARCHAL RECOVERY

Before men and women can move forward together with dignity and respect, however, we need to explore the concept of patriarchal recovery. What I mean is that having an *awareness* of patriarchal trauma is not enough. We need to *confront* the trauma in order to move forward in a manner that is empowering to all women.

According to Ann Filemyr, president of Southwestern College in Santa Fe, New Mexico, in order for women to recover from patriarchy, they must first understand what she calls the patriarchal wound. Filemyr defines this wound as "ancestral suffering and intergenerational trauma caused by the power imbalance between genders."[12] This is essentially the generational trauma I have explored earlier in this chapter. And in order for women to recover from this ancient form of trauma, they must acknowledge it before they can reclaim their authentic selves.

I don't want to give the impression that only women need to recover from the trauma of patriarchy. As I've noted, it is safe to say that men have also internalized thousands of years of intellectual, psychological, and emotional manipulation. Just as women's cultural value in the world has been defined in relation to men, so, too, has men's frame of reference been defined in relation to women. Men have been subject to the greatest cultural hoax of all time—namely that they are inherently superior to the other half of the population. One might argue that this has created a privileged system. And obviously what men suffer from patriarchy is not remotely similar to women. I'm in no way suggesting otherwise.

What I am suggesting is that men have internalized patriarchy in such a way as to distort and corrupt their sense of masculinity. As we noted, men have been taught to embrace a toxic form of masculinity that renders them as two-dimensional beings, incapable of revealing the feminine aspect of their lives. In order for men to recover from the trauma of patriarchy, we as a society must stop encouraging boys to believe they are superior to girls or to become aggressive. We need to break the cycle where gender identity is prescribed at a very young age. We need to put an end to the old, worn-out cultural precept that "boys will be boys."

We need to encourage both boys and girls to expand their gender awareness by allowing them to explore the rich tapestry of identity. Girls must be raised to believe that their sense of worth and value in the world is not in relation to boys; rather, girls need to believe their potential contribution and impact on the world is only limited by their imagination. Patriarchal recovery cannot happen unless we fundamentally redefine our cultural paradigm of what it means to be male and female.

PATRIARCHAL INJURY

In addition to the patriarchal trauma that all women are burdened with, there is also an emotional injury that manifests itself in ways that we may not be fully conscious of. Although the term patriarchal injury does not exist in the literature, it might be helpful to begin our discussion with a simple definition of injury. According to *Merriam-Webster*, injury is defined as "1. Hurt, damage, or loss sustained; 2a. an act that damages or hurts, 2b. violation of another's rights for which the law allows an action to recover damages."[13] Notice that at the heart of the meaning behind injury is a certain level of hurt and a violation of rights.

Now, the obvious question is this: How is injury different from trauma? While there are different types of traumas, such as acute, chronic, and generational trauma, the one constant that ties them all together is "the long-term effects on the person's well-being."[14] In other words, trauma, particularly generational trauma, is deeply ingrained in the collective psyche of women. Injury, on the other hand, can heal much faster.

Patriarchal injury is a triggering mechanism that brings to our consciousness how patriarchal power structures shape how we interact in the world. While patriarchal injury affects both men and women, women are impacted at a far deeper level. Imagine for a minute that you are an executive in a large corporation. Imagine further that you are in charge of an upcoming meeting where other executives from different regions and countries will be attending. You are aware that the CEO and CFO—both are men—will be in attendance. You are naturally nervous, but you are fully prepared for this important meeting.

After you make your presentation, you open the meeting for discussion. Everything seems to be going fine until several male executives begin to question your presentation. Feeling confident, you defend your team's research and push back. The arguments begin to heat up, but you are still in control of the meeting. Now imagine a senior executive, say the CEO or CFO, says, "Look, sweetie, you gave an excellent presentation, but it's just not the direction we are willing to go right now." Did you notice the injury? The senior executive called you "sweetie." That's the patriarchal injury. If you are a man, you may have missed it. But it's obvious to every woman. Let's examine the psychological free fall you feel upon hearing this seemingly harmless term.

Your mind is now focused on that one word. Your confidence is shaken, and your ideas and the team you assembled to conduct the research are now in doubt. You keep quiet while others monopolize your time. The injury also triggers all sorts of images of how women are marginalized. You may think of your childhood and the struggles you had to endure to rise to this position of what you believed to be power. Your stress level goes up. You want to yell at the senior executive who referred to you as "sweetie," but you hold your tongue. You don't want to come off as being difficult or not a team player.

The example above is just one kind of injury that unleashes deep-seated emotions beneath our conscious awareness. Before you say to yourself that what I'm describing are simply emotional states and not injuries, consider the fact there are physical manifestations to the stress brought upon by patriarchal injuries. According to the Cleveland Clinic, stress is the "body's reaction to any change that requires an adjustment or response. The body reacts to these changes with physical, mental, and emotional responses."[15] Stress can manifest itself in the following symptoms:

- Dizziness
- General aches and pain
- Headaches
- Indigestion or acid reflux
- Loss of appetite
- Problems sleeping
- Racing heart
- Trembling and shaking[16]

It's common for women to experience patriarchal injuries. If you are a woman reading this book, think of the time you were in high school or college or at your place of employment. How often were you reminded of your gender? How often were you spoken to in a condescending manner? How often did your teacher or professor make you feel that you are not smart enough? How often were you passed over for a raise? How often did you feel that you had to work harder than the men to prove your value? If you can identify with any of these questions by affirming that you have often experienced unfair treatment due to your gender, or any general question where gender was linked to your ability to contribute, then you've suffered from patriarchal injury.

While the vast majority of women experience patriarchal injury, we don't all respond to it the same way. Some women freeze when faced with stepping beyond traditional norms—stepping into power, speaking out, making a lot of money. Others have a fight-or-flight response. They may be able to brave the spotlight, but they pay for it. Regardless of how patriarchal injury is physically manifested, these injuries always trigger something from our individual or collective past.

We might remember the boys at school teasing us that because of our gender they are stronger or smarter than us. We may also remember our parents and grandparents who were bound by the rigid masculine and feminine roles of their time. A host of unpleasant memories take hold of us, bringing with them the pain and doubt we may have felt in the past.

Let me share with you some of the injuries—both subtle and overtly humiliating—that were inflicted upon me throughout my career. Fresh out of college, I was fortunate to have landed a position at one of the largest insurance companies in the world. As I learned the insurance business, as well as basic investment strategy, I started to move up the corporate ladder and firmly believed that I was a valued member of the company. What I didn't realize early on was that I was in a male-dominated financial culture or, more importantly, the implications of such a reality.

As I look back now, I realize there were numerous micro injuries that I may have overlooked or dismissed—suggestive glances and inuendo, condescending and dismissive attitudes, and constant reminders that I should be grateful that I have a job. I dismissed these micro injuries because I was driven. I was determined to show these poorly mannered men that I would never be defined by their sophomoric behavior.

This kind of toxic behavior is neither trivial nor benign. Micro patriarchal injuries—similar to what psychologists call microaggressions—can have a profound impact on women. According to Kevin Nadal, professor of psychology at Jon Jay College of Criminal Justice, microaggressions are defined as "the everyday, subtle, intentional—and oftentimes unintentional—interactions or behaviors that communicate some sort of bias toward historically marginalized groups."[17]

As one of the most marginalized groups in history, women have to deal with microaggressions, or what I call micro injuries, on a daily basis. Part of what makes this form of aggression so subtle and yet powerful is "that people who commit microaggressions might not even be aware of it."[18] Simply, men have been engaging in such hurtful behavior for so long that they are no longer aware of the emotional and psychological injuries they cause. Over time, however, these micro injuries reinforce negative stereotypes about women. They are difficult to overcome, as I know from the mountain I had to climb to achieve financial success for myself.

After spending several years working for the insurance company, I decided to take the knowledge and experience I'd gained and open up my own financial advisory business. During my first few years, I had to endure a chorus of negative noise: "She doesn't know what she's doing," I heard, along with "Women don't belong in finance." That last comment, which was repeated ad nauseam, was hurtful, but I knew that if I was going to make it in this business, I had to develop a thick skin.

After the stock market crash of 2002, when so many of my clients lost money, all the negative comments, condescension, and dismissive attitudes I had encountered had a profound psychological impact on me. For a time, I found myself frozen in place, unable to make sense of the financial situation, and I began to believe the voice in my head that perhaps I didn't belong in the male-dominated financial world. Patriarchal injury and trauma caused me to feel doubt and uncertainty.

How did I come back? The first step of my journey to overcome the toxic effects of patriarchal injury and trauma was grieving. Grieving "allows us to 'free up' energy that is bound to the lost person, object, or experience—so that we might re-invest that energy elsewhere. Until we grieve effectively, a part of us remains tied to the past."[19] Grieving helped me move forward by helping me let go of the patriarchal injuries and traumas that were defining my life. I first had to confront my past. Then I had to transform all of the negative energy that was confining me to the past and preventing me from realizing my full potential. Over time, and with the help of others, I developed six steps to overcome the oppressive forces of patriarchy:

- Awareness
- Acceptance
- Reconciliation
- Liberation
- Dignity
- Destiny

From a psychological perspective, awareness is defined as "the state of being conscious or the quality of being perceptually knowledgeable. It is also the ability to perceive, feel, know, or be cognizant of events."[20] More simply, awareness is the capacity to understand yourself in relation to the world around you. When something jolts us out of our comfortable reality, our awareness increases. You cannot grieve for something if you are not aware of the underlying injury or trauma. Awareness must lead to acceptance.

People often confuse acceptance with surrender. However, acceptance "simply means being willing to acknowledge what is, without resisting or denying it."[21] Let me elaborate a bit on this idea. If you are one of the millions of people who have and continue to benefit from Alcoholics Anonymous, you will be familiar with the Serenity Prayer. The prayer states, "God, grant me the serenity to accept the things I cannot change, the courage to change the things I can, and the wisdom to know the difference."[22] It might be easy to assume that acceptance is a passive emotional state. (We simply acknowledge the patriarchal reality around us and move on.) This is not the case, though. Acceptance is active and ongoing, as in the part of the Serenity Prayer that states "the courage to change the things I can." Acceptance does not mean we run away from the daily patriarchal micro injuries and aggressions; rather we accept that they are there and collectively gather the courage to change them.

Our capacity to acknowledge that patriarchal injuries happen all around us and our ability to do something about them is why reconciliation is profoundly important. The word "reconciliation" comes from two Latin words—*re*, which means "again," and *conciliare*, which means "to bring together."[23] To bring an end to patriarchy, both men and women need to come together with resolute courage to change the injustice that women continue to endure.

I believe that men and women can, and must, come together to confront the remaining power structures that continue to favor men over women. When I mention men, I'm not talking about an abstraction; I'm talking about the men in our lives—our husbands, significant others, fathers, and sons. Part of reconciliation is to engage men in an ongoing conversation about the patriarchal injuries women endure all the time. With this kind of cultural reconciliation between men and women, we can liberate women from the ugliness of patriarchy.

MATRIARCHAL LESSONS

The idea of liberating women from the ugliness of patriarchy is not a new idea. The 18th-century English writer and early feminist Mary Wollstonecraft argued that "a revolution in female manners" was necessary. The revolution she was describing had nothing to do with etiquette or how to sit at the dinner table. Wollstonecraft wanted to "overthrow the system of socialization that made men and women prisoners of each other's tyranny, rather than the virtuous companions whom they were meant to be."[24] In other words, both men and women have become prisoners of their own mind and imagination. She felt that in order to achieve social liberation for women, we need to liberate our minds from the poisonous ideas that women are inherently inferior.

Wollstonecraft was well aware of the important distinction between social and individual liberation. Throughout her writing, she "targeted literary and intellectual giants—John Milton, Jean-Jacques

Rousseau, Edmund Burke—for propagating absurd and destructive ideas about the innate inferiority and natural subordination of women to men."[25] Amazing to think that here we are in the 21st century and these absurd and pernicious ideas persist. What men and women need to do, in the spirit of reconciliation, is to individually challenge these ridiculous ideas about women. This type of liberation is the first step to achieving a broadly defined cultural liberation. Now, the not-so-obvious question is this: Where does liberation take us?

On a self-evident level, liberation means freedom from the historical chains that have marginalized women for countless generations. On a more personal level, liberation is the process of reclaiming both our dignity and self-respect. There is an inherent human desire for dignity that transcends all of our differences. Dignity is the "shared desire to be seen, heard, listened to, and treated fairly; to be recognized, understood, and to feel safe in the world."[26] Dignity is our existential capacity to recognize and acknowledge our shared humanity, to treat each other as ends rather than as a means to some ulterior motive. Once women reclaim their dignity, both individually and culturally, they will be able to embrace their destiny as free agents who will change the world.

Our world today is governed by a powerful patriarchy that affirms the dominance of men in the social, political, and economic spheres of cultural interaction. Patriarchy has become so ingrained in our collective imagination that the roles of men and women have become a part of the cosmological order. And when something becomes a part of the cosmological order, many of us forget it was once merely a construct created by those in power and generationally transmitted to the rest of us. Given this stubborn and persistent reality of a male-dominated social order, it might be difficult to understand there was once a time when society was defined in terms of matriarchy. According to Peggy Reeves Sanday, emeritus professor of anthropology at the University of Pennsylvania, "matriarchy has never been theorized in and of itself. From the start its meaning was fashioned by analogy with 'patriarchy' or 'father right.'"[27] In other words, matriarchy has always been understood only in relation to patriarchy. If patriarchy is considered as a male-dominated social rule, then matriarchy becomes the female variant.

Under patriarchy, women have always been defined in relation to men. This oppositional approach has created the kind of generational trauma that is with us today. Let me explain what I mean. If men define themselves as strong, then women must be the opposite of strong—that is, weak. If men are superior, then women are inferior, and so on. It was Simone de Beauvoir, in her groundbreaking work *The Second Sex*, who introduced the idea of oppositional meaning. Beauvoir points to Aristotle and St. Thomas as defining women in terms of the "negation of what the male affirms. It was Aristotle who said: 'The female is a female by virtue of a certain lack of qualities; we should regard the female nature as afflicted with a natural defectiveness,' while St. Thomas called woman an 'imperfect man' and 'incidental.'"[28] His point was that for thousands of years, women have been looked upon and treated as incidentals, an afterthought.

Yet there was once a time when women were defined as the *equal* sex. They were viewed as self-definitional agents in the world. There was a time prior to patriarchy, between 40,000 and 10,000 years ago, which is often referred to as the Golden Age, when *matriarchy* existed. However, "if one is looking for a society in which women take the 'ruling' role of men," then such societies did not exist.[29] The anthropological research reveals instead that matriarchal societies were "not based on domination by any gender, but upon maternal values which will exhibit as caretaking and nurturing negotiation-oriented communities, with complementary equality for women and men."[30] Instead of conquest, matriarchy was about unity and preservation.

The following graphic represents the various stages of culture, from the earliest hunter-gatherer societies where matriarchy developed to the rise of patriarchy. You will notice that matriarchy existed for a much longer time period than patriarchy.

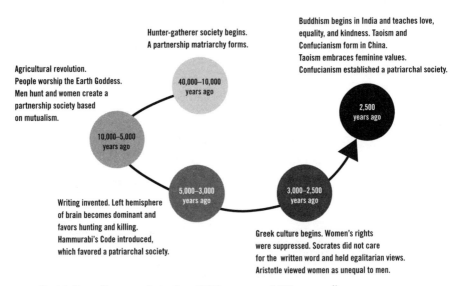

Fig. 3.1. Chart of human evolution from 40,000 years ago to 2,500 years ago.[31]

In fact, matriarchy has not completely disappeared. Heide Göttner-Abendroth, a philosopher and pioneer of women's studies, has argued that "abundant evidence" proves that matriarchal societies do exist even today in Asia, America, and Africa. These "gender egalitarian societies" have "no hierarchies, classes, nor domination of one gender by the other."[32] There are two important concepts here to understand—egalitarian societies and domination. Egalitarianism is "characterized by belief in the equality of all people, especially in political, economic, or social life."[33] Domination, of course, is the capacity to exert power over others.

The idea of gender domination is the theme of Riane Eisler's book *The Chalice and the Blade: Our History, Our Future.* Eisler argues that "there are two basic ways of structuring the relations between the female and male halves of humanity. All societies are patterned on either a dominator model—in which human hierarchies are ultimately backed up by force or the threat of force—or a partnership model, with variations in between."[34] Dominator societies are what we've all been accustomed to over the past several millennia.

Given that fact—that patriarchy has existed for thousands of years— there are those who believe that the second-class status of women is a biological reality rather than a social construction with origins that go back to the advent of agriculture and the ownership of land. One of the most dramatic finds in archaeology is the ancient city of Çatal Hüyük (pronounced *cha-tel hoo-yek*), which is today located in southwest Turkey. Although this region of Turkey today is a rocky desert, 9,000 years ago this patch of land was fertile and filled with an abundance of water. Sometime around 7500 BCE, nomadic hunter-gatherers settled near a river. According to historian and biographer Amanda Foreman, an ancient town "grew until it had 8,000 residents living in some 2,000 houses. They had primitive agriculture, domesticated sheep, dedicated tools, and a culture that produced both art and religious iconography."[35]

This ancient culture seemed to be more enlightened than our technologically sophisticated world, since one of the striking discoveries at Çatal Hüyük was evidence of true gender equality. Skeletal remains revealed that "both sexes ate the same diet, performed the same work, and spent the same amount of time outdoors. In life, they inhabited the same physical space; in death they were given the same kind of burials."[36] In this formulation, matriarchy has been defined as part of an inclusive, participatory, and gender-neutral form of a partnership society.

Çatal Hüyük, of course, was not the only ancient settlement to embrace an inclusive kind of matriarchy. Nomadic tribes started to settle in various villages throughout the Middle East, particularly the Fertile Crescent region, which is today Iraq. These settlements were "from the start a woman's world."[37] It was the women who were the foragers and gatherers and likely developed horticulture, which was an early form of agriculture. Women planted einkorn, a wheat-like grain. Women marked the fields for planting and harvesting. It is important to understand that these early settlements farmed the land only for subsistence, while men hunted to supplement the harvests and were away from the village for long periods of time.

LANGUAGE AND THE RISE OF PATRIARCHY

In hunter-gatherer culture, mythology and religion had centered on two deities who symbolized the partnership of men and women working in harmony: the Mother Goddess, who brought all life into existence, and the Horned God, who was the god of the sun, masculinity, and hunting.[38] These masculine/feminine projections of the ancient world would undergo a gradual transformation toward a male-centered religious belief system.

These religious beliefs or mythologies offer us a cosmological frame of reference for those times. In other words, ancient belief systems shaped how men and women understood the world and their place in it. For the hunter-gatherer societies of the Stone Age, belief in gods and goddesses established egalitarian societies.

Then, sometime around 5,000 years ago, city-states emerged in Mesopotamia, Egypt, and the Indus River Valley. These city-states led to what is commonly referred to as the rise of civilization: Temples were built, kings rose to power and proclaimed they had a divine right to rule, writing was introduced, social classes were created, wars were waged, and private property became the source of men's power. Importantly, these historical forces converged to fundamentally undermine the matriarchal order.

The question to ask now is this: How did these historical forces come together to create a broadly defined male-centered worldview? One answer has to do with the control of nature. As the hunter-gatherer society was replaced by an agriculturally based one, land became valuable. Labor roles were gradually linked to gender. Men typically worked in the fields and women were responsible for child-rearing and other domesticated duties. Although this simple division of labor might be interpreted as part of the natural order, it was not. Once the division of labor was defined along gender lines, a hierarchy would emerge over time, thus giving men power and control over women. Although the agricultural revolution created a power imbalance between men and women, it also introduced "broader social and class stratification that had also never existed before."[39] In this sense, the need to control nature and divide labor were instrumental in creating a power imbalance. But this is an incomplete analysis of why patriarchy took hold.

Another force that led to a male-centered worldview might actually surprise you. It was an invention that had far-reaching implications: the introduction of written language.

Think about how you come to understand the world. You use an alphabet-based symbolic system of communication, otherwise known as language. An alphabet system is sequential and linear, which helps us understand the logical sequence of ideas, mathematics, and science. What made language possible was the evolutionary development of the human brain.

Our brain is divided into two separate and yet connected hemispheres. The left brain is responsible for the analytic understanding of the world. Our abilities to analyze, dissect, perceive numbers and quantity, and develop language occur in the left brain. The right brain understands the world in a much more holistic manner. The right hemisphere of our brain is where emotions happen. It's the seat of intuition and a deep awareness of our existence.[40]

Women, it turns out, are right-brain dominant, while men are left-brain dominant.[41] Now, what does this have to do with the transition from matriarchy to patriarchy? According to author and surgeon Leonard Shlain, in his groundbreaking book, *The Alphabet Versus the Goddess: The Conflict Between Word and Image*, the development of a sequential and linear alphabet favors those with a dominant left brain and, by extension, men. According to Shlain, the benefits of having a written language set humanity on a path toward progress, but there was a price to pay:

There exists ample evidence that any society acquiring the written word experiences explosive changes. For the most part, these changes can be characterized as progress. But one pernicious effect of literacy has gone largely unnoticed: writing subliminally fosters a patriarchal outlook. Writing of any kind, but especially its alphabetic form, diminishes feminine values and with them, women's power in the culture.[42]

Prior to the introduction of language, Shlain proposed, a holistic and synthetic view of the world characterized a feminine perspective, while a sequential and reductionist way of thinking defined the masculine outlook.

Fig. 3.2. Taoist symbol of yin and yang.

These two forces, the feminine and the masculine, can work as complementary means of comprehending reality. This harmony between the energy of the feminine yin and the masculine yang is perfectly captured by the Taoist circle of symmetrical integration. That concept is at the heart of the Taoist philosophical tradition, which started some 2,500 years ago in China and which embraces the fundamental idea that we are neither man nor woman. Instead, our primordial essence is a harmonious balance between masculine and feminine essence. "One cannot exist without the other, indicating equality between the masculine and the feminine. They are understood to be two sides of the same coin."[43]

As a religious practice, Taoism is gender neutral, emphasizing the equality of men and women. According to Shlain, this balance was disrupted with the advent of language, which favored the more analytical left brain.

Now it was not the case that an alphabet-based language was introduced and women were immediately denied this new form of knowledge. There was a period of time, over centuries, when language and the visual image governed by the right brain intersected and overlapped as a way of comprehending the world. But as language spread and became more dominant, the power of the visual image decreased, while our analytical ability (left brain) increased. Moreover, according to Shlain, written language "shaped both the development of the human nervous system and the social dynamics of gender relations."[44] The gradual introduction of an alphabet-based language system, he says, actually changed the wiring of our brains in such a way as to favor men.

According to Shlain, we are all born "with a unique set of genetic instructions, we enter the world as a work-in-progress and await the deft hand of the ambient culture to sculpt the finishing touches. Among the two most important influences on a child are the emotional constellation of his or her immediate family and the configuration of his or her culture. Trailing a close third is the principal medium with which the child learns to perceive and integrate his or her culture's information. This medium will play a role in determining which neuronal pathways of the child's developing brain will be reinforced."[45]

What does this mean? He's saying that for thousands of years, the cultural medium that integrated the world was visual images, which neurologically favored women. Then, over a long period of time, the gradual introduction of an alphabet-based language gradually favored men on a neurological level.

This, coupled with the agricultural revolution, meant that the status of women gradually diminished and patriarchy emerged as an all-consuming cultural force that would marginalize women for millennia. The good news today is that the digital revolution is fundamentally changing the world once again. The visual medium of our digital technology is allowing women to flourish, which is why women will thrive under this new paradigm. That fact, along with the increasing economic power of women (which we saw in the introduction and which we'll revisit later), along with a push for their greater financial literacy (which we will examine in part II) will help fuel feminism's fourth wave.

PART II:

MOVING BEYOND PATRIARCHY

4

THE PERSISTENCE OF PATRIARCHY

"If you want something said, ask a man;
if you want something done, ask a woman."

—MARGARET THATCHER

We are all born into patriarchy. It forms the very fabric of our world. And as we've seen in the previous chapter, it has left a legacy of trauma and injury that continues to impact our world.

To recap the definition as I see it, patriarchy is a socially constructed system that forms the foundation of human interaction based on gender, dominance, control, manipulation, separation, submission, alienation, and a host of other deeply ingrained irrational projections of masculine superiority. Patriarchy asserts itself in public places. We see male dominance in the workplace; in how we worship; in the media, academia and financial awareness; and in the surrounding space of our cultural life.

To better understand how women have become so marginalized, it's helpful to explore the relationship between women's contributions and how history remembers and records such contributions. Gerda Lerner, who was one of the founders of women's history as an academic field, argued in her book *The Creation of Patriarchy* that women have actually played a critical role in shaping society. The problem, however, is that their contributions have been ignored, undermined, forgotten, and considered unworthy of a historical footnote. Lerner writes that the importance of women and the central role they play in society is often contradicted by the men who write history and that these historians have systematically left out the contributions of half the population in order to maintain a patriarchal image of masculine superiority. She also notes that the disconnect will push women to take action.

> The contradiction between women's centrality and active role creating society and their marginality in the meaning-giving process of interpretation and explanation has been a dynamic force, causing women to struggle against their condition. When, in that process of struggle, at certain historic moments, the contradictions in their relationship to society and to historical process are brought into the consciousness of women, they are then correctly perceived and named as deprivations that women share as a group. This coming-into-consciousness of women becomes the dialectical force moving them into action to change their condition and to enter a new relationship to male-dominated society.[1]

ARISTOTLE AND THE INFERIORITY OF WOMEN

When you consider that the Western intellectual tradition took hold in ancient Greece, you begin to realize just how powerful history is in shaping our understanding of the world. It was the Greeks who first introduced democracy; formalized the study of philosophy, science, and mathematics; made significant advances in engineering, literature, and history; and created an elaborate mythological view of the world. Ancient Greece was also a patriarchal society. Women were controlled by men at every stage of life. They had no political or economic rights. Their social role was to bear children, preferably male children, and to run the household. The mythological depiction of women played a central role in influencing and justifying how women were to be treated. Given that mythology was produced by men, "the associations between mythological portrayal of human characters mirrored the patriarchal society to which the folklore belonged, maintaining gender relationship already imbedded in the cultures that created them."[2] Mythology mirrored reality in the sense that it offered a powerful framework to justify the cruel treatment of women.

Greek mythology portrayed women as deceitful, manipulative, and responsible for the downfall of men. Female characters in Greek mythology were often described as shameful, vindictive, and irrational. Women were seen as a necessary evil, however, because they were necessary to reproduce the social order, which was constructed by men.[3] I'm sure many of you have heard the story of Pandora's box, a present that, upon opening, becomes a curse. According to the Greek poet Hesiod, when Prometheus (a trickster and a god of fire) stole fire from heaven, Zeus (the king of the gods) punished the thief by sending Pandora to Prometheus's brother, Epimetheus. She brought with her a jar that, when opened, would release sickness, death, and unspeakable evil upon humanity.[4] In this context, women were characterized as evil and bent on the destruction of mankind.

Mythology is both a projection and reflection of cultural attitudes and norms, artistic sensibilities, and religious beliefs, among other things. Over time, mythology gave rise to other areas of human inquiry, such as science, mathematics, history, politics, literature, and philosophy. Philosophy speaks to us with authority and carefully reasoned arguments, and a culture's philosophical traditions are expressions of its ethics, ideals, and archetypes.

The formal introduction of Greek philosophy can be traced to Socrates, though he himself wrote nothing. What we know of him comes from his student, Plato. Socrates's ideas about women were radically different from the prevailing cultural view. He had a high view of the female sex, often mentioning foreign women as his teachers. He claimed to have learned rhetoric—the art of public speaking—from Aspasia of Miletus, who was the mistress of the Athenian general and statesman Pericles.[5]

Socrates, unfortunately, paid a price for his philosophical views. His trial in Athens is one of the most famous in Western civilization. The philosopher was charged with disrespecting the gods and the corruption of youth. To better understand these charges, we need to discuss how Socrates engaged his students in philosophical inquiry. He had a dialectical approach to learning, which meant that he would ask his students questions and encourage conversation and contradiction in order to arrive at a higher level of truth. Once Socrates started to challenge the Greek conception of polytheism [the belief in many gods] and other myths, the Athenian government brought charges against him.[6] He was found guilty and, under the Athenian system of democracy, asked to propose his own punishment. When Socrates joked that he should be rewarded for his effort to enlighten the youth, the Athenians were not amused. They sentenced him to death by drinking hemlock, a poisonous plant. Although the Athenians gave Socrates every opportunity to escape, he refused on the principle that by escaping he would be admitting his guilt. He drank the hemlock and died in 399 BCE.

Plato, who was perhaps the philosopher's most brilliant student, witnessed the death of his master and resented the Athenians who, in his mind, murdered Socrates. In fact, Plato rejected the idea of democracy and would write extensively about it in his major work, *The Republic*. Most of Plato's writing was in the form of a dialogue, in which he often used Socrates as the mouthpiece for his own views. What Plato did was redefine the prevailing Greek conception of human beings. At the time, humans were defined by their physical body: Men were physically stronger and, therefore, responsible for protecting their families. Women, on the other hand, given their biological differences, were suited to produce and raise children.

Plato, influenced by Socrates's more positive view of the sexes, rejected this prevailing idea and argued that human beings exist as a duality—a soul and a body. The body exists for a brief period and dies. The soul, however, survives the body. And given that knowledge resides in the soul and not the body, Plato placed women on an equal footing with men.

In place of democracy Plato envisioned a system of government that would rule with absolute authority. It would be made up of philosopher kings who would undergo a rigorous education. Plato also believed that women could belong to this elite group of philosopher kings—or queens in this case—who would rule with enlightened awareness. And although Plato did believe that women by nature were twice as bad as men, he attempted to reconcile this contradiction by suggesting that giving women access to education would overcome this natural impediment.[7]

Plato's greatest student and disciple rejected these ideas on women, however. Aristotle, considered the most influential thinker of the pre-modern world, had an influence so profound that in the *Inferno*, by Italian poet Dante Alighieri, he is referred to only as "The Master."[8]

Aristotle's contribution to the Western intellectual tradition is broad and awe inspiring. He wrote on such varied and seemingly disparate topics as metaphysics, ethics, logic, literature, poetry, politics, rhetoric, theater, mathematics, physics, medicine, biology, agriculture, and zoology. He systematized, categorized, and catalogued philosophy, science, and the humanities. He introduced the syllogism, in which a conclusion is drawn from two assumed propositions or premises.[9] In short, our understanding of the world today—our embrace of science, logic, mathematics, literature, political theory, and, of course, patriarchy—can be traced back to Aristotle.

Despite his extraordinary intellect, Aristotle was unable to escape the patriarchal views of his time. The arguments put forth by Socrates and Plato were not sufficient to either shape his views on women or change his deep-seated hostility toward them. A few quotes from his book on political philosophy, *Politics*, make the case. In book I (the equivalent of chapter 1), Aristotle said the following:

The male, unless constituted in some respect contrary to nature, is by nature more expert at leading than the female, and the elder and complete than the younger and incomplete.

The relation of male to female is by nature a relation of superior to inferior and ruler to ruled.

The slave is wholly lacking the deliberative element; the female has it but it lacks authority; the child has it but it is incomplete.[10]

Now, scholars of history and philosophy may argue that we cannot judge Aristotle's views from the perspective of the modern world. According to this argument, the philosopher's demeaning language must be assessed against the backdrop of his time. However, Aristotle's teacher, Plato, and his teacher's teacher, Socrates, espoused positive views of women. Aristotle's views of women reflect his own massive shortcomings rather than anything that is meaningful or intelligible.

If you find it disturbing to read about Aristotle's misguided and cowardly views, keep in mind that today they are obsolete. Take a moment to breathe, and rather than give way to anger, listen to your powerful inner voice that affirms your value and dignity in the world. And remember that understanding the past, however painful, will give you the strength to embrace your femininity and achieve your own boundless potential.

WOMEN IN THE EARLY CHURCH

Christianity emerged from within the Roman Empire, which was a patriarchal society. Jesus both challenged and undermined the social conventions of his time. His was a radical message: He "addressed women as equals, gave honor and recognition to children, championed the poor and the outcast, ate and mingled with people across all class and gender lines, and with bold rhetoric attacked the social bonds that held together the patriarchal family."[11] This is one of the reasons why women gravitated toward Jesus. Women embraced Christ's message as a form of liberation and salvation from the oppressive nature of their marginalized existence.

Women played a pivotal role in the development of the early church, but their contributions have largely been ignored. According to the Book of Acts in the New Testament, women during the time of Christ's ministry included "Mary Magdalene, most likely an upper-class woman of means instead of the prostitute label still wrongly attached to her, but there is also Mary and Martha, the sisters of Lazarus, Mary the mother of Jesus, the Woman at the Well in Samaria, the Woman Taken in Adultery, and many others who are referenced warmly at times in the epistle even when women, in general, are given second-class status."[12]

In addition to these women, who helped frame the foundation of Christianity, there were others who helped spread Christ's message during the religion's first 300 years. There was Perpetua (c. 181 to c. 203 CE), who refused to renounce her Christian faith and was arrested and executed by the Roman emperor Septimus Severus. Her father, a pagan in good standing with the Roman authorities, pleaded with Perpetua to renounce her faith, but she refused. It's interesting to note that, according to I. M. Plant, a lecturer in ancient history at Australia's Macquarie University, scholars believe the account of Perpetua's imprisonment and execution was written by her, which would make it the earliest Christian text written by a woman.

Another powerful woman who helped spread Christianity was Amma Syncletica of Alexandria (c. 270 to c. 350 CE). Born to wealthy parents in Alexandria, Egypt, Syncletica turned down several suitors because of her devotion to Christ. Upon her parents' death, she, along with her younger sister, took to the desert to live in solitude and prayer. She went on to teach others about Christianity. Her story—possibly recorded by Bishop Athanasius of Alexandria—would later inspire European monasticism.[13] These are just two of the women who, tragically or triumphantly, helped spread the message of Christ.

This short period of women leading the church would soon come to an end. Beginning with St. Paul (c. 5 to 67 CE), and continuing with other New Testament writers, women were regarded as inferior to men and their service to the church was eventually banned. St. Paul connected women to Eve and the Fall of Man by implying that if Adam had been left to his own devices, he would have happily remained in the Garden of Eden.[14] With this narrative—which was shaped by ideas from Greek and Roman culture—St. Paul would seal the fate of women for 2,000 years.

Many early church fathers were influenced by the Aristotelian argument that women lacked the capacity for rational thought. This idea was buttressed by a deliberately misinterpreted verse from Genesis 2:18: "The Lord God said, 'It is not good for the man to be alone. I will make a helper suitable for him.'"[15] The word "helper" was often used to underscore women's inferior status. The result was a patriarchal religious system that would assert power and authority over women everywhere. If you actually read the Bible, you will find 21 different references to the word "helper." The word itself comes from the Hebrew word *ezer* (pronounced ay-zer), which means "to help" or "to rescue." In 16 different cases, the word "helper" is used to refer to God as our helper or rescuer. God, of course, is not subordinate to his creation. Similarly, women are not subordinate to men. In fact, one might argue that women were created to be the rescuers of men.

Although it may be difficult for our modern mind to fully comprehend the unimaginable treatment of women throughout history, it is important to understand that the views of Aristotle, as well as the male-dominated early church, framed the narrative of women for over 2,000 years. This definitional framework forced women to exist in a world removed from men. In other words, the public space for women was nonexistent in the sense they had no voice or mechanism by which to challenge the power structure of their time. This is why I argue it is a moral imperative that both men and women understand the historical forces that came before in order to move forward with a spiritual impulse toward social, political, and economic equality.

Some men reading this book might feel that what I've written so far about the role of the church in marginalizing women is unfair and one-sided. I would respond by asking men to consider what the Catholic Church had to say about the treatment of women throughout its long history. On April 2, 2019, Pope Francis made a remarkable statement on the history of male domination and sexual abuse of women. His message was that the church must repair its reputation with young people or risk becoming "a museum."[16] In a 50-page apostolic exhortation, Francis wrote about, among other things, the sex abuse scandal that has plagued the church for decades. He also made this acknowledgment: "A Living Church can look back on history and acknowledge a fair share of male authoritarianism, domination, various forms of enslavement, abuse, and sexist violence. With this outlook, she [the church] can support the call to respect women's rights, and offer convinced support for greater reciprocity between males and females, while not agreeing with everything some feminist groups propose."[17] One significant proposal these feminist groups are referring to is the addition of women to the priesthood. One thing is clear: While acknowledging historical mistakes is a significant step forward, Pope Francis needs to do more to empower women to realize their agency within the church and beyond.

Although Pope Francis appointed women to positions of greater power and authority, the Vatican remains a largely male-dominated institution. Part of the reason is that the ceiling for women has been predefined for centuries. For example, women cannot rise to the level of priest and certainly cannot become bishops. Despite this arbitrary glass ceiling, women are gaining greater power. Consider that as of 2019, "Twenty-four percent of employees at the Holy Sea were women, compared with 17.6 percent in 2010, continuing a gradual increase that began in earnest after the Second Vatican Council."[18] These new positions for women are not simply window dressing; rather they represent substantive change. In 2020, Pope Francis appointed six women to the once all-male Council for the Economy.

The significance of the sweeping change happening in the Catholic Church today can only be understood in the context of the historical trauma that women endured for centuries. I'm not suggesting the emotional and psychological abuse that defined women is the fault of men, but rather the systemic and physical abuse that was justified by the grotesque views of religious men. Such abuse was normalized for centuries, and the remnants of this toxic form of patriarchy are with us today. This is partly why systemic change is difficult. The dense layers of history are unwieldy and difficult to remove. In order to embrace a future where men and women can work together to create a world of equality, transparency, and mutual understanding, we need to confront the ugliness of our past.

THE RULE OF THUMB

The patriarchy of the Middle Ages succeeded in not only marginalizing women but also traumatizing that half of the population with institutionally sanctioned use of violence, leaving millions of women scarred for countless generations. According to Elizabeth Gould Davis, an author and librarian, "men were exhorted from the pulpit to beat their wives."[19] Gould offered an example from a medieval morality tale regarding the appropriate punishment for a nagging wife. Her graphic description of violence and brutality is shocking to the modern mind, but it is worth quoting in full, as it offers a powerful testimonial of what daily life was like for women:

> Here is an example to every good woman that she suffer and endure patiently, nor strive with her husband nor answer him before strangers, as did once a woman who did answer her husband before strangers with short words; and he smote her with his fist down to the earth; and then with his foot he struck her

in her visage and broke her nose, and all her life after she had her nose crooked, which so shent (spoiled) and disfigured her visage after, that she might not for shame show her face, it was so foul blemished. And this she had for her language that she was wont to say to her husband, and therefore the wife ought to suffer, and let the husband have the words, and to be master, for that is her duty.[20]

The religious justification for the abuse of women came from monks who held a unique position within the church. The monastic tradition was designed to leave the materiality of this world behind in order to establish a vertical axis connecting the sacred with the profane. In simple terms, the purpose of monastic life was to leave the world behind and to connect with God through prayer and solitude. During the mid-15th century, traveling friars (monks) moved from village to village preaching the word of God. One important brother, Friar Cherubino of Siena, in north central Italy, formalized the rules of marriage.

Addressed to men, since women were often considered property, the rules served as a guide to help men restrain themselves from too violently beating their wives. According to Terry Davidson in his book *Conjugal Crime*, men were counseled in this way by a monk whose mission was to mediate God's divine grace to others:

> When you see your wife commit an offence, don't rush at her with insults and violent blows. . . . Scold her sharply, bully and terrify her. And if this still doesn't work . . . take up a stick and beat her soundly, for it is better to punish

the body and correct the soul than to damage the soul and spare the body. . . . Then readily beat her not in rage but out of charity and concern for her soul, so that the beating will redound [contribute] to your merit and her good.[21]

Although I acknowledge that we're looking at the 15th century through a 21st-century lens, it is difficult to reconcile such oppression and cruelty toward women on the part of men who looked to God for guidance and wisdom. And if this was the advice from a man of God, then how deeply embedded was the violence toward women? A husband was given permission to bully, terrify, and beat his wife with a stick in order to correct her soul. In fact, the stick that Friar Cherubino mentions would live on in folklore, be codified into British common law, and brought to America as the "rule of thumb." This rule stipulated that a husband could only beat his wife with a "rod not thicker than his thumb."[22] William Blackstone, an 18th-century British jurist, had this to say about the rule of thumb: "For, as [the husband] is to answer for her misbehavior, the law thought it reasonable to intrust [sic] him with this power of chastisement, in the same moderation that a man is allowed to correct his apprentices or children."[23]

It is important to keep in mind that society creates the moral rules and laws—the norms—that we follow. And social norms change over time, that what was accepted in the past may no longer be true today. The rule of thumb may have been widespread in the past, but today it's unacceptable, though you might be surprised at how long it lasted in the United States.

In 1824 the Mississippi Supreme Court, in *Bradley v. State*, agreed with the argument that part of a man's role at home is to be a disciplinarian. It ruled that the law should not interfere with such an important role, ruling, "Let the husband be permitted to exercise the right of moderate chastisement, in cases of great emergency, and use salutary restraints in every case of misbehavior, without being subjected to vexatious prosecutions, resulting in the mutual discredit and shame of all the parties concerned."[24] There is quite a bit to say about this disturbing quote, starting with the concept of "moderate chastisement."

The word "chastisement" refers to an act of scolding or a strong verbal reprimand. This was not the type of chastisement the Mississippi Supreme Court was talking about. Most of the colonies allowed physical chastisement, which was a euphemism for wife beating. An extension of the rule of thumb allowed men to chastise their wives, as long as the physical beating did not inflict permanent damage.

When the Mississippi Supreme Court affirmed that a husband must use "salutary restraints," it meant that he could beat his wife in the spirit of correcting her misbehavior without fear of prosecution. Remember, this was in 19th-century America, an age of scientific and technological progress that celebrated reason and rationality. Much of the superstition from the Middle Ages had been swept under the proverbial carpet in favor of a more enlightened view of the world. What is particularly disturbing is that despite our collective enlightened exterior, a vicious patriarchy would simply not go away.

The glaring cultural contradiction between the ideals of progress and antiquated, cruel patriarchy came at the expense of women who were ridiculed in public spaces and beaten in private homes. Men continued to be looked upon as the masters of their own home, and the courts were complicit in upholding unjust laws. A case in point is an

1864 North Carolina high court ruling in *State v. Jesse Black*. In this case, a man was accused of physically abusing his wife after she directed profanities at him. Ruling on behalf of the husband, the court argued the following:

> A husband is responsible for the acts of his wife and he is required to govern his household, and for that purpose the law permits him to use towards his wife such a degree of force as is necessary to control an unruly temper and make her behave herself; and unless some permanent injury be inflicted, or there be an excess of violence, or such a degree of cruelty as shown that it is inflicted to gratify his own bad passions, the law will not invade the domestic forum, or go behind the curtain.[25]

Beyond the barbarity of this ruling, the language was vague enough to include a multitude of crimes committed by men. A husband could use "a degree of force" necessary to control his wife's temper and correct her behavior, provided he did not inflict permanent injury or derive sadistic pleasure. One need not be a legal scholar to ask some pointed questions. What constitutes a degree of force necessary to control women? Is it a slap across the face? What if a husband picks up a wooden stick (not thicker than his thumb) and breaks his wife's arm? Let's remember that unless there is permanent injury, any form of violence was permitted.

Although by the end of the 19th century the courts affirmed that a husband was no longer legally permitted to beat his wife, thousands of women had no legal recourse against their husbands. It was up to the state to bring charges, which was done only rarely. The chastisement laws gradually became a thing of the past, yet throughout the 20th century husbands continued to beat their wives with impunity, and violence against women continues to this day.

The authorities did intervene in exceptional cases. But generally, the men who assaulted their wives were "often granted formal and informal immunities from prosecution, in order to protect the privacy of the family and to promote 'domestic harmony.'"[26] The idea of domestic harmony deserves some attention. Once the chastisement laws were removed from legal proceedings, the concept of the family would change. The rule of thumb (punishment) was replaced with the rule of love.

Ideally, the rule of love was a virtuous approach to correct the mistakes of past generations. The only problem was that battered women were forced to stay in abusive relationships. Instead of punishing the men who beat their wives, social workers, prosecutors, and judges encouraged couples to reconcile for the sake of domestic harmony. Physical assault was often "viewed as an inappropriate expression of emotions; wives and husbands needed to learn how to rechannel those emotions."[27]

By the late 1970s, feminists began to challenge the idea that a family is a private affair since it offered little or no protection for abused women. Despite changes, violence in the home continued. In fact, according to the US surgeon general, from 1970 to 1990 "[the] battering of women by husbands, ex-husbands or lovers '[is] the single largest cause of injury to women in the United States.'"[28]

A CONTRADICTION OF IDEALS

Underlying the issue of violence to women is the persistence of patriarchy. Given some of the ideals that were expressed with the founding of the United States, it's important to ask how patriarchy gained a foothold in the new world.

For hundreds of years America stood as a symbol of hope for millions who dreamed of a better tomorrow. The phrase "a city upon a hill" has long been invoked to characterize America as a place for everyone who yearned for freedom and opportunity.

The phrase itself originated in the Bible. In Matthew 5:13–14, Christ tells his disciples the following:

> You are the salt of the earth. But if the salt loses its savor, how can it be made salty again? It is no longer good for anything except to be thrown out and trampled by men. You are the light of the world. A city on a hill cannot be hidden.[29]

In 1630 John Winthrop, one of the founders of the Massachusetts Bay Colony, reminded his fellow Puritans that their new community would be a city upon a hill and the world was watching.[30] More recently presidents John F. Kennedy, Ronald Reagan, and Barack Obama also invoked this powerful symbol. But if the United States was founded on noble principles, then why did patriarchy persist?

Part of the answer, of course, is that though America was initially settled by Europeans who came to the new world in search of economic opportunity, freedom of worship, and a new sense of identity, their hopeful narrative didn't apply to women. Freedom and opportunity were elusive for women who toiled in isolation and for whom the new world was defined by strict rules and boundaries.

In early America "women had no defined legal identity as an individual. Women grew to resent being repressed socially and legally with the constant law changes restricting the liberties permitted to their gender."[31] The fact that women lacked legal status meant that their identity was defined by the male-dominated hierarchy of the religious groups who migrated to the new world. Religious control would later translate to social and political dominance, with women excluded from public discourse.

Male religious dominance in the colonies would ripple through history down to our own time. If only men were able to speak in houses of worship, then it was only logical they would also speak in matters of public interest. It was men who received an education, became political leaders, wrote books, conducted commerce, challenged their status as colonies of England, and waged war.

Famously, Abigail Adams, the wife of John Adams, who would become the second president of the United States, advised her husband during the meeting of the Continental Congress that "his fellow legislators should 'Remember the Ladies,' for 'all Men would be tyrants if they could.'"[32] Adams responded to his wife with contempt, comparing his wife's brazen request "to the current prevalence of rebelliousness among dependents like children and servants, which mimicked the larger struggle against Great Britain."[33]

Although women were ignored and silenced in early America, there was one bright spot. The founding documents of this nation—the Declaration of Independence and the Constitution—were flexible enough and sufficiently forward-looking that the seeds of change were imbedded in them. When women and other marginalized groups demanded change, they used the language of these revered documents to argue for equality.

We have seen sweeping change over the past century, and the good news is that more change is coming. As you will see in the following chapters about the waves of the feminist movement, women have broken through numerous patriarchal barriers. Now women are on the verge of dramatic change that was unimaginable only a generation ago. Our vulnerabilities are indeed being transformed to become our greatest strengths.

5

FIRST-WAVE FEMINISM

"Turn your wounds into wisdom."

—OPRAH WINFREY

There are punctuated moments in history where the necessity for change is both revealed and apparent. Change itself, if it is to be meaningful and enduring, must be transformational. In a broad sense, the feminist revolution over the past 230 years occurred in successive waves that brought sweeping change. The philosophical seeds of those changes began with the Enlightenment. Philosophers and other intellectuals such as John Locke, David Hume, Jean-Jacques Rousseau, Immanuel Kant, Adam Smith, Montesquieu, and others celebrated the power of ideas over and above irrational beliefs. While history remembers and celebrates these men for their cultural contribution, there were many women who contributed original ideas that would spread throughout Europe and beyond.

These women include Marie Paulze Lavoisier, who presided over one of Paris's most influential salons, frequented by such notable guests as Benjamin Franklin and James Watt; the astronomer Caroline Herschel, who was the first woman to discover a comet; and Mary Somerville, who contributed to our understanding of magnetism and light.

While these women might not be household names, they contributed to the very blueprint of the modern mind. Perhaps one of the most compelling women to emerge from the Enlightenment period was Mary Wollstonecraft, whom we've mentioned before and who is often considered a seminal figure in the history of feminism. Wollstonecraft was an English writer and philosopher. In addition to her considerable intellectual output, Wollstonecraft was also the mother of Mary Shelley, author of the classic novel *Frankenstein*.

During her brief life (she died at the age of 38), Wollstonecraft wrote novels, treatises, and a historical account of the French Revolution. Her most significant book was *A Vindication of the Rights of Woman*, published in 1792. In this groundbreaking work of feminist philosophy, Wollstonecraft argued that the subordinate position of women was the result of a flawed educational system that deprived women of the same knowledge that men aspired to cultivate.

A CUP OF TEA: HOW THE SUFFRAGE MOVEMENT CHANGED THE WORLD

On July 9, 1848, Jane Hunt, a well-to-do Quaker and reformer invited a few notable women to her home in Waterloo, New York. Hunt and her husband, Richard, were known to support human rights causes, particularly the abolition of slavery. Given their philanthropic work, when Jane learned that the well-known Quaker minister Lucretia Mott of Philadelphia was visiting her sister, Martha Wright, in nearby Auburn, New York, she decided to invite her to tea. Mott accepted the invitation and brought Martha, as well as Mary M'Clintock and Elizabeth Cady Stanton. It would be during this historic gathering of these five pivotal figures that an organized women's movement in the United States started.

During this fateful afternoon, the women discussed the numerous injustices committed against their sex. During this time women couldn't obtain an education or vote, and their economic livelihood was dependent on men. Women lived under an oppressive moral code that expected them to be subservient wives and perfect mothers. But the five women at Hunt's tea party were independent thinkers who rejected the moral paradigm of their time. Lucretia Mott and Elizabeth Cady Stanton had known each other since the 1840 World Anti-Slavery Convention in London.

Following their discussion over tea, the women issued a public call for a women's rights convention in the local newspaper. It would be held in the Wesleyan Chapel at Seneca Falls, New York, on July 19 and 20, 1848, and would serve as a watershed moment in the history of the women's rights movement. It was there that Stanton wrote and delivered one of the most impassioned speeches in the history of the women's movement.

She patterned her Declaration of Sentiments after the Declaration of Independence. Given the profound significance of this document, it is important to quote the opening:

When in the course of human events, it becomes necessary for one portion of the family of man to assume among the people of the earth a position different from that which they have hitherto occupied, but one to which the laws of nature and of nature's God entitle them, a decent respect to the opinions of mankind requires that they should declare the causes that impel them to such a course. We hold these truths to be self-evident; that all men and women are created equal; that they are endowed by their Creator with certain inalienable rights; that among these are life, liberty, and the pursuit of happiness.[1]

It has been estimated that 300 women and men attended the convention, with 68 women and 32 men signing the Declaration of Sentiments.[2] The declaration itself was nothing short of genius, both in style and the logical sequence of arguments. The philosophical framework accepted the truths of the Declaration of Independence and endeavored to apply those same moral principles to women.

Following the Seneca Falls convention, the suffrage movement would continue to struggle and push for women's right to vote. The next several years were not easy, given the tensions within the suffrage movement, particularly when it came to strategic direction and race. The suffragists, led by Susan B. Anthony, Stanton, and Lucy Stone, had lent their support to the abolitionist movement, but after the Civil War they split over the proposed 15th Amendment to the Constitution, which would give the vote to Black men, but not women. Stanton's and Anthony's refusal to support ratification led to a public break with abolitionist Frederick Douglass and alienated many of the Black suffragists.

In 1872, a dozen women, including Anthony, were arrested in Rochester, New York, for illegally voting in the presidential election. Anthony unsuccessfully fought the charges and was levied a fine of $100, which she never paid.

One of the stains on the early suffrage movement was the racism that existed within the White suffrage movement. For example, Black suffragists were barred from attending conventions. In 1896, Black suffragists organized their own national group, which included such towering figures as Harriet Tubman, Frances E. W. Harper, Ida B. Wells-Barnett, and Mary Church Terrell. The group, the National Association of Colored Women Clubs (NACWC), advocated for equal pay, educational opportunities, job training, and access to child care for Black women.

At the turn of the 20th century, suffrage was still out of reach, but progress was being made. By 1913, Alice Paul, who was the vice president of the National Woman's Party, created a militant group that would fight for federal action. She led a march on Washington in which 5,000 to 10,000 women marched on the day of President Woodrow Wilson's inauguration. In 1916, Jeanette Rankin of Montana became the first woman elected to Congress. Two years later President Wilson changed his position and supported the suffrage movement. And in 1919, both the House of Representatives and the Senate finally passed what would become the 19th Amendment, which allowed for the ratification process to begin. That was completed on August 18, 1920, when Tennessee provided the final vote necessary. Women finally had the vote.

Once the 19th Amendment passed, there was a dramatic change in terms of the women in public life. Throughout the 1920s, women embraced their new role in society. Dramatic changes "took place in politics, the home, the workplace, and in education."[3] Of these changes, the most powerful was political change. The idea of men and women existing in separate spheres was set aside, as more women entered public life. By the end of the 1920s, women were represented in local, state, and national politics.

Technology would also change how women lived. Electricity and indoor plumbing revolutionized housework. The introduction of vacuum cleaners, washing machines, irons, and modern kitchen appliances reduced the workload at home, which gave women more time to do other things. Education expanded, giving women access to the same knowledge that men enjoyed. Women became a part of the consumer culture. Advertisers targeted women by appealing to their sense of fashion and style. Even smoking represented a new freedom for women. Nevertheless, despite all this dramatic and concentrated change, the goal of most women was marriage. A job for women was considered a temporary thing until the ultimate goal of marriage was achieved.

There was an exception to this—a woman of singular achievement and historical significance. Frances Perkins ignored all of the social norms of her time by shattering glass ceilings before such a term existed. She rose to the highest levels of government and became a tireless advocate of workers' rights. She led by example, showing women that it was very much possible to not only enter male-dominated professions but also thrive there. Her story serves as inspiration to all women who dare to dream.

On March 7, 1933, newly elected President Franklin Roosevelt convened his first cabinet meeting. All of the cabinet members were male, with an average age of 59, with one glaring exception. Sitting in the room with these accomplished men of power was Frances Perkins, who was appointed by Roosevelt to be the US secretary of labor. At a time when patriarchy governed accepted norms, Perkins forged her own path, and, in doing so, paved the way for other women. Her accomplishments are awe inspiring and breathtaking. She was a sociologist who advocated for workers' rights. She was the first woman appointed to the cabinet. She was also the longest-serving secretary of labor (1933–1945). She was one of the architects of Roosevelt's New Deal programs. Perkins was responsible for implementing the Civilian Conservation Corps, Public Works Administration, National Industrial Recovery Act, and the Social Security Act.

Perkins succeeded in establishing unemployment benefits, pensions for elderly Americans, and welfare for the poorest Americans. She helped craft laws against child labor and established the first minimum wage and overtime laws. She established the 40-hour workweek. After she'd served as labor secretary for 12 years, President Truman asked her to serve on the United States Civil Service Commission. One of the first things she did as a member of this commission was to speak out against the practice of government officials requiring secretaries and stenographers to be physically attractive. After leaving government service at the age of 72, Perkins went on to become a lecturer at New York State School of Industrial and Labor Relations at Cornell University. She continued to teach and lecture until her death at the age of 85. Her name lives on. In 1982, Perkins was inducted into the National Women's Hall of Fame. The US Department of Labor is now called the Frances Perkins Building. And the liturgical calendar of the Episcopal Church has honored her with a feast day on May 13.

To better understand and appreciate Perkins's extraordinary contributions, it's useful to have a frame of reference. Born Fannie Coralie Perkins in 1880, she would come of age during a period of technological and social change. Between 1900 and 1920, the world saw innovations like vacuum cleaners, air-conditioning, radar, radio broadcasting, electric washing machines, Ford's Model T, stenotype machines, and sonar, to name just a few. Culturally, this was the Progressive Era. Women continued to fight for the vote and they turned the traditional label of women as mothers and homemakers on its head. Such women started to identify themselves as "municipal housekeepers," which meant that they would enter the public sphere in order to clean up politics. Under the mantle of motherhood they created a form of maternal activism, which resulted in the creation of the bureaucracy behind New Deal programs. Many of the women who filled these newly created positions considered themselves maternal activists.

Born to well-educated parents in Boston, Perkins attended Mount Holyoke College, where she majored in chemistry and physics. The school offered her the intellectual environment to thrive and opened her eyes to the possibilities of her own contribution to the world. Mount Holyoke was founded by Mary Lyon in 1837, and its mission was that women should "go forward, attempt great things, accomplish great things."[4] One of Perkins's professors, Annah May Soule, would have a profound influence on the young Perkins. Soule, who taught history and political economics, assigned her students to tour factories to witness the horrible working conditions there. This experience of observing how the working class struggled to make ends meet shaped the direction Perkins would take in life. After graduation, her parents expected her to stay at home and teach until a suitor came along. She, of course, had other ideas and instead accepted a teaching position at Ferry Hall, an elite school for girls in Lake Forest, Illinois, near Chicago.

To further assert her independence, Perkins joined the Episcopal Church in 1905. Part of what attracted her to the Episcopal faith was the social gospel movement, which applied Christian ethics to social problems. Perkins would embrace this aspect of Episcopalian belief, particularly when it came to economic inequality, child labor, lack of unionization, poverty, alcoholism, and racial tensions. She had a desire to be a voice for marginalized people everywhere. Of her spiritual awakening she said, "I had to do something about unnecessary hazards to life, unnecessary poverty."[5] In addition to teaching, Perkins volunteered at Chicago Commons and Hull House, two organizations that served the poor and unemployed. This work reaffirmed her vocational choice. The epiphany about her calling in life, coupled with a spiritual drive to serve the underprivileged, would help change the course of American history.

Perkins had a mission to speak on behalf of not only women but also all of humanity. In 1907, at the age of 27, she accepted the position of general secretary of the Philadelphia Research and Protective Association, whose goal was to stop the horrific practice of forcing young immigrant girls, as well as Black women from the South, into prostitution. If all this was not enough to keep her busy, in 1907 she enrolled at the University of Pennsylvania's prestigious Wharton School, where she studied economics. She went on to Columbia University in 1910, graduating with a master's degree in sociology and economics. That same year, she became the executive secretary for the Committee on Safety of the City of New York. Some of her accomplishments at the time included "sanitary regulations for bakeries, fire protection for factories, and legislation to limit the working hours for women and children in factories to 54 hours per week."[6] In 1911 a tragic fire at the Triangle Shirtwaist Factory in New York would bring her to the attention of former president Theodore Roosevelt.

It was the morning of March 25, 1911, when Perkins was having tea with friends in New York City's Washington Square. Suddenly, she and her friends heard the wailing sirens of fire engines. Perkins ran outside to discover that a building was engulfed in flames. Forty-seven factory workers would jump to their deaths; nearly 150 in all would die. The trauma of witnessing such a tragedy would reaffirm Perkins's belief that much more needed to be done to protect workers. She would later describe that day as "the day the New Deal was born."[7]

After that tragic event, Roosevelt recommended Perkins to become the executive secretary of a committee whose broad mandate was to investigate the unsafe conditions of industrial workers, including the prevention of future factory fires. Perkins was responsible for championing the most ambitious and far-reaching change in the history of workplace safety.

A few years later, although the 19th Amendment had not yet been ratified, the State of New York allowed women to vote in the 1918 gubernatorial election. Frances Perkins would help deliver the women's vote for her good friend Al Smith, who, when he took office, appointed her to a vacant seat on the New York State Industrial Commission. It was one in a series of what would become firsts for Perkins: She became the first woman appointed to a position in New York, and, with an annual salary of $8,000, she also became the highest-paid woman to hold a public office in the Unites States.[8] Al Smith would go on to win four terms as governor, and, in his final term, he appointed Perkins as the chairwoman of the commission. She was about to have a date with destiny that would change her life forever.

It was a cold February night in 1933 when Perkins found herself waiting to meet her next employer at his residence on East 65th Street in New York. The man waiting for her was Franklin D. Roosevelt. She had brought with her a few scraps of paper, where she scribbled some notes, and after some good-natured bantering, the conversation turned serious. Perkins had known Roosevelt for more than 20 years. He had succeeded Smith as governor of New York, and Perkins had worked with him when she was in Albany, New York, as part of the industrial commission.

Now Roosevelt had been just elected president and was forming his cabinet. He wanted to appoint her to become his secretary of labor, but she had conditions. The year 1933 was, of course, a challenging time for any administration, particularly an incoming president. The United States—indeed, the world—was in the middle of the Great Depression with no end in sight. The economy was a top priority for Roosevelt, and he needed someone like Perkins, with her extensive experience in labor, to attack the problem of mass unemployment and other economic issues.

As Perkins stood with notes in her hand, Roosevelt motioned her to name her conditions. Think about this: It was unheard of for women during this time to rise to the highest level of government. But here was the newly elected president of the United States trying to convince a woman to accept a position in his cabinet. Perkins went through her list of items, some of which were practical and doable, others radical in their daring: a 40-hour workweek, a minimum wage, worker's compensation, unemployment benefits, a federal law banning child labor, Social Security, health insurance, and so on. There were other items on her list, but she paused to gauge Roosevelt's demeanor. He had a habit of choosing political expediency over radical change. She looked at Roosevelt and said to him, "Nothing like this has ever been done in the United States before. You know that, don't you?"[9] Roosevelt accepted her conditions. He trusted her and gave her the power to carry out her vision.

What Perkins was proposing was revolutionary in the sense that many of her ideas went against the conventional wisdom of the time. Of course, today we take for granted the benefits of Social Security, unemployment insurance, and health insurance, but back in the 1930s, these programs were innovative. Roosevelt was taking a huge gamble not only by nominating Perkins for labor secretary but also for supporting her sweeping proposals.

Perkins was fully aware of the monumental task ahead of her, made particularly more difficult because of her gender. She had spent decades working in a man's world. She had observed the way men think, behave, and act. She kept a journal and called it *Notes on the Male Mind*. Perkins asked Roosevelt if she could have some time to think about it. Later that day, Perkins went to visit her husband in a sanitorium. She had married in 1913, but her husband, Paul Caldwell Wilson, who was an economist, suffered from mental illness and was frequently institutionalized.[10]

She told her husband about Roosevelt's offer. He worried that she may not have time to visit him. Once she assured him she would visit him every weekend, however, he gave his blessing. Nevertheless, the decision was agonizing for her. She cried at night, as she knew the job would change her forever. She was entering uncharted territory, and it was frightening. There would be media scrutiny, harsh criticism, and the inevitable cry of "never put a woman in a man's job." In the end, she accepted the offer and became the first woman to hold a cabinet position. As a cabinet member, Perkins also became the first woman to be in the presidential line of succession.

As soon as Roosevelt was sworn in as the 32nd president of the United States, he had to deal with an economic mess. Half the country's banks had failed, and unemployment was 20 percent, which translated to 15 million Americans out of work. Industrial production had dropped by half. Bread lines and soup kitchens became common. To make matters worse, severe droughts and high winds from Texas to Nebraska forced the mass migration of people from farmland to cities in search of work.[11]

One of the first things Roosevelt did upon taking office was to announce a four-day "bank holiday," which required banks to close, while Congress stabilized the banking system. The Emergency Banking Act allowed the 12 Federal Reserve Banks to issue additional currency so that banks could meet the demand. The situation was so dire that Roosevelt decided to address the nation directly over the radio, in what would be affectionately labeled his "fireside chats." The president understood the gravity of the situation and the challenge of the moment. He knew the free-market system would not fix the economic mess he inherited. His predecessor, Herbert Hoover, believed the economy would rebound after the stock market crash of 1919. Hoover, who was a Republican, believed that the government should not directly intervene in economic affairs, nor was the government responsible for creating jobs or offering economic relief to its citizens.[12] Under Hoover's leadership the economy only got worse.

By the end of the first hundred days of Roosevelt's first administration, Perkins had become a tireless advocate of unprecedented public works programs to bring people back to work. Once Congress passed legislation establishing the Civilian Conservation Corps, Roosevelt asked Perkins to oversee its implementation. Before Roosevelt submitted his national recovery legislation to Congress, Perkins persuaded him to allocate $3.3 billion for public works programs, including the building of schools, roads and highways, housing projects, and postal offices. This program alone employed 1.5–2 million people.[13] In 1934, Roosevelt appointed Perkins to head a committee on economic security. That would be her most enduring accomplishment. Perkins created the blueprint for legislation that would become the Social Security Act. Signed into law by Roosevelt, the Social Security Act was a system that offered pensions for retirees, unemployment compensation, and disability benefits.

In 1938, Perkins helped draft legislation for the Fair Labor Standards Act, which eliminated child labor and established the 40-hour workweek and a minimum wage. Roosevelt died in April 1945, but Perkins had become the longest-serving labor secretary in history and one of only two cabinet positions to serve the entire length of Roosevelt's presidency. A year earlier, an article in *Collier's* magazine described her accomplishments as "not so much the Roosevelt New Deal, as . . . the Perkins New Deal."[14] She had succeeded in accomplishing all the items she had on her list in 1933, with the exception of universal health care. In June 1945, the Labor Department gathered all 1,800 employees in the department's auditorium to honor the woman who had changed the face of America.

While there have been several attempts to acknowledge her, many Americans are not aware of her towering achievements. If you are today working on a 40-hour-a-week cycle and paid overtime for hours in excess of 40 hours, if you are one of the millions who collect Social Security or plan on collecting those benefits, if you are collecting unemployment or disability benefits, then you have Frances Perkins to thank for that.

Fig. 5.1. President Franklin D. Roosevelt signs the Social Security Act on August 14, 1935.

You may notice immediately, in the photo of Roosevelt signing the Social Security Act on August 14, 1935, that in a room full of men, one stoic-looking woman stood behind Roosevelt. Perkins's tireless, almost superhuman effort to not only draft that legislation but also lobby Congress is remarkable. We need to remember that in 1935 Congress had only 8 women serving—1 senator and 7 representatives—out of 535 members. Perkins had to use her considerable skills of persuasion and charisma to enable the Social Security Act to pass. Throughout her professional life, Perkins towered over others to achieve the kind of change that endured. She represents the very best of us and, despite extraordinary obstacles, touched the sky so that we, men and women alike, might emulate her courage, tenacity, and wisdom.

The first wave of feminism is full of women in history who fought for equality and justice. We remember these women, such as Susan B. Anthony or Elizabeth Cady Stanton, as giants who hammered away at the patriarchy that made them feel less than, inferior to, weaker than, and alienated from their identity as multidimensional human beings who could impact the world.

Frances Perkins led by example, showing the rest of the world how hard work, courage, perseverance, dedication, sacrifice, and a determination to fight for the common man and woman could reshape the world. We are all in her debt, not only because she was a woman and a pioneer but also because she helped to lead our nation out of economic collapse. Perkins transcended the patriarchy of her time to become an eternal symbol for men and women working together to elevate humanity. She is an inspiration for all women who ever felt sidelined, marginalized, ignored, condescended to, harassed, objectified, and alienated under a male-dominated system. Frances Perkins was a powerful transitional figure who anticipated second-wave feminism, which is the subject of the next chapter.

6

SECOND-WAVE FEMINISM

"You must be the change you wish to see in the world."

—MAHATMA GANDHI

The advent of World War II would act as one of those watershed moments that would help give rise to second-wave feminism. Prior to the war, women primarily worked in the clerical and services sector. However, that all changed as the war created opportunities in heavy industry and wartime production plants. These changes were symbolized by Rosie the Riveter, who was "a strong and self-assured woman rolling up her denim shirtsleeve to reveal her right bicep as she confidently exclaims 'We Can Do It!' She was one of 19 million women who worked for wages during the war, five million for the first time."[1]

Fig. 6.1. Rosie the Riveter.

The fact that women started to work alongside men gave rise to difficulties, as men felt threatened by women becoming the breadwinners. By the end of the war, millions of women returned to the home, while those who wanted to stay in the workforce had limited opportunities. Employers pushed women out by giving them lower wages for the same work that men performed. Throughout society there was a desire to return to the idea of "separate spheres," where men resumed their masculine defined roles and women once again were kept out of public life.

By the 1960s women were largely educated but confined to the home. Much of the progress of obtaining the vote and working during the interwar years was lost. This would lead to a second wave of feminism, which was inspired in part by the American feminist writer and activist Betty Friedan and her book *The Feminine Mystique*. Published in 1963, the work was the result of a survey that Friedan was asked to conduct of her former Smith College classmates. The survey revealed that many of Friedan's classmates, 15 years after graduating from Smith College, were unhappy with their lives as housewives. Following her survey, Friedan decided to conduct in-depth interviews with suburban housewives. She initially wanted to write a magazine article about her findings, but she was turned down by every reputable magazine editor in the country. Instead, she expanded her article into a book, which became the best-selling nonfiction book of 1964, with over a million copies sold.

Friedan chose the phrase "feminine mystique" to show the irony of women's lives during the 1950s. Women had a socially imposed and self-referencing mystique that glamorized marriage, housework, and raising children as the highest form of feminine fulfillment. Friedan, of course, rejected this fairy tale, partly out of the sheer boredom she experienced being a housewife. After she graduated summa cum laude with a major in psychology from Smith, Friedan went on to do graduate work at Berkeley, studying under the famed psychologist Erik Erikson.[2] In her memoir, Friedan claimed that her boyfriend at the time pressured her to turn down a PhD fellowship and abandon her academic career. She eventually married, had children, and became a housewife. It would be this suffocating domestic life that created her feminist awakening. She rejected the socially prescribed domestic arrangement that women belong in the home.

Women in the 1960s were defined almost exclusively in relation to men. Their sense of identity and value in the world was understood only in reference to masculine superiority. In areas from education to employment, women were either denied entry or paid a fraction of what their male counterparts earned. The honor of attending an Ivy League college belonged almost exclusively to men. With few exceptions, women couldn't attend Ivy League colleges until 1969; they attended associated women's schools. "Yale and Princeton didn't accept female students until 1969. Harvard didn't admit women until 1977 (when it merged with the all-female Radcliffe College). . . . Brown (which merged with women's college Pembroke), Dartmouth and Columbia did not offer admission to women until 1971, 1972, and 1981, respectively."[3]

The 1963 Kennedy Commission on the Status of Women produced a report that revealed that in the workplace women earned 59 cents for every dollar that men earned. Although an amendment to the 1964 Civil Rights Act made it illegal to discriminate on the basis of gender, women continued to experience rampant discrimination in the workplace.[4]

The media, however, began to play a role in confronting these issues. During the 1960s, television would both project and amplify second-wave feminism to the rest of America. Prior to the more recent digital revolution, in which social media spreads ideas, information, and social awareness instantly, television was the most powerful medium to connect us. In the 1960s and '70s, the three major networks—CBS, NBC, and ABC—dominated the airwaves. These three networks offered Americans a powerful shared experience of the racial and gender injustice that unfolded all around them. The "network news coverage of feminism was a surprising mix of positive and negative reporting. Most reports, for instance, treated abortion rights and the ERA (Equal Rights Amendment) as reasonable, even commonsensical, demands. The National Organization for Women's focus on public gender discrimination generally resonated with journalists who understood demands for equality because of their experience with civil rights protest."[5] Television coverage accelerated the process of change by raising the consciousness and awareness of women's marginalized status.

RUTH BADER GINSBURG: A TOWERING GIANT

When Sir Isaac Newton was asked how he was able to accomplish so much in mathematics and physics, he responded with this timeless quote: "If I have seen further, it is only because I was standing on the shoulders of giants."[6] Giants, of course, come in all shapes and sizes, which is why you should never be fooled by Ruth Bader Ginsburg's diminutive stature. Ginsburg was a towering legal and intellectual force who tirelessly fought for women's rights. Her personal battles alone are sufficient to secure her place in history as a powerful force for women. She fought sexism, both at the micro and macro level, to achieve the improbable. She was one of only nine female students at Harvard Law School in 1957, enduring indignities it's hard to imagine today. Consider this: "The women were refused access to the library (the same fate that befell Virginia Woolf at Cambridge decades earlier); they were not called upon in class; and were asked by the dean to explain, one by one, why they had enrolled at the university and taken a place from a man."[7] When her husband, who was a lawyer himself, took a job in New York, Ginsburg transferred to Columbia Law School and graduated as valedictorian in 1959.

Intellectual brilliance alone was, of course, no guarantee of breaking into the male-dominated legal profession of the 1960s. Ginsburg, despite her credentials, was initially rejected in her efforts to find work as a law clerk. In 1960, Harvard Law School professor, and later dean, Albert Sachs recommended Ginsburg, his most gifted student, to Supreme Court justice Felix Frankfurter. After admitting that Ginsburg's record was impressive, Frankfurter replied to Sachs by telling him "he just wasn't ready to hire a woman and so couldn't offer a job."[8] Ginsburg would persevere and would go on to become a law clerk for Judge Edmund L. Palmieri of the US District Court for the Southern District of New York, a position she held for two years.

In 1963, Ginsburg went on to become a professor at Rutgers Law School. This was, of course, a historic breakthrough. At the time there were fewer than 20 female law professors in the United States.[9] But just as she was making giant leaps forward, society found a way to remind her that she was not the equal of men. When Ginsburg was hired as professor, she was informed she would be paid less than her male colleagues. The reason the university gave is beyond belief today: The university pointed to the fact that her husband was a well-paid lawyer. Again, this did not deter Ginsburg's drive to rise to the top. From 1972 to 1980, she taught at Columbia Law School, where she would go on to become the first tenured woman and where she co-authored the first law school casebook on sex discrimination.

Ginsburg was making a name for herself by using the judicial system to bring about meaningful and enduring change for women. During the early 1970s, she co-founded the *Women's Rights Law Reporter*, which was the first law journal to focus on women's rights. She also co-founded the Women's Rights Project at the American

Civil Liberties Union (ACLU) in 1972 and within a year became the general counsel of the group. Ginsburg went on to spend a year as a fellow of the Center for Advanced Study in the Behavioral Sciences at Stanford University from 1977 to 1978. Her reputation for her knowledge of the law and eloquence of speech was spreading far and wide.

It's useful to look at the political and judicial environment of those times. In 1971, President Richard Nixon was preparing to make two appointments to the Supreme Court. Although Nixon had once told an aide, "Thank God we don't have any [women] in the Cabinet,"[10] political necessity meant he still was considering naming a woman to the nation's highest court. Nixon was hoping to gain a few crucial women's votes, but nonetheless then chief justice Warren Burger informed Nixon that if he nominated a woman, he would resign. In the end, Nixon nominated, and the Senate confirmed, Lewis Powell and William Rehnquist.[11]

It was this cultural context that Ruth Bader Ginsburg had to navigate. She lived in a world of two unequal spheres—a world where men were naturally accepted in public life and women were looked upon as an irrelevant afterthought. Believing that gender discrimination of any kind was unconstitutional, Ginsburg took on a case that defended men's rights.

In 1972, Ginsburg argued before the Tenth Circuit Court, in the case of *Mortiz v. Commissioner*, that section 214 of the IRS code, which only allowed women to take caregiver deductions, was unconstitutional. Charles Mortiz of Denver needed someone to help him take care of his elderly mother. He elected to take the deduction under section 214. The IRS ruled that the deduction did not apply to Mr. Moritz because he was not a woman and not married. Ginsburg argued that it was not for the government to decide that only women could serve as caregivers for members of their family. The court agreed and ruled that section 214 of the IRS code was "'an invidious discrimination and invalid under due process.'"[12] This was an example of Ginsburg's strategy to choose cases that methodically chipped away at the gender-based discrimination that characterized the patriarchy of her time.

By 1980 Ginsburg was nominated, and confirmed, to a seat on the DC Circuit appeals court, sharing that bench with conservative judges Robert H. Bork and Antonin Scalia. In 1993, President Clinton nominated Ginsburg to the US Supreme Court. Once confirmed, she became the second female justice and the first Jewish female justice.

After she joined the high court, she volunteered to write the opinion for *Reed v. Reed*, which led the US Supreme Court to expand the Equal Protection Clause of the 14th Amendment to women and prohibit discrimination based on sex. The significance of this case was nothing short of historic for women's rights since it provided a mechanism by which women could achieve legal equality with men.

In *Reed v. Reed*, an Idaho couple, Sally and Cecil Reed—who were married but separated—couldn't agree on who would become the designated administrator of their deceased son's estate. The probate court in Idaho appointed Cecil administrator under an 1864 law that declared that "if more than one person claimed to be equally entitled to be trustee, 'males must be preferred to females.'"[13] Agreeing with Ginsburg, the Supreme Court justices unanimously ruled that the Idaho law favoring men was arbitrary and unconstitutional.

In 1996, Justice Ginsburg wrote the majority opinion in *United States v. Virginia*. The United States challenged the admission policies of the Virginia Military Institute, which barred women. In the majority opinion Ginsburg wrote, "Neither federal nor state government acts compatibly with equal protection when a law or official policy denies women, simply because they are women, full citizenship stature—equal opportunity to aspire, achieve, participate in and contribute to society based on their individual talents and capacities."[14]

In the 2007 *Ledbetter v. Goodyear Tire & Rubber Co.* case, Ginsburg not only wrote the minority dissent but she read her dissent from the bench, which gave it extra force. The case involved employees who were suing their employers over allegations of wage discrimination. In her dissent, Ginsburg said, "In our view, the court does not comprehend, or is indifferent to, the insidious way in which women can be victims of pay discrimination."[15]

Ruth Bader Ginsburg was one of those rare, once-in-a-generation figures who challenged the status quo to address the systemic injustice of women. She used the law as an instrument to address the cruelties of patriarchy across every level of society. Her own personal struggles would serve as a road map to other women. Whenever a door was closed to her, she found a way to open it. If Betty Friedan was the cultural architect of second-wave feminism, then Ruth Bader Ginsburg was its legal architect, who opened countless doors for future generations of women. She stands today as an inspiration for women everywhere. She reminds us that women can conquer any force that denies them agency in the world.

Second-wave feminism did not occur in a vacuum; rather it was part of the broad cultural movements of the 1960s, which included the civil rights movement and the domestic upheaval around the Vietnam War. Today, the word "intersectionality" has gained currency in relation to the Black Lives Matter movement and racial unrest. The term was first introduced by Kimberle Williams Crenshaw, a lawyer, civil rights advocate, and professor at Columbia Law School and UCLA School of Law. Intersectionality simply means that our sense of identity—based on our gender, race, class, and so on—is the result of intersecting forces that contribute to privilege and different forms of discrimination. For example, at the time of the rise of second-wave feminism, it wasn't only feminists who demanded change in terms of social inclusion and acceptance. African Americans were also advocating for their rights.

By the 1990s, feminism entered a third wave where it addressed the ugly side of patriarchy. We'll examine those developments in chapter 7.

7

THIRD-WAVE FEMINISM

"Go inside the house, and attend to your work, the loom and the
distaff, and bid your handmaidens attend to their work
also. Talking is men's business, all men's business."

—THE ODYSSEY *BY HOMER*

While there is disagreement as to when third-wave feminism began, it
is generally accepted that Anita Hill's congressional testimony in 1991
was the defining event. A generation before the #MeToo movement,
Anita Hill's testimony during the Clarence Thomas Senate Judiciary
Committee hearing "sparked an avalanche of sexual harassment com-
plaints, in much the same way . . . [as the] Harvey Weinstein accusations
were followed by a litany of sexual misconduct accusations against other
powerful men."[1] The following year, 1992, was called "the year of the
woman," as 24 women were elected to the House of Representatives and
three more women won Senate seats.

It was also in 1992 that feminist writer and activist Rebecca Walker coined the term "third wave." In an article for *Ms.* magazine, Walker wrote what might be described as a feminist manifesto: "To be a feminist is to integrate an ideology of equality and female empowerment into the very fiber of my life. It is to search for personal clarity in the midst of systemic destruction, to join in sisterhood with women when often we are divided, to understand power structures with the intention of challenging it."[2] It would be this integration of empowerment into "the very fabric" of women's lives that would come to define the latest iteration of feminism.

On July 1, 1991, President George H. W. Bush nominated Clarence Thomas for the Supreme Court of the United States. He was confirmed by the Senate to succeed Thurgood Marshall and become the second African American to serve on the high court. The confirmation hearings, however, were bitterly contested as a result of a sexual harassment allegation made by Anita Hill. Hill's testimony marked the first time that a woman publicly shared her story of workplace harassment on the national stage, and Americans were riveted by the spectacle of lurid, sexually charged questions posed to her by an all-White, all-male Senate Judiciary Committee.

Marcia Greenberger, founder and co-president of the National Women's Law Center, has reflected upon the significance of the hearing: "I think women saw play out, in the most human terms, Anita Hill—credible, and very much reflecting the experiences of so many other women—being demeaned, being dismissed and being mistreated by an array of male senators."[3] It was this sense of outrage at being demeaned, mistreated, harassed, assaulted, ignored, belittled, objectified, and dismissed that defined feminism's third wave.

One would imagine that following the Anita Hill testimony, and subsequent demonstrations, systemic change would take place. Unfortunately, changing a patriarchal system that is thousands of years old is a maddeningly slow process. In the late 1990s, another sexual misconduct story exploded on the national scene. On August 17, 1998, President Bill Clinton, after months of denial, admitted on national television to having had an inappropriate relationship with a 21-year-old White House intern. Clinton's affair with Monica Lewinsky, in which every salacious detail was revealed to the public, exposed the dark side of patriarchy. Although the affair was "consensual," the power imbalance between a 21-year-old intern and a 49-year-old president of the most powerful nation on earth served as a stark reminder of how women were, and continue to be, taken advantage of by men in positions of authority and influence.

It is important to remember that a power imbalance between men and women exists in every industry—from politics to Hollywood, from white-collar to blue-collar jobs, and everything in between. It would only be a matter of time before other nationally recognized men were exposed as sexual predators.

One of the first scandals to hit Hollywood was centered on Bill Cosby, who was found guilty of three counts of aggravated indecent assault and sentenced to three to ten years in state prison for allegations of rape that went back several decades. Bill Cosby had been the star of one of the most popular television shows in history, *The Cosby Show*, which spent five consecutive seasons as the number one rated show on television during the 1980s.[4] On-screen, Cosby was Dr. Heathcliff Huxtable, a loving husband and father who was dedicated to his family and well respected in his community. Off-screen, too,

Cosby "was a moral authority known for scolding some of his fellow black fathers. He was an Emmy and Mark Twain Prize Winner, and the face of Jell-O Pudding, Coca-Cola and U-Mass (The University of Massachusetts). In short, he was 'America's Dad.'"[5] Nicole Weisensee Egan, an investigative journalist, wrote that "many Americans were slow to accept that, quote, 'the man who left an entire generation wishing he was their father was also a monster.'"[6]

Cosby had it all: money, power, fame, and the narcissistic belief that he could have any woman he wanted. When news first broke in January 2005 that he had drugged and raped Andrea Constand, Cosby was "in the midst of a national tour in which he lectured African American parents on personal responsibility. The *Washington Monthly* had just put him on a list of presidential contenders for 2008."[7] Although other allegations of sexual assault poured in, the story did not get much attention outside of Cosby's hometown of Philadelphia. Eventually Constand filed a civil suit in March 2005, and Cosby settled the case and paid Constand $3.8 million. But everything changed for Cosby when a comedian's comments went viral.

In 2014, Hannibal Buress did a stand-up comedy routine in Philadelphia in which he attacked Cosby's self-righteous admonition to African Americans to pull themselves up. "He gets on TV, 'Pull your pants up black people, I was on TV in the '80s! I can talk down to you because I had a successful sitcom!' Yeah, but you rape women, Bill Cosby, so turn the crazy down a couple notches."[8] Buress went on to ask the audience to Google "Bill Cosby Rape," to learn of the truth behind this so-called model of virtue. After Burress's comments went viral, dozens of women came forward with their own horror stories of being raped by Cosby. In total, more than 60 women accused

Cosby of sexual assault spanning decades. His downfall would serve as a watershed moment in third-wave feminism, though it recently had a disturbing reversal: In June 2021, Cosby's conviction was overturned on a technicality and he was released from prison.

Cosby's case, of course, was not an isolated instance. In 2016, the Fox News journalist and co-anchor of the morning show *Fox & Friends*, Gretchen Carlson, brought a sexual harassment lawsuit against Fox News chairman and CEO Roger Ailes. This set off a wave of sexual harassment claims against Ailes. Megyn Kelly, who was a rising star at the network, was among the more than 20 women who reported being harassed by Ailes. Ailes was forced to resign in July 2016 and died the following year. What Carlson, Kelly, and other women at Fox News exposed was not simply an isolated case of male power and privilege; rather they revealed a toxic culture of "misogyny and one of corruption and surveillance, smear campaigns and hush money, with implications reaching far wider than one disturbed man at the top."[9] Many women endured working in this patriarchal, male-dominated media culture until some had the courage to say enough is enough.

Sexual harassment in the workplace transcends political ideology, right-left politics, religious affiliation, class, race, and ethnicity. On November 29, 2017, NBC announced the termination of its television anchor and co-host of *The Today Show*, Matt Lauer. For more than 20 years, Lauer had been

The marquee draw for a franchise that earned the network hundreds of millions per year. He was the face of the Olympics and the Macy's Thanksgiving Day Parade, "the hunk next door" with a reported salary of $20 million a year, an apartment on the upper East Side, three properties on Long Island (a $36.5 million compound in North Haven, a house in Sag Harbor, and a forty-acre horse farm in Water Mill)—not to mention access to chartered helicopters to whisk him away from his various homes to 30 Rock [30 Rockefeller Plaza, home to NBC's New York studios] and back.[10]

When the news broke that Lauer had an inappropriate sexual relationship with a colleague, many of the executives at NBC said they were shocked at the news of Lauer's behavior. And yet, according to Ann Curry, who was Lauer's former *Today* co-anchor, NBC fostered a "pervasive climate of 'verbal sexual harassment' against women during her 15 years at the Peacock network."[11]

Unfortunately, the toxic work environment that was beginning to be revealed in television news pales in comparison to that of the film industry. In October 2017, *The New York Times* and *The New Yorker* published bombshell reports accusing Hollywood producer Harvey Weinstein of rape, sexual assault, and sexual abuse over the course of 30 years. On February 24, 2020, the disgraced movie mogul was convicted on two counts of criminal sexual assault in the first degree and rape in the third degree. His 23-year prison sentence caps his "precipitous fall from the heights of Hollywood, where, for decades, he brandished his power and influence like a blunt instrument—and allegedly sexually assaulted dozens of young women, intimidating them and others into silence."[12] Weinstein's case exposed to the world how male power and privilege reduced women to disposable objects of sexual harassment and assault.

Before his spectacular fall from grace, Harvey Weinstein had established himself as "the kingmaker of Hollywood."[13] After amassing a small fortune from producing rock concerts in Buffalo, New York, Harvey and his brother, Bob, founded an independent film distribution company, Miramax. Throughout the '80s and '90s, Harvey Weinstein was behind some of the most critically acclaimed movies of that time, including *Pulp Fiction*, *The English Patient*, *Forrest Gump*, and *Good Will Hunting*, among others. He was considered "a brilliant movie mogul, and this was evidenced by the many accolades, key relationships, and 81 different Academy Award wins."[14] As he rose to prominence in an industry where sexual harassment was rampant, Weinstein had the power to make or break the careers of both men and women. Rumors of sexual harassment and sexual assault circulated in Hollywood for decades, but either people were too afraid to speak or if they did speak, no one heard them. Weinstein was a sexual predator who was enabled, insulated, and protected by power, male privilege, and a culture that found it easier to look the other way than to confront such shocking behavior.

Shortly after the allegations of sexual assault were made against Weinstein, the #MeToo movement started trending on Twitter in October 2017. Social media gave women a platform to say in one collective voice that they too had been sexually violated, harassed, or assaulted. Women's voices were no longer going to be suspect or buried by a society that gave men the benefit of the doubt. Within a year, as a result of the Weinstein allegations and the #MeToo movement, "at least 200 prominent men have lost their jobs after public allegations of sexual harassment."[15] Some of the men who had a dramatic public downfall include actor Kevin Spacey, comedian Louis C. K.,

US senator Al Franken, television host Charlie Rose, director and producer Bryan Singer, president and CEO of CBS Corporation Leslie
Moonves, US representative John Conyers Jr., actor Jeffrey Tambor,
co-founder of Def Jam Recordings Russell Simmons, playwright Israel
Horovitz, and dozens of others.[16] Nearly half of the jobs that were lost
by men were filled by women.

Patriarchy, of course, exists in every imaginable field of human
activity. One field in particular, the financial industry, continues to
be dominated by men. Consider that women accounted for 23.3 percent of certified financial planners (CFPs) in 2020, according to the
Certified Financial Planner Board.[17] To illustrate how old and tired
social constructs continue to fester in this male-dominated profession,
let's look at one of the most successful people in the industry. Ken
Fisher is an investment analyst and founder of Fisher Investments. He
is the author of 11 books, and his *Forbes* column, Portfolio Strategy,
ran from 1984 to 2017, making it the longest continuously running
column in the magazine's history. Fisher today has $100 billion under
management, and *Forbes* has him listed as one of the 400 richest
Americans. By all accounts, Fisher achieved extraordinary success. He
started his firm in 1979 with $250 and became one of the largest inde-
pendent money managers in the world. In 2011, he was considered to
be one of the top 25 influential figures in the financial world. The only
problem with this narrative is that the success of Fisher Investments
came at the expense of women.

On October 8, 2019, Fisher spoke at the Tiburon CEO Summit.
This summit brings together senior executives from across different
sectors of the financial world to discuss the future of banking, brokerage, and investment management businesses. CNBC obtained audio

recordings of Fisher's statements, as well as statements he made at a previous conference. In the audio recording, Fisher compares winning new clients to picking up women at a bar. He says, "It's like going up to a girl in a bar . . . going up to a woman in a bar and saying, hey I want to talk about what's in your pants."[18] Shortly after his remarks were posted online, Fisher issued a statement that said, "While I said words he cited I don't think he heard me correctly and clearly misconstrued my meaning and certainly my intended meaning."[19] When his comments reverberated across the industry, Fisher issued an apology, stating, "Some of the words and phrases I used during a recent conference to make certain points were clearly wrong and I shouldn't have made them. I realize this kind of language has no place in our company or industry. I sincerely apologize."[20] His apology, of course, failed to contain the firestorm that was coming.

The short-term fallout "cost Fisher Investments more than $3 billion in divestitures from institutional investors in less than three weeks."[21] Tiburon Strategic Advisors managing partner Charles "Chip" Roame said that "the comments lacked dignity and respect that should be expected by any Tiburon CEO Summit speaker. I further barred the speaker [Ken Fisher] from ever attending again."[22] Sonya Dreizler, a financial planner and founder of Solutions with Sonya in San Francisco, offered, "I've never seen a reaction like this before or seen it get national attention."[23] One might think Ken Fisher's attitude toward women is an isolated event, but this is the persistent reality that women face in the industry. Sonya Dreizler's reaction went beyond a simple condemnation. In fact, "sexual harassment, discrimination and racial bias are pervasive enough in the financial advice industry that Dreizler has rounded up dozens of anecdotes from women in the profession and shared them in her blog titled 'Do Better.'"[24] One positive that came out of Fisher's offensive comments is that a national spotlight was focused on the financial industry.

With every wave of feminism, women have inched closer to becoming fully realized, rational agents in the world. Women today are active participants in shaping and directing their own destiny. Young girls today are growing up in a world where they can dream and aspire to become anything they want to be, free from arbitrary gender bias and limitations. The final bricks of patriarchy are crumbling under the weight of their own self-inflated value in the world.

Now let's look ahead. What we need today is not another wave but a fundamental change in the power dynamics between men and women.

The economic and financial power men have wielded over women has long been the force behind patriarchy. It is this financial force, which has been generationally transmitted, that has enabled men to exert their power over women. In order for patriarchy to completely disappear, women need to be powerful agents of their own financial destiny. Gone will be the days when women needed men for financial security and stability. Women need to conquer this last bastion of male dominance. As I've stated in *Redefining Financial Literacy*, knowledge is power. In effect, what we need today is a financial revolution that will empower women to not only improve their financial literacy but also become autonomous financial agents. The good news is that this revolution is just beginning, and women everywhere will soon benefit from equal pay, financial awareness, generational wealth, retirement planning, and the freedom that comes from being financially independent of men.

8

THE FOURTH WAVE

"Being financially literate is a powerful thing, especially for women."

—OTEGHA UWAGBA

As I outlined in the introduction, though men still control the majority of household wealth in this country, women are making gains in higher education, in earning advanced business degrees, in holding corporate positions, and in becoming successful leaders. Yet there is much more to be done.

WOMEN, MONEY, AND POWER

Let's talk about women, money, and power. According to Allianz Life Insurance Company of North America, one of the largest insurance companies in the world, women today, as compared to past generations, "[are] more educated, earn a significantly higher income, and assume a more powerful role in the workplace."[1] I would also add that women today have more political power than ever before. If this is the case, then the question becomes, why is money important? The simple answer is that money is power. Despite the extraordinary advancements women have made over the past century, many women continue to be dependent on men for their financial security. Money gives all of us, men and women, the power to control the narrative of our personal lives. Money is the medium that facilitates our self-determination in the world. Without money, we become beholden to others, and women, in particular, become beholden to men.

One of the reasons that women have historically lacked agency in the world has been the lack of money. It is not that women did not have money; rather they lacked the knowledge to control and expand wealth. In other words, the lack of financial literacy has been at the heart of women's disenfranchisement. There is a popular word used today to describe the financial disparity between men and women—engagement. Historically men have engaged with money or, if you like, been exposed to money at a much earlier age than women. Men have always internalized their economic role from within a patriarchal framework. In other words, they've accepted the tacit social contract that men are the breadwinners and women are the homemakers. Over time, this created an engagement gap between men and women.

This simply means that "women don't engage with their money as much as men and are less confident managing their money than men. They also start managing their money later."[2] The result translates to a lack of substantive power. Power is important here because it allows people to shape the direction of their lives. It is precisely because of the engagement gap that I'm claiming a fundamental financial shift is needed to achieve full gender equality. And it is why Allianz argues that "money and investing is in many ways the last—and perhaps the most important—frontier in gender equality."[3] The fourth, and perhaps final, wave of feminism must include money and the requisite knowledge needed to increase it as the central theme of full equality.

The power of financial equality can offer women certain psychological benefits, which include the following:

- Financial freedom: This freedom translates to a debt-free future, retirement planning, and the capacity to live comfortably. In other words, the materiality of your life will be dramatically improved by simply having financial freedom.

- Less anxiety: While it is true that money can't buy happiness, it is the case that money can offer you a sense of control, which reduces the stress of everyday life.

- Room to dream: You cannot dream of infinite possibilities for yourself and your loved ones when you feel that you exist under a seemingly immovable burden of debt.

- Increased fulfillment: Having the knowledge to manage money gives you the confidence to look for fulfillment by taking risks. Having money also gives you the freedom to make choices about how you want to spend your time.

- A reinforced sense of resilience: Having money empowers you by giving you the resilience to confront sudden hardships, such as divorce, the death of a loved one, or unexpected disability. For example, how many of you reading this book were prepared for the COVID-19 pandemic?

- Higher self-esteem: Having money, and the knowledge to manage it, gives you a sense of self-accomplishment, which in turn gives you a powerful sense of autonomy and the freedom to direct your own life.[4]

One of the disturbing ironies of the past half century is that despite women's participation in the labor force, there has been a lag in financial awareness. Here is an interesting statistic that many women reading this book will appreciate. According to TD Ameritrade, "about two-thirds of men say they make their household's investment decisions . . . and almost 6 in 10 women said they wished they had more confidence in their financial decision making."[5] We already know about the primary wage gap between men and women, where women consistently, and across professions, make less than men. What is less known is the secondary wage gap, which has to do with the difference in men's and women's financial literacy.

Both the primary and secondary wage gaps for women have a cumulative effect. Catherine Azeles, CFP and investment consultant at Conrad Siegel, points out that there is actually a compound effect over a lifetime. Men may rationalize the primary wage gap as "just a little bit of money now, but that thinking fails to take into account the impact that the pay gap will have over a lifetime."[6] To exacerbate matters, the secondary pay gap (the financial literacy gap) magnifies the retirement discrepancy between men and women.

According to the National Institute for Retirement Security (NIRS), women continue to be at a disadvantage in terms of retirement savings. Some of the more compelling findings of a recent NIRS study state this:

- Women earn roughly $0.80 on the dollar throughout their careers compared to men, reducing the amount women can save for retirement.
- Women live longer than men, which means they have to stretch less in retirement savings over longer periods and are more likely to end up widowed.
- Women are more likely to leave the workforce or take part-time jobs to accommodate caregiving responsibilities, resulting in lower Social Security payments and lower total retirement income.
- Years spent out of the workforce for caregiving responsibilities—for children, spouses, and aging parents—significantly impact women's total retirement savings and income.
- Female caregivers younger than 50 have 30 percent less retirement wealth than non-caregivers (compared to 14 percent less for men). Female caregivers 50 or older have 58 percent less retirement wealth than non-caregivers (compared to 48 percent less for men).
- Women 80 and older are most likely to experience retirement income challenges due to the prevalence of widowhood and higher health-care costs.
- Divorce and timing of divorce can have an outsized impact on women's overall retirement assets.[7]

As you can see, the lack of financial literacy for women is costly, particularly when it comes to retirement. Women "have about $123,000 less in retirement savings on average than men, and are nearly twice as likely to not have any retirement savings at all."[8] In terms of having a backup or emergency fund, men have nearly double the amount, $9,820 versus $5,493 for women. This kind of financial discrepancy is not going unnoticed by women. According to data from Laurel Road (a national online lending company) and Wakefield Research, 85 percent of women believe that personal finance education should be a graduation requirement in high school.[9] Given the critical importance of financial literacy, particularly when women are on the verge of a financial revolution, we need a fundamental change in our educational approach. We need to reconcile the disconnect between the female acquisition of wealth and the knowledge necessary to expand such wealth.

Future generations of women are expected to inherit 70 percent of the wealth in America. This does not include the increasing amount of money women earn on their own. In addition, "women already own more than half of the investible assets in the U.S., and by 2030 it's estimated that women will possess about two-thirds of the nation's wealth."[10]

As recently as 2016, a report by Bank of America showed that 16 percent of millennials aged 18–26 were optimistic about their financial future. Yet, during the same year, an article in *Fortune* offered the disturbing statistic that two out of three Americans can't pass a basic financial literacy test. Change is slow and uneven. In 2018, only 17 states required high school students to take a course in personal finance.[11] However, by 2020, 25 states required high school students to take an economics course to graduate.[12]

I've said it before, and I'll say it again: What we need in this country is a financial revolution for women, a revolution that affirms our dignity by empowering us to become financially savvy. We cannot reduce financial literacy to a perfunctory high school course in finance or economics. I love that word, "perfunctory," which simply means to go through the motion of doing anything in this world.

Let me ask this: When you were going through your K–12 education, how many years did you take an English course? How many years did you take a history course? How many years did you take a mathematics course? The answer is undoubtedly the same across the board; you studied these subjects all the way through your senior year of high school.

In civil society, studying English, mathematics, and history are fundamental to our understanding and awareness of the world. Courses in finance and economics need to be elevated to the same status. Students, particularly young girls, need to be exposed to financial concepts at an early stage. Ideas about money, savings, and investments need to be integrated across the curriculum. The financial literacy revolution must include the following:

- Financial literacy courses need to match the status of English, mathematics, and history.
- Financial concepts need to be taught at every stage of academic development, from kindergarten to the 12th grade.
- Financial literacy needs to be integrated across the curriculum so that students can be exposed to financial and economic concepts while studying English, history, and, of course, mathematics.
- All high schools across the country need to make economics/finance a requirement for graduation.

- All colleges need to add economics and finance as a graduation requirement regardless of major.
- Technology needs to be integrated into school curriculums so that students can apply what they learn to the real world.

If we as a society commit to these big-picture changes, women will begin to take charge of their economic power and direct their own financial future. For too long women had to depend upon men for their own financial well-being. According to Suze Orman, women who are happily married, or in a committed relationship, cannot allow love to cloud their judgment by surrendering major financial decisions to the men in their lives. Love, for Orman, "does not mean saying you trust someone to do what is smart and right. Love does not mean you have the luxury of letting someone else handle the stuff you find boring and confusing."[13] Orman's point, which is powerful and compelling, is that women need to begin relying upon themselves for their own financial future. The more women understand the financial world, the more they will begin to take charge of their future.

Beyond education, there are other big-picture changes that are absolutely necessary. Politically, we need more women in Congress to address such topics as the gender pay gap, corporate hiring practices, sexual harassment, and other issues relevant to women. Consider that as of 2021, there are only 119 women from 36 states serving in Congress. In other words, of the 535 members of Congress, only 26.7 percent are women.[14] What these disturbing numbers should tell you is that unless more women are represented, the political and economic narrative of women will continue to be controlled by men. As you continue to read, you will realize that the fourth wave of feminism is critically important to the economic and financial well-being of women.

With each successive wave of feminist change, women found themselves closer to realizing their full potential. The first wave gave us a public voice with the vote. The second wave shattered the illusion that women were happy and fulfilled by domestic work. The third wave exposed the ugly side of patriarchy as women brought global attention to the toxic work environments created by certain men in power. The fourth wave, which I'm calling the financial revolution, will empower women to realize their financial destiny.

Financial literacy will help women demand wage equity, plan and invest for their retirement, and no longer depend on men for their financial well-being. The financial revolution that I'm calling for is critical for women to stand on their own two feet. Financial knowledge will give women the power to overcome any and all obstacles that stand in their way. Our vulnerabilities will become our greatest ally to help us embrace a future with limitless possibilities.

In addition to the six steps outlined above, which will help women achieve a high level of financial literacy, there are also actionable steps women can take now to set themselves on a path of financial freedom.

- Set goals and stick to them. Actually, setting goals is easy. It is sticking to our goals that proves to be the difficult part. Setting short-term and long-term goals helps you to focus on clearly defined targets. In addition, you need to create an action plan that will help you achieve your goals. An example of a short-term goal might be to create an emergency fund.

- Establish a budget. Today, there are numerous budgeting apps available on your smartphone. These apps will help you create a clear budget that easily tracks your expenses. People are often amazed by how much money they overspend on products and services they do not need. For example, you might be surprised how much money you spend on lattes and cappuccinos every month. Remember, the purpose of a budget is to identify areas of overspending, which in themselves are signs of poor financial habits.

- Create an emergency action plan. When the COVID-19 pandemic hit us in 2020, millions of Americans found themselves completely unprepared. In fact, 40 percent of Americans don't have $400 in the bank for emergencies.[15] But unexpected events can—and do—happen. A good rule to follow is to have at least six months of expenses saved. But an emergency fund is more than just how much money we save. Women need to consider protecting themselves by obtaining an umbrella insurance policy that includes life insurance, renter's or homeowner's insurance, and health insurance. Think of an emergency action plan as a network of support that can help you withstand sudden emergencies.

- Consider avoiding credit card debt. It seems that credit cards are designed for one thing only—immediate gratification. Credit cards and lines of credit are easily available to us, but some problems with having credit cards, aside from the fact they tempt us to overindulge, include paying interest on everything you purchase. This can leave you with unnecessary monthly debt that prevents you from saving for an emergency fund and may result in poor credit scores and poor budgeting. A good rule to consider is to "use no more than 10 percent of your credit line and make regular payments to avoid paying too much interest."[16] If you want to improve your credit and also save money, do yourself a favor and limit your credit card usage.

- Invest your money. One of the things I always tell my clients, particularly women, is that investing your money is an excellent way to potentially build wealth—since there's the potential to lose principle when investing. Let's look at some of the reasons you should think about investing your money:

  ° Potentially grow your money

  ° Save for retirement

  ° Possibly earn higher returns

  ° Work toward financial goals

  ° Build on pretax dollars

  ° Qualify for employer-matching programs

  ° Conceivably reduce taxable income

  ° Support others[17]

Of all the reasons to invest your money, though, retirement is perhaps the most important, which leads us to the next bullet point.

- Plan for retirement. Today people "are living longer and want to thrive in retirement. Retirees need more income for a longer time, so they will need to save and invest accordingly."[18] Retirement today does not look like the retirement of your parents or grandparents. Today it's more important than ever to prepare for retirement, as pensions and Social Security may no longer guarantee a comfortable income. Here is something you need to consider: According to the 2020 Social Security Board of Trustees' annual report, "the surplus in the trust funds that disburse retirement, disability and Social Security benefits will be depleted by 2035."[19] The greatest single gift you can give yourself today is to sit down with an experienced and qualified financial planner to plan for your retirement.

ESTATE PLANNING

Let's define estate planning as the "preparation of tasks that serve to manage an individual's asset base in the event of their incapacitation or death."[20] Estate planning involves how your assets, such as cash, stocks, bonds, real estate, and other investment holdings, will be preserved, managed, and distributed after you die or if you are incapacitated. An estate plan is one of the most important things you can do to protect your assets and personal property. People often assume that estate planning is for the rich, which is absolutely false. Some of the reasons why everyone needs to consider having an estate plan include the following:

- Protecting your beneficiaries
- Avoiding creating a tax burden for your loved ones
- Avoiding family conflicts

Creating a will, which is a "legal document that sets forth your wishes regarding the distribution of your property and the care of any minor children," will help your adult children, or the ones you love, avoid costly court costs.[21] If you don't have a will, you will leave the distribution of your assets to probate court. Estate planning could also reduce the amount of federal and state taxes your heirs pay. However, perhaps the most important reason to have an estate plan is to avoid family conflicts, particularly between siblings. Having a will in place will help to avoid such conflict, or you may want to create a trust, which establishes a "fiduciary relationship in which one party, known as the trustor, gives another party, the trustee, the right to hold title to property or assets for the benefit of a third party, the beneficiary."[22] In other words, a trust allows you to legally designate someone, a family member or a legal firm, to distribute your assets.

As women become more financially independent, they will need to become knowledgeable about, and comfortable with, estate planning. One of the consequences of women being excluded from the financial world is a disconnect between having power over money and knowing what to do with that power. Given that women live on average 5.4 years longer than men, they are the ones who become responsible for the decisions regarding the transfer of wealth.[23] This is why it is critical for women to understand not only financial planning but also estate planning. According to Gina Nelson, senior vice president and head of fiduciary services at Chilton Trust Company, women continue to fall behind their male counterparts when it comes to the legal profession's specialization in estate planning.

Nelson's experience is worth recounting. In 2002, she attended an estate-planning conference. She was fresh out of law school and working for an attorney who specialized in trusts and estates. Although some 200 lawyers attended the conference, Nelson "realized that in that room of approximately 200 people, I could count the number of other women attendees on two hands."[24] In the 20 years since, the number of women estate-planning lawyers has continued to fall behind. This, of course, is unacceptable. We need to have more female attorneys who understand that it is often women who ultimately control the disposition of wealth for their family.

One of the things that I do as a financial planner is to offer regular lectures for both men and women where I focus on financial literacy, including estate planning. I'm often surprised by the women in the audience who, when it comes to estate planning, defer to their husbands. Women need to fundamentally change their mind-set when it comes to their financial responsibility. This area of financial planning is so important that I refer all my clients to experienced estate-planning attorneys. While it is possible to create your own will or trust, the process is complex. I recommend that you have a lawyer do it for you. But it is possible to educate yourself on the basics of financial literacy. That is the focus of part III.

PART III:

FINANCIAL LITERACY FOR WOMEN—A PRIMER AND MORE

9

FROM HIDDEN FORCES
TO HIDDEN ACTORS

"A rich understanding of human psychology, a reasonable appreciation of financial theory, a deep awareness of history, and a broad exposure to current events all contribute to the development of well-informed portfolio strategies."

—DAVID SWENSEN

In *Redefining Financial Literacy*, I made the argument that Americans have a narrow view of financial literacy, which has traditionally been defined in terms of our "ability to understand and effectively apply various financial skills, including personal financial management, budgeting, and investing."[1] This rather simple definition needs to be broadened to include historical, social, political, and economic forces that directly impact our financial planning. What is urgently needed today is the kind of financial literacy that transforms our mind-set from passive spectators to active participants. Women, in particular, need to broaden their financial awareness in order to make informed, fact-based decisions when it comes to their hard-earned money. Perhaps the greatest single gift women can give themselves today is wealth accumulation. In previous chapters of this book, you read about the generational trauma women endured as a result of patriarchy. The reason financial literacy is critically important to women is to increase generational wealth.

Wealth transfer from one generation to the next helps secure a level of financial freedom and autonomous control of money that protects women from depending on men. As I wrote earlier, "a great wealth transfer is coming, passed down from the baby boomer generation, and women may emerge as the biggest beneficiaries. Approximately $30 trillion in wealth is set to change hands in the next decade and women are poised to inherit a sizeable share."[2] What is even more significant is that women are also accumulating their own wealth. Despite the glaring wage gap that persists, women are "intentionally accumulating their own wealth by climbing the career ladder."[3] Here is the caveat: Women need to improve their financial literacy, both at the macro and micro level, in order to expand their wealth accumulation. According to Malia Haskins, vice president of wealth strategies at RBC Wealth Management, "women are attaining financial roles and responsibilities that are taking them beyond simply controlling the household budget."[4] This is why it is absolutely critical that women understand the hidden forces that shape their financial reality.

These hidden forces are not merely abstract concepts; they have a direct impact on your financial future. For example, the Social Security system that our parents and grandparents enjoyed may become insolvent if Congress fails to enact reforms. The pensions that past generations have relied upon to carry them through retirement are becoming extinct. Consider this: "The practice of companies sending monthly retirement checks to their former workers is headed for extinction, and remaining pension funds are in tough financial shape."[5] Despite the fact that there are hidden forces that seem to be out of our control, there is something you can do about them. If you broaden your understanding of these hidden forces, you could be in a position to better prepare and plan for your retirement. One of the hidden forces I've mentioned earlier is historical. You might remember taking history classes in high school and asking yourself, "Who needs history?"

What you must realize is that a meaningful understanding of the financial world must include its history. History is not just some abstract and pedantic study that is removed from our lives. It affects us in ways that impact how we plan our future. As the saying goes, "Those who cannot learn from history are doomed to repeat it." As recent history has shown us, this is precisely what has happened over the past century.[6] But we don't have to acquiesce to the inevitable; we can use the knowledge of past events to shape our own future. This is especially true for women, who now hold more than half of the personal wealth in the United States.[7] What we choose to do will depend on our capacity to think critically about the decisions and choices that came before us. For example, let's look at the Gilded Age and our failure to learn from the systemic inequality that resulted from greed and corruption.

THE GILDED AGE

The Gilded Age in America, the period between 1876 and World War I, was characterized as a time seemingly covered with glitter on the surface but corrupt underneath. It was a time of "greed and guile: of rapacious Robber Barons, unscrupulous spectators, and corporate buccaneers, of shady business practices, scandal-plagued politics, and vulgar display."[8] By 1890 more than 70 percent of America's wealth was concentrated and controlled by the top 10 percent of the population. Although it is tempting to believe that our world is far more egalitarian today, it is in fact less so—in 2016 the top 10 percent of families controlled 76 percent of the total wealth.[9] Despite the fact that we are 150 years removed from the original Gilded Age, the economic reality today is just as bifurcated and iniquitous as it has ever been. The American Dream continues to elude many Americans, and generational wealth favors only a small percentage of the population.

The Gilded Age coincided with the industrial revolution, in which factory work replaced farming as the leading source of employment, the railroad introduced a national transportation system, and the rise of corporations revolutionized capitalism. The Gilded Age witnessed a period of unprecedented technological breakthroughs, too, including the telephone, the phonograph, the radio, the electric light bulb, the automobile, and countless other innovations. It marked the beginning of the consumer economy, where technology and culture converged to create popular culture. For example, by the turn of the 20th century, the rise of the mass-circulation newspaper and the monetization of leisure, including sports and entertainment, fundamentally changed how we lived. As a consequence of this dramatic change over a very short period of time, an economic chasm opened between the privileged few and everyone else.

Some of those who accumulated vast amounts of wealth became known as robber barons. These robber barons created a closed loop in which wealth, greed, and corruption shaped and defined the political and economic reality of their time. These captains of industry succeeded by paying workers low wages, exploiting children and immigrants, and avoiding government regulations. Men such as John D. Rockefeller, Andrew Carnegie, and J.P. Morgan amassed sufficient wealth to both control and manipulate the economy.

Andrew Carnegie, for example, made his fortune in the steel industry. He "engaged in tactics that were not in the best interests of his workers";[10] in 1892, in response to Carnegie's attempts to lower wages, his workers went on strike. The Homestead Steel strike, also known as the Homestead massacre, ended in violence and numerous deaths. This treatment of workers with disdain and contempt was the result of a lack of government regulations, as well as monopolistic practices.

John D. Rockefeller, who owned Standard Oil, controlled 90 percent of the oil infrastructure in the United States. In the area of banking and finance, J.P. Morgan "invested in Thomas Edison and the Edison Electricity Company, helped to create General Electric and International Harvester, formed J.P. Morgan & Company, and gained control of half of the country's railroad mileage."[11] The amount of power these men wielded, particularly in politics, was extraordinary.

I'm sure you noticed that the Gilded Age was largely defined by men. It was the men who were the robber barons. And it was the greed and corruption of men in the political and economic arenas that contributed to greater inequality. This growing divide between an elite few, who controlled the vast majority of wealth, and everyone else was both glaring and offensive.

In general, there was a lack of a spiritual awareness or any moral compass to guide the unprecedented change in American society. The vacuum was filled by early feminists who formed the temperance movement to confront a culture of excess. Although the temperance movement was successful in passing the 18th Amendment, which prohibited the manufacture, sale, or transportation of alcohol, its philosophical foundation can be traced to transcendentalism. Intellectual giants such as Ralph Waldo Emerson, Henry David Thoreau, Margaret Fuller, and Elizabet Palmer Peabody believed in the "essential unity of all creation, the innate goodness of humanity, and the supremacy of insight over logic and experience for the revelation of the deepest truths."[12] The idea of "supremacy of insight over logic" is essentially what I've called "the mystery of intuition." This tension between the robber barons and transcendentalism continues to shape and inform what is commonly referred to as the second Gilded Age.

THE SECOND GILDED AGE

Many economists and historians identify the digital revolution as "the Gilded Age 2.0." Indeed, the parallels between the Gilded Age and today are both striking and disturbing. Both periods experienced unprecedented technological change. Today the telephone is being replaced with the smartphone; the phonograph is now digital music apps, through which we can hear music whenever and wherever we want. Newspapers and books have been replaced with instantaneous access to information in our pockets or on our wrists. The internal combustion engine is disappearing in favor of clean electric vehicles. The Vanderbilts, Morgans, Rockefellers, and Carnegies of the past find their modern counterparts in Jeff Bezos, Steve Jobs, Mark Zuckerberg, Elon Musk, and Bill Gates.

Another similarity is that our new Gilded Age is beautiful to look at on the outside, but if we inspect it more carefully, we will find massive inequity between those who are on the forefront of the digital revolution and everyone else. In terms of the trappings of wealth and the ostentatious display of material excess, the wealthy elites of today evoke those of a time long past, yet they are ineluctably connected to the failure of capitalism.

Although historians may look back to the second Gilded Age as beginning around 1990, nothing epitomizes the unabashed projection of wealth and corruption as much as the current political and economic climate. *USA Today* characterized the 2016 election of Donald Trump as personifying "the second Gilded Age as much as robber baron industrialists and financiers did the first."[13] Boston College historian Patrick Maney declared, "It's as if J.P. Morgan had been elected president. Donald Trump puts an exclamation point on this Gilded Age."[14] To further illustrate some of the similarities between the two historical periods, consider this: In 1894 unemployed workers, known as Coxey's Army (named after Jacob Coxey, a politician from Massillon, Ohio), marched to Washington, DC, to demand that Congress allocate funds to create jobs for the unemployed. In 2011 the Occupy Wall Street movement marched in New York's financial district to protest the preferential treatment of the top 1 percent of the nation. In both cases, the protestors failed to achieve their objectives.

During the Gilded Age, wealthy industrialists dominated entire industries. Today "almost half of U.S. industries are dominated by the four largest companies" and "Google . . . accounts for 87% of all internet searches."[15] The men who are on top in this second Gilded Age did not make themselves out of thin air. Like those earlier titans of industry who were shaped by beliefs about manifest destiny, today's billionaires also believe in their own capacity to reshape the world and to bend history to their will. They believe in punctuated historical moments, that their actions will help humanity take leaps forward. The only problem is that when you combine money and power, you inevitably produce greed and corruption, with the inescapable outcome of marginalizing both the middle class and the working class.

The parallels between today's wealthy elites and those of the Gilded Age are uncanny. In fact, I believe the power elites of today are tone-deaf when it comes to the other 99 percent of the population. These individuals live in a separate world, removed from the rest of us. And once again men are behind this latest cycle of wealth concentration. The reason wealth concentration is a problem is that it contributes to the ever-growing bifurcation between the rich and everyone else. From government to corporate America, income inequality is growing: The majority of lawmakers in 2020 are millionaires.[16] In addition, wage inequality is getting worse. Think about this for a minute: The bottom 90 percent of Americans are trapped in a $30,000 income range, while the top 0.1 percent earn more than $1 million on average.[17] Another glaring outcome of male-dominated wealth concentration is the temptation of greed and corruption.

It is evident that the cycle of male-concentrated wealth and corruption keeps repeating itself. The good news is that this cycle will soon come to an end. As more women enter politics and climb the corporate ladder, we can look forward to less greed and corruption. A recent study by Virginia Tech economist Sudipta Sarangi found that "corruption is less prevalent in countries where there is a greater number of women in political leadership roles, both at national and local levels."[18] The study also revealed that women in corporate leadership, such as CEOs and other executive positions, engage in less corrupt activity when compared to men.[19]

But can we be sure that because more women are climbing the corporate ladder, there will be less corruption and greed? We have long assumed that greed is a vice that tempts both men and women. What if greed is a by-product of biology?

According to the Oxford Languages dictionary, greed is defined as an "intense and selfish desire for something, especially wealth, power, or food."[20] But we probably don't need a formal definition for us to grasp its meaning. At an intuitive level, we all seem to be able to identify greedy behavior. Children at play have an almost innate grasp of greediness. In some respect, greed is the antithesis of sharing. And women, it turns out, are much better at sharing than men. According to a 2017 study by a group of psychologists, economists, and neurologists from the University of Zurich, men's reward system was sensitive to selfish behavior, while women were sensitive to sharing.[21] How did they determine this? It turns out women experienced a higher level of dopamine, which is a neurotransmitter associated with pleasure and reward, as a result of sharing, while men had elevated levels of dopamine when they behaved in a selfish manner.

Although the researchers clearly showed a biological difference in our response to selfish behavior, they could not conclude that biology was the only factor. Part of the reason is that the dopamine system in our brains is also responsible for learning. In other words, the concept of sharing may have a basis in biology, but it is also shaped by gender stereotypes. Women have been taught to share, while men have been taught to be greedier.[22] While the psychology of greed is interesting and eye-opening, it does seem a bit abstract.

In the world of finance, greed can become a destructive force. It can make us irrational and blind us to the dangers of our actions. We have seen this happen numerous times: There was the stock market crash of 1929, which ushered in the Great Depression; the tech bubble of the late 1990s and the subsequent stock market crash of 2002; and more recently the housing bubble of the mid-2000s, which brought about a global financial meltdown. Each of these historical events involved rampant greed. One might argue that greed and capitalism go hand in hand, which is why I believe that capitalism itself is broken.

BEYOND THE GILDED AGE: WOMEN'S PUSH FOR ECONOMIC EQUALITY

On the face of it, women today hold a different social, political, and economic status than their counterparts during the first Gilded Age. Women today are not only far more educated than the women around the turn of the 20th century but also more educated than their male contemporaries. In fact, according to Statista.com, 38.3 percent of women in the United States have completed four years or more of college in 2020 compared to 36.7 percent of men.[23] Although the types of jobs for women during the first Gilded Age were limited to clerical work, switchboard operators, and typists, today women can be found in every field of human endeavor. From medicine to law, politics to science, women have proven they belong in historically male-dominated positions. If this is the case, then why bother even comparing women today to the inequalities of past generations?

The answer is quite simple. Many of the inequities that existed over a century ago continue today. As I've pointed out, while women are more educated than men, they continue to earn substantially less than men for the same work. According to the Bureau of Labor Statistics data, "women's annual earnings were 82.3 percent of men's, and the gap is even wider for many women of color."[24] While women have made significant improvements in the workplace, they continue to lag behind men when it comes to promotions to senior executive positions, otherwise known as the C-suite. In fact, for every 100 men promoted to managerial positions, only 85 women were promoted. This gap widens for women of color, where just 58 Black women and 71 Latinas were promoted.[25] To exacerbate matters, as a result of COVID-19, as many as two million women are considering leaving the workforce, which means there will be fewer women in leadership roles.[26]

It is difficult to fully comprehend the implications of a gender pay gap until you put that in the context of how long it will take women to achieve parity with men. Prior to the COVID-19 pandemic, it would have taken 100 years to achieve global gender parity with men. If you think this was unacceptable, then consider this: The World Economic Forum predicts that as a result of the pandemic, it will now take women 135.6 years to achieve parity.[27] In other words, the pandemic set women back 36 years. What is tragically ironic about the second Gilded Age, with all of its glamorous technology, is that we have built an economy that favors men while leaving women behind.

This is unacceptable. It is preposterous to think that women will wait for 136 years to achieve pay parity with men.

There are, of course, actionable steps that both government and the private sector can take to ameliorate this glaring gap. The government, regardless of political polarization, must become a leader in this area. First, the Biden administration needs to relaunch a presidential task force whose mission is to devise different strategies to combat pay inequality. This task force, which was initially started by the Obama administration, needs to address such issues as enforcing equal pay, reviewing contractor pay practices, and combating pay discrimination for women of color. Other measures the government can take is to reinstate the collection of pay data from large corporations. This information, which breaks down salaries by race, ethnicity, and gender, will help enforcement officials identify companies who continue to engage in rampant pay disparities.[28]

One glaring area where gender and racial pay gaps can be eliminated is the federal workforce. The reason I use the word "glaring" to describe the wage gap in the federal workforce is that the federal government needs to be a model of gender equality. Rather than being a leader in gender equity, the federal government is part of the problem. According to the Office of Personnel Management (OPM), an estimated 2.1 million people work for the federal government.[29] Although there is only a seven-cent federal pay gap between men and women—which is much smaller than the overall pay gap—OPM needs to do more to create parity within the federal workforce.

Perhaps the greatest obstacle to bridging the pay gap is secrecy. Many companies who contract with the federal government often engage in retaliatory practices against employees who disclose, or otherwise discuss, their pay. Although the Obama administration issued an executive order in 2014 prohibiting such practices, the Office of Federal Contract Compliance Programs needs to do a better job of identifying federally contracted companies who continue to engage in gender pay discrimination.[30]

There is so much more they can do: Businesses need to track pay across race, gender, and other demographics to identify areas of pay inequity. There should be an annual pay audit in relation to race and gender. Technology platforms such as Pipeline.com can be utilized to "report on equitable decision making across hiring, pay, performance, and potential promotion."[31] Other measures include addressing bias in corporate culture in order to permanently close the pay gap, changing the gender balance in leadership by promoting more women to senior executive positions, and providing salary ranges so that women are in a better position to negotiate. Finally, we as a society need to hold corporations accountable for the ongoing pay gap. Social media can be used to expose and shame companies who continue to marginalize women through antiquated gender preferences.[32]

We have seen so far that both Gilded Ages have brought extraordinary innovation and technological comforts to our lives. However, such progress came at a high cost. Despite the progress made during both Gilded Ages, women and other minority groups continue to endure systemic discrimination, while White males continue to benefit disproportionately from our economic gains. It is the systemic nature of the gender pay gap that suggests there is something very wrong with our capitalist system.

BROKEN CAPITALISM

The free-market capitalism that marked the Gilded Age benefited a small elite group who manipulated the political system in order to perpetuate their economic dominance. The government failed to intervene when greed and excess, which came at the expense of the vast majority of Americans, went out of control. These hidden forces would continue to dominate the economic landscape well into the 1920s.

In the 1920s, greed captured the imagination of both banks and the individual investor. Banks engaged in speculative investing by lending money to people who wanted to buy stocks. At the time there were no regulations, which led to a market bubble, and in 1929 the stock market crashed under the weight of its own irrational exuberance. On October 28, 1929, which is remembered today as Black Monday, the Dow Jones Industrial Average plunged nearly 13 percent. On the following day, Black Tuesday, the market fell an additional 12 percent.[33]

President Herbert Hoover advocated for laissez-faire economics, which is the idea—first developed by the philosopher and economist Adam Smith—that governments should take a hands-off approach to the market. Hoover believed "that economic assistance would make people stop working. He believed business prosperity would trickle down to the average person."[34] This noninterventionist approach would lead to the greatest economic disaster in American history, as well as to Hoover's defeat by a landslide in the 1932 presidential election. By the time Franklin Roosevelt took office on March 4, 1933, "unemployment had risen from 3% to 25% of the nation's workforce. Wages for those who still had jobs fell. U.S. gross domestic product was cut in half, from $103 billion to $55 billion, due partly to deflation."[35] By the end of his first 100 days in office, Roosevelt had introduced numerous government programs called the New Deal, many of which were introduced or implemented by Frances Perkins. But in addition to the New Deal programs, Roosevelt wanted to address the fundamental causes of the financial collapse.

Let's remember that before the stock market crash of 1929, retail banks used depositors' funds for the purpose of investing in initial stock sales, otherwise known as initial public offerings. Many banks facilitated risky mergers and acquisitions and operated their own hedge funds without any governmental oversight. In response to the near collapse of the banking system, Congress passed the Glass-Steagall Act in 1933, which removed and separated investment banks from retail banks. This act "restored confidence in the U.S. banking system. It increased trust by only allowing banks to use depositors' funds in safe investments. Its FDIC (Federal Deposit Insurance Corporation) insurance program prevented further bank runs. Depositors knew the government protected them from a failing bank."[36] Over the next several decades, the banking industry fought to repeal what they believed to be excessive government regulations.

Over time, grounded in a misguided philosophy of corporate and individual self-interest, the philosophy of neoliberalism would help defend the greed and corruption of the late 20th century. Once again, it was the men who were behind the economic philosophy that favored the rise of a select few corporations and individuals over and above the average American. In time, neoliberalism helped usher in the second Gilded Age, which, as we've seen, restricted the American Dream.

HIDDEN ACTORS: THE RISE OF ECONOMISTS

Our economy today is dominated by economists. Whenever you watch a financial news program on Bloomberg, CNBC, or Fox Business, you will often see economists analyzing market trends and other economic activity. Economists today are the rock stars of the financial world. Consider that "about 37% (776) of all Ph.D. economists who work for the federal government are employed by the Federal Reserve System—roughly half at the Board of Governors and half at the 12 regional Fed banks."[37]

One would think that economists have always wielded extraordinary power, but that is not the case. Although the field of economics has been around since 1776, the year the Scottish philosopher Adam Smith published his groundbreaking work, *An Inquiry into the Nature and Causes of the Wealth of Nations*, it is only during the past 50 years that the field has risen to prominence. In fact, the first Nobel Prize for economics was handed out in 1969. Difficult as it may be to believe, there was a time when economists were dismissed as irrelevant bureaucrats.

During the late 1940s and early 1950s, economists played a marginal role in shaping economic decisions. There is an interesting story about the economist Paul Volcker, who became chairman of the Federal Reserve in 1978. In the early 1950s, when he was a young economist, he worked in the basement of the Federal Reserve. His job was to crunch numbers for the people who made decisions. At the time, Volcker told his wife that he saw little hope of ever moving up, since the leadership of the Federal Reserve was made up of bankers and lawyers. There wasn't a single economist.

The Fed chairman then was William McChesney Martin, a former stockbroker. Martin once told a visitor "that he kept a small staff of economists in the basement of the Fed's Washington head-quarters. They were in the building, he said, because they asked good questions. They were in the basement because 'they don't know their own limitations.'"[38] This early contempt for economists was shared by President Franklin Roosevelt, who dismissed John Maynard Keynes, arguably the most important economist of his generation, as "an impractical 'mathematician.'"[39] Eisenhower, too, would later urge Americans to keep "technocrats" (economists) from power.

So widespread was the contempt for economists that Congress rarely consulted them, and the courts often ignored economic evidence as irrelevant. Despite these humble beginnings, a revolution was coming. It would only be a matter of time before economists sat at the seat of power, where they not only advised policy makers but were also responsible for shaping policy.

The one figure who epitomized the rise of the economist was Milton Friedman of the University of Chicago. Although Friedman refused to take a job in Washington, his ideas shaped the thinking of presidents from both political parties. The Nixon administration, for example, embraced Friedman's idea that the markets should determine the exchange rates between the dollar and foreign currency. Both liberal and conservative economists, despite their disagreements in certain areas of public policy, shared the belief that markets tend toward equilibrium. This shared belief meant there was little interest in involving the government in rectifying economic inequality from economists on both sides of the political spectrum.

As an example, Charles L. Schultze, President Carter's chairman of the Council of Economic Advisors, fought for efficient policies, "even when the result is significant income losses for particular groups—which it almost always is."[40] In 2004, Robert Lucas, who was a Nobel Prize–winning economist, argued against any effort to reduce inequality by suggesting that of any steps taken "that are harmful to sound economics, the most seductive, and in my opinion the most poisonous, is to focus on questions of distribution."[41] This approach to income inequality was rationalized by blaming globalization or technological change.

Some economists were simply willing to accept inequality as an inevitable by-product of capitalism, and policy makers followed suit, embracing efficiency and encouraging the concentration of wealth. As you will read in the next chapter, baby boomers would contribute a great deal to income inequality and take greed to an entirely new level.

MILTON FRIEDMAN AND NEOLIBERALISM

By the early 1970s, a new economic philosophy was starting to take hold. Neoliberalism embraced laissez-faire economics, which is "an economic theory from the 18th century that opposed any government intervention in business affairs."[42] One of the early architects of neoliberalism was Milton Friedman. In a little-known *New York Times Magazine* article published in 1970, "The Social Responsibility of Business Is to Increase Its Profits," Friedman offered a framework for corporate behavior. He wrote, "There is one and only one social responsibility of business—to use its resources and engage in activities designed to increase its profits so long as it stays within the rules of the game, which is to say, engages in open and free competition without deception."[43] In other words, the government should not interfere with free-market competition by imposing regulations that interfere with it. Eventually neoliberalism would contribute to the repeal of the Glass-Steagall Act.

In 1971, a Virginia attorney by the name of Lewis Powell wrote a memo in support of businesses coming together to defend their corporate interests. Powell argued, "Business must learn the lesson . . . that political power is necessary; that such power must be assiduously cultivated; and that when necessary, it must be used aggressively and with determination—without embarrassment and without the reluctance which has been so characteristic of American business."[44] This one fateful memo would catch the attention of President Nixon. Two months later, Nixon nominated Lewis Powell to the US Supreme Court. Powell's memo was, in effect, a call to arms for businesses to defend their mission of free and open competition without government regulations. Both Milton Friedman and Lewis Powell set the stage for less government regulation, which would contribute to the second Gilded Age.

ROBERT BORK AND CORPORATE SUPREMACY

If Milton Friedman was the architect behind the political ideology of neoliberalism, then Robert Bork was the legal scholar who justified corporate greed and corruption by advocating for corporate mergers and monopolies. President Reagan nominated Bork to the Supreme Court in 1987, but the nomination was contentious, prompting heated debates in the Senate. Because of his stated desire to roll back civil rights, Bork is one of only four Supreme Court nominees (along with William Rehnquist, Samuel Alito, and Brett Kavanaugh) to be rejected by the American Civil Liberties Union.[45] Many Democrats opposed Bork because of his opposition to the authority claimed by the federal government to impose voting fairness standards on individual states. Bork also advocated for the executive branch's having far more power than the legislative or judicial branch.

Despite the fact that Bork never became a Supreme Court justice, his influence on antitrust laws was extraordinary. He played a "critical role in recreating the antitrust laws of the original Gilded Age. During that period, antitrust enforcers largely allowed corporations to merge and control markets in, for instance, chemicals, steel, telegraphs, and tobacco."[46] Bork's 1978 book, *The Antitrust Paradox*, has shaped antitrust laws for several decades. For example, "the Department of Justice and Federal Trade Commission today mostly leave Google, Walmart, and other businesses across the economy alone and seek to suppress the collective action of workers in the service economy."[47]

Think of antitrust laws as laws that promote or maintain market competition. In fact, in Europe these laws are called competition laws. Throughout American history, the concept of competition called for a balancing act between individual liberty and excessive economic power. For example, the Sherman Antitrust Act of 1890—named for its principal author, Senator John Sherman, and signed into law by President Benjamin Harrison—was designed to prohibit anticompetitive agreements and monopolies from stifling competition.

You may be wondering where the word "antitrust" comes from. The concept of a legally binding trust first arose almost 1,000 years ago in England. It is defined as a "fiduciary relationship in which one party, known as a trustor, gives another party, the trustee, the right to hold title to property or assets for the benefit of a third party, the beneficiary."[48] You can broaden this definition to include corporations.

Corporate trusts were first used in the United States in 1882 when Samuel C. T. Dodd came up with the idea in order to allow John D. Rockefeller to consolidate control of the numerous acquisitions of the Standard Oil Company, which at the time was the largest corporation in the world. Think of it in these terms: Standard Oil was big enough, and powerful enough, to purchase smaller companies. Through the "trust agreement," the shareholders of several smaller corporations agreed to convey their shares to the trust, and Standard Oil ended up owning 14 corporations outright and exercised majority control over 26 others. Rockefeller himself held 41 percent of the trust certificates.[49]

The idea of corporations developing trusts to take over smaller corporations and gain more power and control over certain sectors of the market would serve as the beginning of legalized greed in American capitalism. The Sherman Antitrust Act of 1890 was introduced to challenge the growing problem of these corporate monopolies.

The Sherman Antitrust Act was used over the years with some success. For example, in 1911, the Standard Oil Company was broken up according to geography; also, in 1911, American Tobacco was split into four companies; and in 1982, AT&T was forced to break up into seven regional Bell operating companies. More recently, Microsoft was sued by the United States for illegally maintaining a monopoly position in the personal computer market, and a settlement was reached in 2001. Microsoft was required to share its application programming interfaces with third-party companies, and a panel of three was appointed to have full access to Microsoft's systems, records, and source code for five years in order to guarantee compliance. Despite these successes, however, corporate monopolistic practices have continued to increase and are indeed a major source of inequality today.

In *The Unmasking of America: A Recent History*, writer and radio host Kurt Anderson describes a

> kind of secret history that happened in broad daylight; starting in the early '70s, a band of conservative economists and pro-business groups, terrified of the progressive movements of the 1960s, drew up plans and blueprints for a version of America in which big corporations and Wall Street would be liberated from regulation and labor unions and antitrust laws, allowing the free market to sort out the winners from the losers.[50]

This vision of American corporate power has largely been realized at the expense of the average person who is trapped under a broken capitalist system that favors the wealthy few.

Neoliberalism in general, along with Robert Bork's legal framework to support corporate monopolies, helped create a world where a mere handful of global corporations control how we interact and consume information in the digital age. While on the surface, we celebrate the marvels of modern technology, upon closer inspection, we are living in a dystopian world where economic power is concentrated in the hands of a few powerful corporations.

Think for a minute about how much you rely upon the services of Apple, Amazon, Google, and Facebook. Consider that

Amazon controls a third of the cloud business, 44 percent of
e-commerce, and a staggering 70 percent of the smart-speaker
market. Google controls 90 percent of search. Facebook has
become a conduit for political disinformation and Apple
a symbol of conspicuous consumption and ruthless brand
protection. As tens of thousands of small and not-so-small
businesses face bankruptcy in the wake of the [COVID-19]
pandemic, all four companies continue to thrive.[51]

In many ways, these four corporations are the face of the second
Gilded Age.

10

HIDDEN RISKS AFFECTING YOUR FINANCIAL FUTURE

"Not ignorance but ignorance of ignorance is the death of knowledge."

—ALFRED NORTH WHITEHEAD

Now that you have a basic understanding of how seemingly invisible forces can have a powerful impact on your financial future, it is time to explore some of the hidden risks and behind-the-scenes actors that may contribute to market uncertainty. You need to understand these forces and the risk they pose to your financial well-being. There are several intersecting and overlapping variables that may influence your financial future. For women, in particular, understanding these risks could mean the difference between financial freedom and economic dependency.

Before I explore the different layers of risk, it would help to have a working definition of the concept of risk itself. According to James

Chen of Investopedia, "risk is defined in financial terms as the chance that an outcome or investment's actual gains will differ from an expected outcome or return. Risk includes the possibility of losing some or all of an original investment."[1] When you invest your money, you have an expectation that your investment will grow in value. Risk is when your actual outcome is different (higher or lower) than what you expected. We all take certain risks whenever we drive a car, walk a flight of stairs, or invest our hard-earned money. Given that risk is inevitable, the question becomes, how much risk can we tolerate? This is known as your risk profile, which is your willingness and ability to withstand risk. There is a general rule in finance that states, "As investment risks rise, investors expect higher returns to compensate for taking those risks."[2] Taking higher risk does not, of course, guarantee higher returns.

What are the different types of risk that can potentially undermine your investment return? Many of these risks do not work in isolation; rather they intersect and overlap with each other. Below are ten different kinds of risks that can negatively impact your investment return.

- Political Risk
- Economic/Globalization Risk
- Federal Reserve Risk
- Corporate Risk
- Correlation Risk
- Regulation Risk
- Longevity Risk
- Ideological Risk
- Social Media Risk
- Gender Risk

POLITICAL RISK

Political risk is the risk that an investment's returns could suffer as a result of political changes or instability in a country. Political risk is also referred to as geopolitical risk and becomes more of a factor as the time horizon of investment gets longer.[3] It is important to understand that political risk may create market uncertainty. Many of the companies whose stocks you may own operate in countries around the world. The political landscape of other countries and the taxes imposed on multinational corporations, regulation, currency valuation, trade tariffs, labor laws, environmental regulations, and so on often have an impact on the stock market.[4] Political risk affects us here at home as well, particularly during national elections.

During periods of contentious presidential elections, political risk increases, which in turn creates higher levels of market uncertainty. If you recall, the 2020 presidential election was contentious to the point that it polarized our nation. In this context, a "contentious political environment fuels uncertainty to the detriment of both consumers and businesses and encourages financial market volatility."[5] Political uncertainty is not limited to decisions on presidents, however. The 2020 election also determined which political party took control of the Senate, and when elections are this close, they create uncertainty, which breeds volatility. This is important to understand because if you are heavily invested in stocks, or even have a 60/40 stock-bond portfolio, you expose yourself to that uncertainty.

Stocks are not the only thing that is affected by political risk. So is the bond market. "Uncertainty is further fueled by concerns the election results could be delayed or challenged and the myriad of variables that have competing influences on bond markets depending on which party claims the White House and/or controls the Senate."[6] If you remember the 2016 presidential election between Hillary Clinton and Donald Trump, you know that most of the political forecasts predicted Clinton would win the election. That, of course, was not the case. Just as political forecasting is difficult, and at times inaccurate, market forecasting is similarly difficult. Given that financial markets are forward-looking, they are constantly assimilating as much information as possible to gauge risk and set bond prices.[7]

How does this affect you? We know that the majority of Americans (52 percent) invest in the stock market, so you are more than likely one of them.[8] There are many others who invest directly, or through their 401(k) plan, into the 60/40 portfolio. If you expose your hard-earned money to a single investment vehicle (stocks), or the binary portfolio of stocks and bonds, you are essentially taking on high political risk. Although the 60/40 portfolio offered relatively strong returns over the past 20 years (about 6 percent), it may no longer continue to do so. Morgan Stanley forecasts that the 60/40 is expected to offer "a 2.8% average annual return over the next 10 years."[9] This does not even factor in the inflation rate. According to the International Monetary Fund, inflation is projected to be 2.24 percent throughout 2021.[10]

ECONOMIC/GLOBALIZATION RISK

In *Redefining Financial Literacy*, I introduced the concept of hidden forces, which converge in such a way as to impact your return on investment. These hidden forces include macro, big-picture political and economic risks that leave investors with little control. The reason

I always stress the importance of financial literacy is that you, the investor, have more control at the micro level by managing debt, savings, and your investment choices.

Economic risk "refers to the likelihood that macroeconomic conditions (conditions in the whole economy) may affect an investment or a company's prospects domestically or abroad."[11] Measuring economic risk is a complicated process, which is why the job of judging the economic risk of a country is done by experts. Just as you have a credit rating to determine the risk factor in lending you money, countries also have credit ratings. Companies such as Moody's and Standard & Poor's publish what is called a sovereign credit rating, which is an assessment of a country's creditworthiness.[12]

There are several economic risk factors, which include the following:

- Unemployment or Underemployment
- Cyber Attacks
- Foreign Exchange Risk
- Failure of National Governance
- Fiscal Crises[13]

Now, if you invest in stocks on your own, understanding economic risk is critical to your research of which companies to invest in and which to avoid. Imagine for a moment that you are considering Company X as an investment for your hard-earned money. As part of your research, you may want to know which countries it operates in. You see, many companies today are multinational, meaning they operate in several countries around the world. What if one, or more, of these countries has a low rating by Moody's? That's when economic risk becomes immediately relevant to you. If Company X is operating in countries with low economic ratings, you may want to think twice before investing in its shares.

Now, what if you are just too busy to deal with all this? I suggest you keep this simple rule in mind. Given that the stock and bond markets are subject to political, economic, and other risks, you may want to limit your exposure. Begin by asking questions. You may want to meet with a qualified and experienced financial advisor to find out how a multi-asset class portfolio can potentially lower your exposure to risks of the stock and bond markets. The following diagram illustrates how knowledge

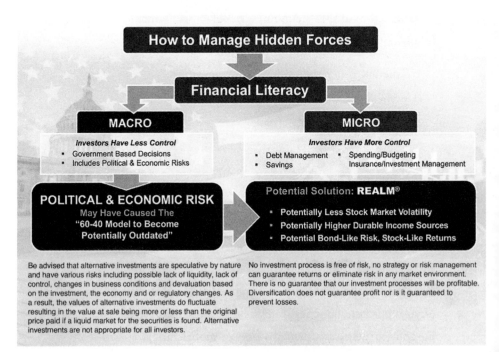

Fig. 10.1. Flowchart of how hidden forces can potentially impact your financial choices.

of hidden forces can help you understand the macro political and economic risks that can potentially affect your investment strategy, and some of the steps you can take to help you improve debt management, savings, budgeting, and investment management. You may also notice in the flowchart how my innovative REALM model can potentially lower your exposure to stock market volatility and offer higher durable income sources.

Within the umbrella of economic risk is globalization risk, which is "the web of relationships between economies worldwide by way of international trade and investments."[14] Let me add to this definition that globalization is the product of technological innovation and the explosive growth of information. While globalization started long before the digital age, today it has become an inescapable fact of life.

Some of the pros of globalization are obvious enough. Consumers have access to greater goods and services due to increased global competition. Countries can come together to form trade agreements and investment opportunities, which can lower the prices of consumer goods. Poorer counties can benefit from globalization by having greater access to consumer goods and increased job opportunities. Some of the disadvantages of globalization include the fact that wealthy nations and transnational corporations can exploit cheap labor from poorer countries. Globalization also causes job displacement. There are some who hold the view that globalization increases the number of jobs, but this is an overly simplistic analysis. In reality, globalization "redistributes jobs by moving production from high-cost countries to lower-cost ones. This means that high-cost countries often lose jobs due to globalization as production goes overseas."[15]

Perhaps the greatest risk of globalization is the increased possibility of a global recession. Here is why: Globalization allows certain companies, which are referred to as transnational corporations, to operate on a global scale. This means that these large corporations have developed the resources and infrastructure to "operate their supply chains and distribution in many countries."[16] This web of interconnectedness increases vulnerability to political and economic forces, which occur on a global scale. The 2007 global financial meltdown is one example of how globally interconnected markets can fail as a result of chain reaction. For example, if there's a housing bubble in the United States, then the ripple effect becomes global.

Globalization risk is real, and it can impact your investment strategy. Let's suppose that you invest in stocks, or your investment is largely locked up in the 60/40 model. If we look back to 1968, an era that parallels the growth of globalization, we can count 21 market corrections and 7 market crashes. A market correction is defined as a drop of less than 20 percent, and a market crash is defined as a rapid market drop of more than 20 percent.

If you look at the chart, you will notice there have been seven market crashes with a duration of 250 days or longer. Clearly globalization risk can have a detrimental effect on your stock portfolio.

Year	% Decline	Duration (in days)
1968-70	36.1%	543
1971	10.7%	103
1971	11.0%	76
1973-74	48.2%	630
1974	13.6%	29
1975	14.1%	63
1976-78	19.4%	531
1978	13.6%	63
1979	10.2%	33
1979	17.1%	43
1980-82	27.1%	622
1983-84	14.4%	286
1987	33.5%	101
1990	10.2%	28
1990	19.9%	87
1997	10.8%	20
1998	19.3%	45
1999	12.1%	91
2000-02	49.1%	929
2002-03	14.7%	104
2007-09	56.8%	537
2010	16.0%	70
2011	19.4%	157
2015	12.4%	96
2015-16	13.3%	100
2018	10.2%	13
2018	19.8%	95
2020	33.9%	33

Fig. 10.2. Yardeni Research Inc.[17]

FEDERAL RESERVE RISK

One of the ways the government can affect investing is through the Federal Reserve's raising or lowering the national interest rate, which is the rate at which banks lend money. When interest rates are low, people tend to borrow more and buy more things, which increases spending, thus increasing GDP. This works for stocks, too: People borrow to buy more stocks, although this process has the potential to lead to stock bubbles, which eventually burst.

When interest rates drop, that's a signal that the Federal Reserve wants to stimulate spending, to raise the GDP. The end result is that the stock market typically goes up. However, when interest rates go down, bond prices go up; lower interest rates make bonds pay out less. If you buy a $500 bond at 1 percent, you will make less over the same amount of time as a $500 bond at 4 percent, so the investment costs more in lost returns.

This lost money can make other investments more attractive; even if investments initially cost more, if their returns are higher, they may negate that extra cost. If stocks are more attractive, more people want to buy them, which pushes their cost up. This can cause stocks and bonds to move in the same direction—the prices of stocks and bonds both increase or decrease, instead of one rising as the other falls. When stocks and bonds move in the same direction, you have little to no protection when the market declines sharply or even crashes, as we've seen over the last 40 years; it is a possible sign of trouble on the horizon.

There are three key factors that may cause stocks and bonds to trend together. These factors include political, social, and economic forces, which may converge to create more risk and less return for the average investor. The political factors occur when the government intervenes in the market by artificially keeping interest rates low in order to boost the economy. The practice of keeping interest rates artificially low is known as quantitative easing, and it causes broad social concern and uncertainty, particularly among millennials, who now represent the largest demographic. In my experience, many millennials don't care for high-risk investments, which can cause downward pressure on both stocks and bonds, strengthening their correlation—but in the wrong direction. The economic consequences can be increased global debt, slower growth, falling productivity, and inflation, which further affect stocks and bonds, creating a dangerous cycle.

CORPORATE RISK

As you've already read, the Federal Reserve has extraordinary power to influence the economy. It can impact inflation, employment, and economic production by setting monetary policy. It can affect the money supply by setting the federal funds rate. The Federal Reserve can also offer its own stimulus program, independent of Congress, which includes direct cash aid to corporations.

In response to the COVID-19 pandemic, the Federal Reserve has approved a program to "provide hundreds of billions in emergency aid to large American corporations without requiring them to save jobs or limit payments to executives and shareholders. Under the program, the central bank will buy $500 billion in bonds issued by large companies."[18] Now, on the surface, one might argue that the pandemic has created an extraordinary situation, particularly affecting the airline industry. However, if you dig deeper, you will find that many corporations have created the mess they find themselves in today. One such company is Boeing.

In 2017, Boeing secured $23.4 billion in military contracts—that's taxpayer money. Additional contracts from both foreign and domestic airlines brought the company's total revenue to $100 billion.[19] In April 2020, Boeing announced a $641 million loss in the first quarter of 2020. In addition, it has "burned through $4.3 billion in cash. Revenues dropped 26 percent from the first quarter of last year, to just shy of $17 billion. It cut payroll 10 percent, through 'voluntary measures' and layoffs in its 160,000-person workforce."[20] As a result of these unprecedented circumstances, Boeing sought $60 billion in relief. Boeing would not need "anywhere as big a bailout as it's likely to get if it hadn't spent almost $60 billion . . . for dividends and stock buybacks from 2014 to 2019."[21]

Here is the problem with corporate buybacks: It contributes to social inequality. The practice of "increasing cash dividend and buying back stock in the open market are classic ways of 'returning money to shareholders,' as Wall Street calls it, and putting upward pressure on share prices . . . [it] keeps not only shareholders happy but often helps enhance top executives' personal wealth and compensation."[22] Once Boeing, and other large corporations, found themselves strapped for cash, the Federal Reserve was ready to step in.

Congress finally woke up to this practice of buybacks when it decided to add conditions to its stimulus package to help businesses during the pandemic. Companies can no longer use federal money to buy back their own stock. President Trump lent his support for this provision in the CARES act of March 2020 by saying, "I don't want to give a bailout to a company and then have somebody go out and use that money to buy back stock in the company and raise the price and then get a bonus. OK?"[23] According to Goldman Sachs stock market analysts, "first, politicians are denouncing repurchases given the impending recession. Second, from a practical perspective, as revenues evaporate firms will be looking to preserve cash."[24] The question, of course, is, why did it take a pandemic for Congress to take action?

Let's remember that although Congress added a provision barring buybacks in its stimulus package, the Federal Reserve's emergency relief program, which was set up jointly with the Treasury Department, has no restriction on how corporations spend the money. There is no directive to companies limiting stock dividends, executive compensation or stock buyback, or to maintain a certain employment level. Without these safeguards, this program permits companies to reward shareholders and executives at the expense of employees who stand to lose the most.

In short, the Federal Reserve has considerable power to influence the movement of the market, which can create higher volatility and uncertainty. During this pandemic, you need, more than ever before, to reevaluate your portfolio in order to protect yourself. It is precisely because of these hidden forces and risks that I developed the REALM model.

CORRELATION RISK

Correlation risk has often been taken for granted. Stocks and bonds are assumed to be inversely correlated assets, which means they are expected to move together—at the same time but in opposite directions—in response to economic cycles. Until recently, this statement was strongly predictive: When stocks rose in value, bonds languished. Conversely, when economic conditions drove stock values down, the value of bonds predictably rose.

This inverse correlation model was bound by certain assumptions, which may no longer hold true. Since 2008 the correlation between stocks and bonds—if it still exists at all—is no longer predictive and no longer meaningfully inverse. This movement away from an inverse correlation negates the very reason we entrusted our diversification strategy.[25] Another way of discussing correlation risk is to describe the correlation as either positive or negative. Economists prefer to use the term "negative correlation" to describe the inverse relationship between stocks and bonds. Part of what made the 60/40 portfolio an attractive investment vehicle was that "for most of the last 20 years,

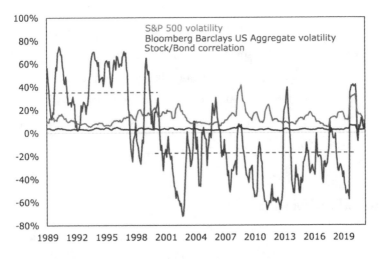

Fig. 10.3. Stock/Bond correlation. Source: Russell Investments[26]

stocks and bonds have been negatively correlated, meaning when stock prices fell, bond prices rose. This was especially helpful during periods of extreme market volatility, such as during the 2008–09 Great Financial Crisis or the COVID-induced bear market."[27] If you look at Figure 10.3, you will see that since 2000, stocks and bonds have shown a negative correlation, which means that investors were protected against higher volatility.

Think of correlation risk this way. If your investment vehicle unnecessarily exposes you to more risk, then you need to find different investment opportunities. I've known for several years now that something was fundamentally wrong with the 60/40 portfolio when stocks and bonds stopped being negatively correlated. This is why I developed my flexible and customizable multi-asset class portfolio. My REALM model potentially reduces exposure to market volatility by spreading risk to more than just three assets (stocks, bonds, and cash). In order for you to become a wise investor, or at the very least ask the appropriate questions, you need to be aware of the different risks that impact your investment decisions.

REGULATION RISK

As you've read in the last chapter, there is a relationship between government regulation and the free-market system. There has long been a debate among politicians and economists regarding the desired amount of government regulation. Republicans and Democrats have always found themselves on opposite ends of this divide, with Republicans favoring fewer regulations and Democrats arguing for more. The Republican argument on behalf of less regulation rests on the idea that "the free market will force businesses to protect consumers, provide superior products or services, and create affordable prices for everyone."[28] Democrats, on the other hand, argue that regulations are "necessary to protect consumers, the environment and the general public claim that corporations are not looking out for the public's interest."[29] While both Republicans and Democrats can find historical examples to support their case, it seems the absence of government regulations has contributed to unbridled greed and corruption.

As we saw in earlier chapters, when markets are left to their own devices, greed and corruption is almost inevitable. During the 1920s, the stock market was booming. At the time banks were not regulated, which created an environment filled with irrational exuberance, speculation, and wanton greed. Banks joined the frenzy by speculating on the stock market using depositors' money. On October 29, 1929, remembered as Black Tuesday, the Dow Jones Industrial Average fell 12 percent, which is one of the largest single-day drops in market history. During the panic sell-off, 16 million shares were traded, thus ushering in the Great Depression. Although there were several causes that contributed to the stock market crash, the absence of meaningful banking regulation proved to be disastrous.

To address this glaring problem, Congress passed the Glass-Steagall Act in 1933, which prohibited "commercial banks from participating in the investment banking business and vice versa."[30] Glass-Steagall would eventually be repealed by the Gramm-Leach-Bliley Act (GLBA), which was named after three Republican senators (Phil Gramm, Jim Leach, and Thomas J. Bliley Jr.) and signed into law by President Bill Clinton. The passage of the GLBA allowed commercial banks, investment banks, securities firms, and insurance companies to consolidate.

I want you to pay attention here to the fact that the political actors here were not simply Republicans or Democrats; rather it was both parties who repealed the Glass-Steagall Act, with dire consequences later.

Within a few short years after the repeal of Glass-Steagall, the dotcom bubble of the early 2000s burst, thus triggering the stock market crash of 2002. Shortly after that, the real estate bubble burst in 2008, causing another market crash. Part of what was behind the real estate fiasco were the subprime loans of the early 2000s, which were offered by banks and other financial institutions. These subprime loans were given to people with a poor credit history, which meant they were more likely to default. It was not simply subprime loans that caused a cascading global financial meltdown; it was also collateralized debt obligations, where different types of real estate debt were repackaged and resold.

The point to remember is that government regulations, or the absence of regulations, may create higher uncertainty and volatility in the stock market. This is one more reason you need to protect yourself by first understanding the different risks of investing by allocating a large portion of your investment to the stock market. Beyond financial risks, you also need to be aware of the financial actors.

LONGEVITY RISK

Another important factor to consider before you invest is longevity risk. Have you ever considered how insurance companies, or pension funds for that matter, view risk? Insurance companies make assumptions about the life expectancy of the people they insure. These companies use mathematical models to help them reduce the risk. If they get it wrong, they have to make higher payouts.

For the individual investor, longevity is a much more emotional risk. The fear of running out of money during your retirement is real and frightening. In fact, 49 percent of Americans cited running out of money as their primary retirement concern.[31] We are generally living longer: Life expectancy for men is 76 years and for women it's 81 years.[32] While this is great news for all of us, it poses difficult financial challenges. As medical science continues to innovate, the average life expectancy for both men and women will increase to 85.6 years by 2060.[33]

The question is, what do you want your quality of life to be during retirement? The longer we live, the more susceptible we are to market corrections and crashes. Longevity risk is one of the reasons I developed my innovative REALM model, which will potentially help mitigate risk while sustaining one's retirement future.

Women, in particular, need to understand how these hidden forces, risks, and actors will help them ask the relevant questions about investment opportunities. For too long women have had to depend on men to make these decisions on their behalf. This must stop now! With better financial literacy, you can—and must—take actionable steps to help you secure a retirement of potentially 20 years or more.

IDEOLOGICAL RISK

As I've stated earlier, hidden forces and risks do not operate in a vacuum; rather they tend to intersect and overlap. One example is the link between political ideology and economic reality. Over the past 75 years, there have been two broadly defined political ideologies that offered contrasting philosophical views of the role of government in economic affairs. Fordism, which I'll explain in this section, advocated for more government intervention in our economic life, while neoliberalism insisted that governments should not intervene in the market. Both of these antithetical views created different types of market risk. Let's begin with Fordism, which was an ideological framework that helped create the middle class and expanded the American Dream.

Following World War II, a new form of economic growth helped give rise to the postwar boom. This mode of growth became known as Fordism, and, broadly defined, it is a system of standardized production in which workers were offered a decent wage to afford the very goods they produced. Fordism offered mass consumption, sufficient wages to support families, job stability, and rising incomes. From the late 1940s to the early 1970s, "Fordism extended well beyond the factory walls; it reshaped the spatial and demographic configuration of cities; it ignited bouts of economic development, industrial concentration, and social conflict."[34] In many ways Fordism gave rise to the American middle class, which, in turn, helped spread the American Dream. Under Fordism a few large corporations dominated key economic sectors by dictating what consumers wanted and needed.

Fig. 10.4. Fordism was managed by a few large corporations that were based on standardization.[35]

In return for democratizing the American Dream, these large corporations demanded loyalty from their workers, which is why they offered workers high wages and health and other benefits and also respected labor unions. By the 1970s, Fordism would gradually collapse under the weight of its mass-production philosophy. The growth potential had slowly been exhausted, and workers complained they felt a sense of alienation. The market became saturated with mass consumer goods, and increased globalization meant that Fordism would either have to evolve or be replaced by another ideology. What came next not only proved to be ineffective but also revealed how selfishness, greed, and corruption can be elevated to a social virtue with disastrous consequences.

As a result of neoliberalism, corporate greed and fraud became fashionable in the 1980s. What neoliberalism's architect, Milton Friedman, failed to realize when he stated that businesses had only one social responsibility (to increase profits while playing within the rules) was that businesses can use their money and influence to rewrite the rules to their advantage, which is precisely what happened. When the Glass-Steagall Act was repealed in 1999, the stage was set for subprime loans, credit-default swaps, and an unsustainable housing bubble that burst in 2007 and triggered a global financial meltdown. My point is that political ideologies can, and do, influence the market.

SOCIAL MEDIA RISK

Today we are living through the unfolding of the digital age, an age of unprecedented technological innovation, as well as unanticipated problems. As I wrote in *Redefining Financial Literacy*, we have a near infinite supply of information and yet our understanding of the world is limited. We cannot possibly consume the amount of information that is at our fingertips, which is why absorbing knowledge is more important today than ever before. One of the unintended consequences of the digital revolution is known as the Dunning-Kruger effect, which is a "cognitive bias in which people believe that they are smarter and more capable than they really are."[36] The massive amount of information that is immediately accessible lulls us into a false sense of overconfidence. Charles Darwin, in his book *The Descent of Man*, observed that "ignorance more frequently begets confidence than does knowledge."[37] The Dunning-Kruger effect tells us that a "tiny bit of knowledge on a subject matter can lead people to mistakenly believe that they know all there is to know about it."[38]

Disconnected and disjointed pieces of information engender in people the illusion of knowledge. The current general lack of financial literacy, coupled with an exaggerated sense of confidence, often causes people to exhibit poor judgment.

The Dunning-Kruger effect was introduced in 1999, which marks the beginning of the digital revolution. Over the past 20 years, social media platforms have exploded. In 2004, Facebook was created, followed by Reddit in 2005 and Twitter in 2006. These platforms and countless others have fundamentally transformed our social landscape. We now live in a world of constant connectivity where echo chambers have become amplified spaces. Therein lies the danger of social media: People tend to react to the collective will of the group without any critical assessment of the facts or information. This behavior could have political and economic consequences. Politically, these online chat rooms can help spread disinformation and conspiracy theories without any critical analysis or factual evidence. Economically, this type of collective behavior, what I call groupthink, poses a new kind of risk to the market.

This form of groupthink recently manifested itself in the case of the popular video game retailer GameStop. During January 2021, members of the popular online Reddit forum WallStreetBets reacted to hedge funds trying to short stocks of the video game company by creating the kind of hype that catapulted stock share prices by more than 400 percent. In comparison, the Dow Jones Industrial Average went up by a mere 1 percent over the same time period. Now you might be thinking this to yourself: Isn't that a good thing? Isn't it about time that average investors come together to stick it to the large hedge funds who have manipulated the market for years? The answer is not that simple. The fact that a group of people in an online social chat room came together to hype the value of a company without any fundamentals to support the hype is itself a form of market manipulation.

This kind of undisciplined financial power that comes from social media speculation creates a kind of irrational exuberance that only causes greater volatility and uncertainty in the stock market. According to Mark DeCambre and Andrew Keshner, writing for MarketWatch, the meteoric rise of GameStop's stock "in the absence of any market-moving news—raises another issue: the distinction between legitimate, totally legal stock-market hype in 21st century social-media chatrooms and market manipulation that enables some investors to cash in on the exuberance of others."[39] We are now in uncharted territory when social media can artificially influence or, if you prefer, manipulate the market. There will be legal and ethical questions to deal with for years to come.

Before you condemn social media for manipulating the market, let's recall that the Federal Reserve's actions also have consequences. When the Fed keeps interest rates close to zero for an extended period of time, the financial markets become flooded with liquidity. In addition, the stimulus checks the government has issued have also created a kind of irrational exuberance that may contribute to greater market uncertainty.

When you factor in the ease with which investors can trade stocks and other securities online with the availability of social media platforms where certain groups come together to create hype, then you begin to understand the potential for market manipulation. Trading apps such as Robinhood and social media sites like Facebook and Reddit are becoming the wave of the future.

Barbara Roper, who is the director of investor protection for the Consumer Federation of America, had this to say about the current investment environment: "As a general rule, people are allowed to make foolish investment decisions. Others are not allowed to fraudulently promote foolish investment decisions."[40] Let's look at an example. Suppose someone comments on an online chat forum that Stock X is the greatest stock ever. While this statement may strike you as hyperbole, it is perfectly acceptable for people to be irrational and excited. However, if someone makes a statement that is factually wrong, like saying a company just received a patent, then this can be viewed as a form of market manipulation.

GENDER RISK

One of the prevailing myths about investing is that women are not as savvy or rational as men. One of the assumptions that helps perpetuate this myth is that women are not as adept at math and therefore are not smart with money. Let me tell you now that this is simply not true. It is a social construct perpetuated for generations. According to Shelley Correll, professor of sociology at Stanford University, "boys do not pursue mathematical activities at a higher rate than girls because they are better at mathematics. They do so, at least in part, because they think they are better."[41] Let's explore a bit what Correll is trying to say.

For many generations, boys have been led to believe they are smarter than girls when it comes to math. Girls, for their part, have internalized the idea that they are simply not as analytical as boys. In early education, boys and girls are treated differently by teachers. Research has revealed a subconscious bias in terms of how teachers relate to boys and girls that is also evident along gender and racial lines. According to Yasemin Copur-Gencturk, professor of math education at the University of Southern California and the lead author of a study in the journal *Educational Researcher*, "both white teachers and teachers of color interpret boys' math ability as higher than girls' and white students' math ability as higher than that of black and Hispanic students, even when the educators had judged students' math performance as equal."[42] What the research suggests is that regardless of actual performance, girls and students of color are looked upon as having inferior math skills compared to White boys.

One of the disturbing implications of this study is that lower teacher expectations make it harder for girls and students of color to be respected throughout their academic career. By high school, girls have already internalized that they are not good in math. In fact, "by ages 13 to 17, only 11% of girls say they plan to pursue a STEM [science, technology, engineering, and mathematics] career, compared to 35% of boys."[43] It should be no surprise then that women in college are underrepresented in STEM majors—"for instance only around 21% of engineering majors are women and only around 19% of computer and information science majors are women."[44]

If you are asking yourself what all of this has to do with investing, then the short answer is this: Everything. At a basic level, the concept of investing one's money is mathematical. There is a field of study known as quantitative analysis that emphasizes "mathematical and statistical analysis to help determine the value of a financial asset, such as a stock or option."[45] In fact, it was the Nobel Prize–winning economist Harry Markowitz who introduced the modern portfolio theory in 1952. He used "math to quantify diversification and is cited as an early adopter of the concept that mathematical models could be applied to investing."[46] If the stereotype has long been that women are not smart enough to perform mathematics, and mathematics is needed for investing, then it follows that women are not very good investors. The logic is both simple and disturbing. It's clear how society has framed women's analytical abilities.

The cultural construct that women are not cut out for investing because of some antiquated notion that they are too emotional or that they are not smart enough to understand mathematics is simply wrong. Part of my motivation in writing this book is to challenge this pervasive bias by exposing the facts about women and investing. This is not an easy task. In the male-dominated financial industry, women are looked upon as "risk-averse spendthrifts" who need advisors (male, of course) to take control over their investments.[47] This view of women as hapless, emotionally driven investors is, of course, false, and the research proves it.

In reality, according to a Fidelity study, "women investors

consistently outperform their male counterparts, which could leave them with hundreds of thousands of dollars more at retirement."[48] Let's look at the facts:

- Female investors earn better returns than men—up to 1 percent.
- On average, women lost 2.5 percent of their stock portfolio value in 2015, while men lost 3.8 percent.
- Women are less confident in their ability than men, though investing confidence increases with age.
- Women stay the course by trading stocks and changing asset allocations less frequently than men.
- Fidelity reports that only 9 percent of women think they make better investors than men.[49]

Despite the fact that women have been led to believe they are poor investors simply as a result of their gender, as you can see, they have managed to outperform men. While this is great news, it can be misleading. As a general rule, having more money to invest leads to more robust wealth accumulation. From this perspective, women are at a significant disadvantage because women only make $0.82 on the dollar when compared to men. This pay discrepancy means there is a "cumulative $1,055,000 lifetime earnings gap between men and women at retirement age."[50] This is a major reason why it is a financial and moral imperative that the gender pay gap is corrected as soon as possible.

The myth of gender risk is the cultural perception that women, due to inferior math skills, are incapable of understanding the complex world of finance and need men to help guide them along. In my experience, both men and women need help understanding the challenges of financial and investment decisions, but to suggest that women are somehow inherently incapable of navigating the financial world is absurd, and it perpetuates a myth that has no place in our discourse. Women need to be aware of this myth and stop internalizing it as truth. Women not only are capable of making rational and informed investment decisions but will also be the face of generational wealth transfer for years to come.

To sum up, there are hidden forces that may be invisible but are ever present and can, and often do, influence your money. It's like gravity: We can't see it, but it is always there, exerting a force on us. In addition to the hidden forces, there are hidden risks that you need to consider when you plan for your retirement. Beyond that, you need to be aware of the actors (some hidden and some not so much)—the Federal Reserve, technological innovation, and social media—that may have a direct impact on your investment strategy.

As the market becomes more volatile, you may want to reconsider the 60/40 investment portfolio that potentially exposes you to unnecessary risk. This is why I urge you to contact a qualified and experienced financial advisor and begin to ask the right questions. For example, you may want to ask about why bonds are paying close to zero or what is an appropriate exposure to the stock market. You may also want to inquire about adding alternative investments to your portfolio. I'll discuss that in greater detail in chapter 12.

Now that we have a better understanding of the hidden risks behind investment dollars, it is time to look at the interaction between them.

11

THE INTERSECTION BETWEEN POLITICAL AND ECONOMIC RISK

"You can think big when you're thinking about macroeconomics."

—CATHIE WOOD

Thus far I've explored different types of hidden risks that can potentially increase uncertainty and volatility. However, these risks, particularly political and economic risks, do not exist in isolation of each other. Rather, they intersect and overlap in such a way as to magnify the impact they have on your money. In other words, it is difficult to think about, or write about, political risk without discussing economic risk. Let's look at some examples from the past 50 years where political and economic risk worked together to simultaneously increase uncertainty and volatility in the stock market while reducing bond yields.

The 1970s was a decade of political upheaval, economic uncertainty, hyperinflation, and the gradual rise of corporate power. The Vietnam War proved to be a political nightmare for the Johnson administration; during the Nixon administration that followed, the Watergate scandal caused additional upheaval. Consider the economic reality for a moment: Unemployment was at double digits, the stock market lost nearly 50 percent over a 20-month period, and interest rates reached as high as 20 percent, which meant that many people could not afford to purchase cars or homes.[1] Politics and economics were so intertwined as to cause a wave of mistrust of government. For example, in 1964 "78 percent of Americans thought that the government could be 'trusted to do the right thing' either 'always' or 'most of the time.' By the eve of Ronald Reagan's election in 1980, however, that figure had plunged to 26 percent."[2] This lack of trust in government would gradually contribute to the rise of corporate power, which was antithetical to government intervention in the economic life of the average American. The question, of course, becomes, how did corporations successfully achieve total control of American capitalism?

According to Kurt Anderson, author of *Evil Geniuses: The Unmaking of America*, and host of the Peabody-winning public radio program *Studio 360*, corporations rose to prominence without most people realizing what was going on. Anderson asked a simple yet profound question: "So how did big business and the very rich and their political allies and enablers manage to convince enough Americans in the 1970s and '80s that the comfortable economic rules and expectations we'd had in place for half of the twentieth century were obsolete and should be replaced by an older set of assumptions and protocols?"[3] The comfortable economic rules

Anderson is alluding to are the Depression-era New Deal programs established by President Franklin Roosevelt. Those programs, coupled with the Fordist idea that every American deserved a decent wage and the opportunity to realize the American Dream, would give way to another, older set of assumptions.

Anderson was referring to the laissez-faire capitalism that existed prior to the Great Depression. This ideology opposes government intervention in business affairs. Beginning in the 1970s and into the '80s and '90s, a paradigm shift occurred almost imperceptibly. According to Anderson, it was "carried out by means of a thousand wonky adjustments to government rules and laws, and obscure financial inventions, and big companies one by one changing how they operated and getting away with it—all of it with impacts that emerged gradually, over decades."[4] Over time, the cumulative effect of these changes would favor wealthy elites and allow corporations to rise to political and economic dominance.

Some of these changes included less regulation for business, less enforcement of antitrust laws, tax changes that favored the rich, and political influence by large corporations that gradually, but effectively, developed the power and the means to rewrite the laws to perpetuate and expand their cultural dominance. This is a perfect example of economic risk intersecting with political risk. As corporate power increased, the political power of the wealthy elites created what I call the corporate state.

What were the consequences of this confluence of events? What was the risk created by these political and economic forces? The consequences have been dramatic and far-reaching. Between 1980 and today, millions of middle-class jobs disappeared, fixed private pensions and reliable health care diminished, college degrees were earned under the burden of stifling student debt and the share of wealth owned by the richest 1 percent doubled. This is just the beginning of a laundry list of other outcomes that have contributed to our broken capitalist system.

There are those who argue that the transition toward a neoliberal economy occurred at the hands of Republicans who engineered a kind of economic coup that largely went unnoticed. And while there is a great deal of evidence to support this argument—from Milton Friedman's neoliberal ideology to Robert Bork's judicial interpretation of antitrust laws—it is important to understand that Democrats also contributed to the creation of the corporate state. It was President Bill Clinton, for example, who signed the Gramm-Leach-Bliley Act in 1999.

THE CORPORATE STATE

America today is dominated by a concentration of corporate power that has fundamentally changed our conception of the American Dream. The rise of the corporate state was gradual. Businesses gained greater power and influence by changing the legal environment incrementally. When Milton Friedman suggested that businesses have a social responsibility to maximize profits while following the rules of the game, he failed to add that the rules were largely written by the very businesses who wanted to maximize profits. Thus, the Friedman doctrine has become a kind of philosophical blueprint for the rise of corporate power.

Not to put too fine a point on it, the problem with a corporate state is that it challenges some of the core concepts of a democratic society.

According to Alan Schwartz, executive chairman of the investment banking firm Guggenheim Partners, "the market society only works if voters can set the right rules. However, because profits can be increased by weakening competition, evading taxes or suppressing climate regulation, Friedman recognized that business would seek to bend and capture the rules of the game."[5] The fundamental problem of the Friedman doctrine is that it concentrates the political and economic power of a few large corporations at the expense of everyone else. It means that "distorting the regulatory structure is one of the key responsibilities of business. In short, the 'Friedman doctrine' means that business has a 'social responsibility' to erode democracy."[6] When wealth and power are concentrated in the hands of a few mega corporations who have the financial means to avoid paying taxes like the rest of us or to remove government regulations that prove to be inconvenient to their mission of maximizing profits, then the very fabric of our democracy is threatened.

The rise of multinational corporations has created a reality where "climate change, tax evasion, human rights abuses and environmental disasters are the order of the day. On the face of it, the rise of corporate power is exerting undue influence and encroaching on democracy, politics and the state."[7]

It is important to understand what a corporation is and the power it possesses so that you can have a better idea of the forces and risks you are up against when it comes to your financial liberation. In many ways, corporations are paradoxical entities. Although the state "creates, recognizes or confers its legal existence, at the same time the corporation appears to be something outside the state, threatening and challenging its power, and lying beyond its control and regulatory competence."[8]

Historically, governments granted certain rights and privileges to corporations in order to achieve certain goals. But it was the state that held the power, while corporations were subordinate and dependent upon it. This political-economic structure worked for several centuries and contributed to the economic growth of our nation and the world. Over the past 50 years, however, as we've seen, there was "a shift away from a stakeholder view of corporate interests and purposes to one dominated by profit and shareholder value maximization."[9]

Today corporate consolidation of entire industries across the globe suggests that a few dozen large companies rule the world. Many of these companies are household names, such as Walmart, Microsoft, Apple, Facebook, Verizon, Chevrolet, J.P. Morgan, Chevron, Alphabet Inc. (parent company of Google), AT&T, Daimler, Samsung, Berkshire Hathaway, Exxon Mobile, Toyota, and Amazon. The values of some of these companies—Microsoft, Apple, Google, and Walmart—actually exceed the gross national product (GDP) of some countries. Apple, for example, which as of 2021 has a market capitalization of $2.08 trillion, exceeded the GDP of Canada, Brazil, and Italy.[10]

At this point you might be wondering what is so bad about corporations dominating the economies of the world. We are, after all, better off as a result of Amazon, Apple, Google, Microsoft, and all the other companies that make our lives easier. But we need to ask the following: On a political level, do we want our government and elected officials influenced by a few large corporations to such a degree that the very fabric of our democracy is undermined? On an economic level, at what cost are we willing to accept the comforts made available by these corporations? The corporate state has created a concentration of wealth and power whose scale is beyond comprehension. How do we begin to grasp the concept of trillions or billions of dollars when the average American is trying to earn a decent wage to have a roof over her head, provide for her family, and live comfortably through retirement?

This intimate connection between corporations and government institutions forms the very structure of how wealth and power move through society. In other words, "the concentration of economic power has reached extreme proportions. This power is evident in major sectors of our economy, such as technology platforms, telecommunications, banks, health care, and retail."[11] From the standpoint of democracy, powerful corporations have become political institutions in their own right. They exert extraordinary power over governments and politicians by spending billions to influence public discourse through both traditional and social media. By concentrating economic power, corporations wittingly or unwittingly contribute to the continued marginalization of historically excluded groups.[12] One of the ways the concentration of economic power has reached extreme proportions is through tax laws that are favorable to corporations.

You might be surprised to learn that multibillion-dollar corporations pay taxes at a lower rate than you and me. There was a time not so long ago—the 1950s—when corporate income accounted for one-third of the total federal tax revenue. However, as of 2019, the total federal tax revenue from corporations dropped to 6.5 percent.[13] That's not all; there are many corporations that pay no taxes at all. For example, "at least 55 of the largest corporations in America paid no federal corporate income taxes in their most recent fiscal year [2020] despite enjoying substantial pretax profits in the United States."[14] These 55 companies enjoyed a combined profit of almost $40.5 billion in 2020, which meant they would have paid a combined $8.5 billion in taxes had they paid the 21 percent corporate tax rate. To add insult to injury, these 55 companies received $3.5 billion in tax breaks, which brings the total amount of tax avoidance and tax breaks to $12 billion. Now imagine for a moment if you could do that on your tax return.

You might be angrily asking yourself who these companies are that made billions and yet paid no federal tax. You are probably familiar with the names of some of the companies on this list. But the more important question is, how is this possible? The simple answer is politics. Thanks to the Tax Cuts and Jobs Act, which was signed into law by President Trump in 2017, the US corporate tax rate was cut from 35 percent to 21 percent.[15] In addition to legally paying a lower tax rate, companies find numerous loopholes to avoid paying taxes at all. For example, corporations will use foreign subsidiaries to shift US profits to countries with lower tax rates. Another tactic is accelerated depreciation, which allows corporations to expense the cost of their capital at a faster pace than that at which it actually wears out.

With all these tax loopholes and many corporations paying little to no taxes, you might think that these multinational companies are trustworthy. Sadly, they are not. Just as countries are rated for their credit worthiness, so, too, are corporations. Credit rating agencies such as Moody's and Standard & Poor's offer ratings of companies so that investors can make informed investment decisions. Credit ratings lie on a spectrum from AAA (the highest rating) on one end to C and D ratings (which are considered junk). These assessments help investors understand "the likelihood of a company defaulting on its debt obligations or outstanding bonds."[16] The fact is that American companies have never experienced the staggering level of debt that they do today. Consider that in 2020, outstanding consumer debt in the US reached $14.88 trillion, according to data from an Experian debt study.[17] Part of the reason corporations are carrying high debt is a decades-long credit binge due to absurdly low borrowing costs.

It's not just the amount of debt that has skyrocketed. Since the global financial meltdown in 2008, the amount of BBB-rated bonds—those that are the very bottom of investment-grade corporate debt—has risen a whopping 200 percent, according to Standard & Poor's (S&P) Global. The value of BBB-rated bonds grew to more than $3 trillion, which today represents 53 percent of the entire investment-grade market.[18] High corporate debt increases the probability that a company will default on its debt obligations. This creates a higher level of risk to investors, since one of the consequences of rising corporate debt is a protracted economic contraction. One of the causes of such a contraction is "the trillions of dollars that major U.S. corporations have spent on open market repurchases—aka 'stock buybacks'—since the financial crisis a decade ago."[19]

In 2018, as a result of the unprecedented profits that resulted from the Tax Cuts and Jobs Act of 2017, major corporations on the S&P 500 Index spent a combined $806 billion in buybacks, which represented $200 billion more than the previous record established in 2007.[20] The magnitude of corporate buybacks is extraordinary, with 465 companies in the S&P 500 Index that were publicly listed between 2009 and 2018 spending a combined $4.3 trillion on stock buybacks. Why do companies engage in such massive buybacks? The reason is that executives are often paid in stock options and stock awards. Stock buybacks are a way for corporations to manipulate stock prices to their advantage. In other words, stock buybacks are designed to enrich hedge-fund managers, as well as senior executives. Of course, all this comes at the expense of employees and shareholders.

WOMEN AND THE CORPORATE STATE

As we've seen, the corporate state did not occur in a vacuum; it was shaped by the convergence of two powerful events—the rise of economists as a political force and neoliberalism as an economic ideology. It should not come as a surprise that women were largely excluded from the economic profession and from corporate boards. And this omission of women in economics and corporate America contributed to the male-centric neoliberal ideology.

It was economists such as Friedrich Hayek, Milton Friedman, James M. Buchanan, Alan Greenspan, and others—all men—who became the architects of the neoliberal ideology that served as the blueprint for the corporate state. All of them, with the exception of Alan Greenspan, were Nobel Prize–winning economist's; yet the ideology they championed created massive wealth for a privileged few, widened the inequality gap, and led to the 2008 global financial meltdown that exposed neoliberalism's disastrous flaws. In fact, Alan Greenspan, who became the chair of the Federal Reserve, admitted before Congress that his ideology (neoliberalism) was wrong.[21]

Former prime minister of Australia Kevin Rudd also declared that the 2008 stock market crash "called into question the prevailing neoliberal economic orthodoxy of the past 30 years—the orthodoxy that has underpinned the national and global regulatory frameworks that have so spectacularly failed to prevent the economic mayhem which has been visited upon us."[22]

Contrast all that with the work of the only two women who have won the Nobel Prize for economics since it was introduced in 1969. In 2009, Elinor Ostrom became the first woman to win the coveted award. Ostrom, a professor of political science and co-director of the Workshop in Political Theory and Policy Analysis at Indiana University, won the Noble Prize for her analysis of economic governance. Ostrom's work explored mechanisms for tackling common problems that faced communities across the world.

In 2019, Esther Duflo became the second (and youngest) woman to win the Nobel Prize in Economics. Duflo, a professor of poverty alleviation and developmental economics at the Massachusetts Institute of Technology (MIT), won the award for her experimental effort to reduce global poverty. The contribution of these women and their recognition speaks volumes about where their focus lies.

What else can we say about women in corporate life? Let's look at some disturbing numbers. The World Benchmarking Alliance identified 2,000 of the most influential global companies in order to determine the gender breakdown of employees. The disturbing result was that on average, these companie's hires are 79 percent men and only 21 percent women. To exacerbate matters, only 15 percent of executives are women.[23]

What about the Fortune 500 companies and their hiring practices? Every year since 1955, *Fortune* magazine has selected 500 of the largest corporations to include on their list that ranks companies by total revenue. In 1955, General Motors, U.S. Steel, and General Electric were ranked at the very top. During the '50s and '60s, the Fortune 500

CEOs were entirely White men. In 1972, Katherine Graham, who took over *The Washington Post* after her husband committed suicide, became the first woman CEO of a Fortune 500 company. It took another nine years until we had the first Latino CEO when Roberto Goizuela became the CEO of Coca-Cola in 1981. Five years later, Gerald Tsai became the first Chinese American to become the CEO of American Can, and Franklin Raines became the first African American to become the CEO of Fannie May in 1999.[24]

One might imagine that if the first woman CEO of a Fortune 500 company assumed her position 50 years ago, then certainly today women would be represented in far greater numbers. Sadly, this is not the case. As of 2021, only 8.1 percent of Fortune 500 companies were run by women.[25] Another way to look at this is that 459 of the Fortune 500 companies are run by men. One of the reasons corporate culture has not changed is that company boards are largely made up of men, but this perpetuation of the old boys club is simply unacceptable.

The gender imbalance in corporate America may finally be a thing of the past. The good news is that the culture of male-dominated boardrooms is changing, thanks to an elite few financial corporations that have an extraordinary amount of cultural clout.

According to David Matsa, professor of finance at Kellogg School of Management at Northwestern University, the recent rise of women on corporate boards has largely been driven by "the Big Three" institutional investment firms—Vanguard, BlackRock, and State Street. These three corporations "manage over $15 trillion, accounting for three-quarters of indexed mutual fund assets. That means these companies hold shares in almost every large firm in the U.S.—in fact, they're the dominant shareholder in 88 percent of firms on the S&P 500."[26] The efforts by these three mega corporations are leading to more women entering the boardroom. The Big Three corporations are succeeding in changing "the conversation around gender in corporate boardrooms."[27]

Let me add this to the conversation: If change is not moving fast enough, then women today have a powerful voice on social media. The corporate boardrooms that are not changing fast enough to include women need to be exposed. If we want to see a more egalitarian representation of gender and races in corporate boardrooms, it behooves us to pay attention to corporate hiring practices and to speak out about them (positively and negatively) on social media.

CONNECTING THE DOTS

The message of this chapter is clear: Political and economic risks do not exist in a vacuum. Rather, they intersect, overlap, and interact with each other in such a way as to increase risk to your hard-earned money. Obviously, it is important to understand these forces, risks, and actors so you can make informed decisions regarding your financial and retirement future. However, there is another important reason to understand the political and economic reality that envelops all of our lives. The more you understand and appreciate how political and economic risks impact your financial future, the more you realize the uphill battle you are up against when it comes to your financial future. That's why saving your money early and investing early is of paramount importance. Most importantly, you must believe in your own ability to evaluate financial risks and make financial decisions.

If women believe the myth that they are not smart enough or rational enough to understand the financial world, then women will continue to exist on the margins of financial success. They will then rely on others to make financial decisions for them. I can't stress this enough: If you depend on others, then you lose your financial freedom. However, you have an opportunity to avoid that.

When corporations rise to the point of becoming so powerful as to manipulate the democratic order, then you need to fight back by investing intelligently. When corporations can manipulate the political process to rewrite the rules that enable them to maximize profits at the expense of the average American, then you need to protect yourself. When corporations pay little to no taxes and engage in corporate buybacks to enrich themselves, then you need to wake up and make stronger investment decisions. To help investors fight back against the political and economic risks we just discussed and to make the most of their investment choices, I spent years developing my innovative multi-asset class REALM model. I'll explain more about it in the next chapter.

12

A REALM OF POSSIBILITIES

"Insanity: doing the same thing over and over again
and expecting different results."

—ALBERT EINSTEIN

Risk is a stubborn fact of investing. There are people who believe they
are better off keeping their cash in the bank or stuffed somewhere
under a mattress. Here is the problem with this belief: Even cash is
not immune from the hidden forces I've described in previous chapters. If you choose not to invest and hold on to your cash, you are
exposing yourself to inflation risk, which is very much tangible. We
all feel inflation when we go to the market and realize the price of
milk or bread has gone up. Inflation can be a deceptive concept, which
is why it merits an example. Suppose you stashed away $1,000 with
the idea of buying a new refrigerator. After waiting a few months, you
go online—it's easier this way because of the pandemic—to buy the

fridge. The only problem is the refrigerator now costs $1,020. The price has gone up by 2 percent. This is inflation eating away at the purchasing power of your cash.

The reason you need to understand inflation risk is to more easily understand the concept of a real rate of return. There are two types of investment return—the nominal rate of return and the real rate of return. The nominal return is the annual amount of money generated by your investment before you factor in fees, taxes, and inflation. The real rate of return is the amount of money your investment makes annually minus external factors such as fees and inflation.[1] It is important to understand these differences, particularly when we look at the 60/40 investment portfolio. This time-honored tradition of investing in stocks and bonds, while profitable in the past, is potentially broken. Why? The world today is vastly more complex and interconnected than ever before. Markets are more volatile, interest rates are kept at an artificially low level, and the inverse correlation between stocks and bonds may no longer hold true.

The 60/40 portfolio approach leaves 60 percent of your investments, the equities, at risk due to volatility—the fluctuations of the market. At any moment, the market could decrease or even crash, and you could potentially lose all or part of your stock investment. On the other hand, if the market surges, you stand to make a windfall profit. That's the point of the 60/40 approach. The 60 percent in stocks moves in jumps and spurts to hopefully earn you a positive return over a long period. The other 40 percent, which you've socked away in bonds, is meant to provide protection for your investment by balancing the stock market's constant volatility with bonds' hypothetically conservative returns for lower risk.

But what if stocks and bonds both have a bad year?[2] The days when bonds could offer you absolute protection against the volatile stock market are long gone. "In the past, investors were able to rely on income provided by their bond investments to support their portfolios during periods of market stress. Unfortunately, today's low-yield environment means the diversification benefit from bonds will not be as large as in the past."[3] Bonds can also be risky when you factor in inflation. If the cost of living and inflation increase, you may actually earn a negative rate of return. And when it comes to corporate bonds, you must realize that such bonds "aren't guaranteed by the full faith and credit of the US government but, instead, depend on the corporation's ability to repay that debt."[4] As you can see, the 60/40 portfolio may no longer be relevant in today's economic climate.

For these reasons, the 60/40 model has been losing traction over the past several years, both in its ability to safeguard a financially sound retirement and—thankfully—in its use by financial advisors. According to Clifford Stanton, CFP, the preponderant opinion of financial experts is that the 60/40 model is broken.[5] Some of the underlying reasons include the lower yields on bonds, market volatility, and the global economy. This is not what the average investor has envisioned for retirement, particularly when we are living longer today than ever before.

One of the criticisms of modern portfolio theory, in general, is that the investment decisions made based on it would work for a static market, but the real-world stock market is constantly in flux, and the theory fails to adapt to those changes.[6] Modern portfolio theory is simply too inflexible to adapt to the ever-changing market landscape of today's complex world. Add to that the inconsistently correlated risk of having 60 percent in stocks and 40 percent in bonds, and this binary model of investing has potentially created a false sense of reality. In fact, since 1938, this type of portfolio "actually went backwards in relation to inflation."[7] A key problem with the 60/40 asset allocation has always been the lack of diversification; it offers only two kinds of assets.

I'm not the only one, of course, who believes the 60/40 allocation is potentially outdated and ineffective. Analysts from major firms like Bank of America, Morgan Stanley, and J.P. Morgan "proclaimed the death of the 60/40 rule in recent years."[8] Their primary reason for the need to replace the 60/40 strategy is lower returns from bonds. High-quality bonds today offer neither yield nor an inflation hedge. For example, "investing in Treasurys is guaranteed to earn a full 1% less than inflation over the coming decade. Investors in Treasurys are guaranteed to lose value as will investors in municipal bonds and even in high-grade corporate credit."[9] There was a time when bonds offered protection against the volatility of stocks, however, "with yields so low, bonds can no longer rally when stocks sell-off."[10]

Given these problems with the 60/40 portfolio, why has it been so popular? Part of the answer is marketing. Many on Wall Street use "a well-crafted marketing pitch [to sell] this over-simplified, excessively aggressive strategy."[11] There are those who might argue that the 60/40 portfolio is likely to repeat some of its strong performance in the past. The only problem is that this is not a likely scenario: "Bond rates are too low, and stocks are near all-time highs. This is a toxic combination not seen since the 1970s, way before 60/40 was a way for investment firms to build scale in their businesses by herding people into a unified asset allocation."[12]

Another part of what makes the 60/40 allocation appealing is its simplicity. There isn't much to think about. According to David Koch, senior wealth advisor at Halbert Hargrove, the simplicity of this binary portfolio is as follows: "Set it, forget it, and rebalance annually."[13] But a limited-asset allocation strategy like 60/40 fails to consider the modern financial landscape of today's investor:

- Increased longevity shifts the focus to growth.
- Diversification potential is limited.
- The market is evolving.
- Investors' needs aren't static.

The 60/40 allocation model is also easy to deal with in retirement—at least in theory. In the 1990s, William Bengen, a financial planner from California, created a straightforward guideline for retirement withdrawals. His rule simply states that you can withdraw 4 percent of your portfolio each year in retirement. The rule allows retirees to "increase the rate to keep pace with inflation."[14]

The problem with the 4 percent withdrawal rule is that it is outdated and does not reflect the reality we are living in with the COVID-19 pandemic. According to Wade Pfau, professor in the PhD program for financial and retirement planning at the American College in Bryn Mawr, Pennsylvania, "the devastating loss of jobs set off by the COVID-19 pandemic is depriving many folks who planned to retire this year of that lever."[15] The economic reality of sudden job losses has dramatically changed the 4 percent rule for retirees. In fact, the withdrawal rate has "shriveled to only 2.4% for investors taking a 'moderate amount of risk.'"[16] As you can imagine, a 2.4 percent withdrawal rate is unlikely to sustain you during your retirement years, particularly when we are living longer than ever before.

QUANTITATIVE EASING

Sometimes economics can present itself as a technical field of study with its own intimidating language. Once you go beyond the sophisticated language, you often find the meaning is rather straightforward. Let's look at the concept of quantitative easing. Think of the word "quantitative" for a minute. It simply means a quantity of something, like five apples or ten tomatoes. You, of course, know what easing means. When you put them together, you arrive at the concept of lowering interest rates. And the responsibility for lowering interest rates belongs to the central bank of the United States—the Federal Reserve. So, we can formally define quantitative easing as "a form of unconventional monetary policy in which a central bank purchases longer-term securities from the open market in order to increase the money supply and encourage lending and investment. Buying these securities adds new money to the economy, and also serves to lower interest rates."[17] To clarify this, let's look at how the Federal Reserve actually acts.

One way for the Federal Reserve to lower interest rates is to purchase government bonds, which both increases the supply of money and lowers the cost of money. This lower cost of money has the effect of lower interest rates. Quantitative easing is "implemented when interest rates are approaching zero because, at this point, central banks have fewer tools to influence economic growth."[18] One of the unintended consequences of quantitative easing is inflation. If the market is flooded with money, and it is easy to borrow money with low interest rates, inflation can occur.

Here is an example of how the Federal Reserve artificially lowers interest rates. During the height of the 2020 COVID-19 pandemic, the Federal Reserve wielded its considerable power: "With a few strokes on a computer, the Federal Reserve can create dollars out of nothing, virtually 'printing' money and injecting it into the commercial banking system, much like an electronic deposit. By the end of the year (2020), the Fed is projected to have purchased $3.5 trillion in government securities with these newly created dollars."[19] In this way quantitative easing influences bond yields, which, of course, impacts the 60/40 strategy.

Let's recap how this works. When interest rates are kept at an artificially low level for an extended period of time, bond yields decline. On July 31, 2020 (during the height of the pandemic), the 10-year Treasury note yield dropped to as low as 0.520 percent, which, according to Deutsche Bank, marked a record low that we hadn't seen in 234 years.[20] In contrast, 15 years ago, on March 22, 2005, the 10-year Treasury bond yield was 4.63 percent, so you can begin to see that bonds are no longer acting as a hedge to stocks.[21] In the 60/40 portfolio, the 40 percent side of the equation—bonds—was designed to protect investors against the risk of a volatile stock market. If bond yields are at historic lows, however, then the protection that was once there has vanished, leaving you, the investor, potentially exposed to higher risk.

To exacerbate matters, the global bond market is now offering negative interest rates. For example, in July 2019, the Swiss two-year bonds yielded negative 0.91 percent, which were "close to their all-time lows below negative 1.0% [back in 2015]."[22] Negative interest rates are spreading, and, as a result of the interconnected nature of global markets, the yields on 10-year Treasury notes could go even lower as investors flood the US bond market.

Consider for a moment that "some $13 trillion in bonds are paying negative interest rates, which means bondholders actually pay for the privilege of holding an issuer's bonds. That represents more than 20% of a total global bond market value of $55 trillion, according to Bloomberg. Other bonds are paying positive rates so low they carry a real (after-inflation) negative yield."[23] The impact of all this is that investors, particularly retirees, are finding it much more difficult to secure low-risk vehicles that pay decent returns. In fact, the possibility of saving cash, which for a long time was the most secure investment option, might also become risky. The important point here is that there are economic consequences—hidden economic forces—that directly impact your investment future either positively or negatively.

A BRIEF HISTORY OF ALTERNATIVE INVESTMENTS

Today, given the numerous risks that can potentially impact the 60/40 two-asset class model, it's clear that a different approach is necessary. Above all, this different approach must offer customizability and flexibility while managing risk. Now I'm sure you are asking, "Are there other investment strategies that are available to the individual investor?" The short answer is absolutely. To unpack this answer, we need to briefly explore the history of alternative investments.

Although alternative investments have gained momentum in the past few years, the historical underpinning of this once-radical approach to investing was established during the early part of the 20th century. Benjamin Graham (1894–1976), a British-born American investor, economist, and professor, is widely known as the "father of value investing," and wrote two of the founding texts in neoclassical investing: *Security Analysis* (1934) with David Dodd and *The Intelligent Investor* (1949).[24] In these works, he explored investor psychology, buy-and-hold investing, fundamental analysis, minimal debt, concentrated diversification, margin safety, and contrarian mind-sets.

Graham is also "an early adopter of the concept of alternative investing: garnering higher risk-adjusted returns than the market by doing things differently, rather than following the crowd."[25] Graham was the first to introduce hedge funds in the 1920s. By the 1940s, Alfred Winslow Jones had "ushered in a new era by launching the first hedge fund which exploited leverage and derivatives to enhance performance."[26] The next several decades would bring regulations and technological innovations that expanded the types of alternative investments available to the individual investor. By the 1980s, university endowments had started to explore alternative investments as a way of investing for the long term. Yale University would begin to incorporate alternative investments in its approach and, in time, would increase its endowment to stratospheric levels.

According to David Swensen, manager of Yale's endowment fund, investing requires "a rich understanding of human psychology, a reasonable appreciation of financial theory, a deep awareness of history, and a broad exposure to current events [which] contribute to the development of well-informed portfolio strategies."[27] Swensen became the fund manager for Yale in 1985 when the fund was valued at $1 billion. By 2019, the Yale Endowment Fund had ballooned to

$29.4 billion. How did he do this? He did it by having an appreciation for the historical, psychological, and economic forces that shape the world of finance. He did it by building a multi-asset class strategy.

Notably David Swensen succeeded by going against the advice of those who lack the necessary knowledge to succeed, and who nevertheless present themselves as the experts. Swensen was a contrarian, which is to say he defied conventional wisdom and in doing so made Yale billions of dollars. Swensen believed that "you have to diversify against the collective ignorance."[28] The point I'm trying to make is that successful investing demands that you understand the hidden forces that influence your money, as well as the actionable habits that you need to change in order to be successful. Swensen used alternative investment vehicles to manage risk while generating enduring wealth for his university.

WOMEN AND ALTERNATIVE INVESTMENTS

For too long, as we've pointed out several times in this book, women had to endure the tired clichés regarding their ability to invest. I'm sure you've heard some of these stereotypical insults: Women are too emotional to invest on their own, women are incapable of making rational decisions, and women need to rely upon the financial expertise of men to guide them. These silly stereotypes, although powerful in their capacity to perpetuate a myth, are false. In fact, research inverts this old and tired construct on its head. According to a 2017 Fidelity study, women's portfolios "performed better than men by 40 basis points, or 0.4%."[29] This may not seem like much, but compounded over time, it is quite substantial. Sadly, there is a disconnect between perception and reality.

Although women outperform men when it comes to portfolio returns, only 9 percent of women believe they are capable investors. The disconnect between what women are capable of and what they believe about themselves is not new. For decades now as far back as the early 1990s, women have been outperforming men in investment portfolios. For example, a study by the University of California, Berkeley, that used data from 35,000 brokerage accounts over a six-year period found that "women generated returns that were 1% higher, on average, than men."[30] My point is that for many years, women have been outperforming men while simultaneously being viewed as emotionally incapable of investing their money. One reason why women have been outperforming men in this field is that men tend to be overconfident.

It turns out that men tend to be "more overconfident than women in decision domains traditionally perceived as masculine, such as financial matters."[31] The problem with overconfidence is that it often leads to irrational exuberance, which is "unfounded market optimism that lacks foundation of fundamental valuation."[32] According to evolutionary biologist Robert Trivers, "a very disturbing feature of overconfidence is that it often appears to be poorly associated with knowledge—that is, the more ignorant the individual, the more confident he or she might be."[33]

The disconnect between reality (women tend to be better investors than men) and perception (women are too irrational) leads to a self-perpetuating cycle where women seek out the assistance of a professional advisor, who is more likely to be male, only to feel unhappy and disrespected. According to a study by The Boston Consulting Group, 73 percent of women were "unhappy" with the service they received from the financial services industry. Similarly, 70 percent of women switch financial advisors within a year of their husband's death.[34] What is important here is that women are more patient investors than men and they are comfortable seeking out the help of a professional advisor, provided they are not disrespected or treated condescendingly. In addition to being more methodical and patient, women tend to explore other asset classes than traditional stocks and bonds.

When I developed my multi-asset class portfolio, which incorporates alternative investments, my goal was not simply to help men, which I believe is important, but also to help educate all women about the potential benefits of alternative assets.

THE REALM MODEL

The word "realm" refers to an area of knowledge or expertise in some field. Knowledge itself is something we accumulate from reading about particular subjects, as well as by experiencing the world. Innovation, however, is the result of epiphanies, which are sudden bursts of insight or inspiration that come to us. Think of epiphanies as "aha!" moments that help us become aware of deeper insights about certain areas of knowledge or a way of doing things. In order for innovation to happen, one must first recognize and understand why the old way of doing things didn't work.

Throughout the 1990s and early 2000s, I utilized the 60/40 portfolio. As I've said, though, the market crash of 2002 hit me hard. I suppose I could have justified the losses as many other financial advisors did, by simply saying, "That's the nature of the market. It's always unpredictable and risky." But that was not me. I couldn't, and didn't, accept the idea that there is nothing one can do when the markets behave in a wild and unpredictable manner. I knew at an intuitive level there was something wrong with the accepted wisdom. I knew there was something wrong with a portfolio strategy that exposed people to 60 percent in stocks and 40 percent in bonds. I spent the next several years engaged in rigorous study of the 60/40 portfolio in order to understand why it was potentially broken.

If the two-asset class 60/40 model was no longer a viable retirement vehicle, I came to realize that a multi-asset class approach would be a sensible alternative. I knew that university endowments had been wildly successful in generating billions in returns while managing risk. The challenge was not only adapting their endowment model, taking into consideration that individuals have a different time horizon and levels of risk, but also making my model adaptable enough and flexible enough for the individual investor.

Another significant difference between my multi-asset class approach and endowment models is that I don't get institutional pricing like the large endowments do. Although adapting the model was a herculean effort, I pushed on. I spent 16-hour days studying different products. For diversification, I added alternative asset classes such as non-traded real estate investment trusts (non-traded REITs), which are not correlated to the stock market, whose goal is to help smooth volatility. I also developed tactical strategies to help diversify their portfolios against market declines.

The architectural blueprint of my multi-asset class strategy was coming into focus. The challenge was not simply finding suitable products; I also had to create an easy-to-understand model for my clients. After years of study and research, my multi-asset class model was born. It rests on three pillars: passive, tactical, and alternative strategies. My model also had to be fluid, meaning it had to be flexible enough to accommodate different levels of allocation based on each client's needs. I didn't want to have a fixed percentage allocated to each of the three asset classes; rather I wanted the flexibility to customize the multi-asset class strategy based on client needs, investment profile, liquidity needs, and financial circumstances.

The next step was naming the model. I needed a name that would convey all the knowledge and research that had gone into the construction of my strategy. I knew my model had endowment-like qualities, with certain allocations in different asset classes. I also knew it was designed for the retail—individual—investor. The acronym was staring me in the face: **R**etail **E**ndowment **A**llocation **L**ike **M**odel (REALM). Once my REALM model was born, I proceeded to undertake the monumental task of meeting with hundreds of my clients to determine if it made sense to convert their portfolios to this model. My Cinergy team and I worked 12-hour days, perhaps more, to make sure my clients held suitable products according to my innovative REALM model.

I believe that the REALM model is a crucial tool for women as they develop their financial literacy and spearhead feminism's fourth wave. All investors should understand no investment process is free of risk. The REALM strategy contains alternative investments, which are speculative by nature and have various risks, such as lack of liquidity, lack of control, changes in business conditions, and devaluation based on the investment, the economy, and/or regulatory changes. As a result, the values of alternative investments do fluctuate, resulting in the value at sale being more or less than the original price paid if a liquid market for the securities is found. Alternative investments are not appropriate for all investors. No strategy or risk management technique can guarantee that this investment model/process will be profitable. Diversification does not guarantee profit nor is it guaranteed to prevent losses.

13

A SPIRITUAL AWAKENING

"That is the real spiritual awakening, when something emerges
from within you that is deeper than who you thought you were.
So, the person is still there, but one could almost say that
something more powerful shines through the person."

—ECKHART TOLLE

Throughout the history of patriarchy, women have been systematically marginalized, ignored, dismissed, negated, preyed upon, and generally reduced to something wholly inferior to men. Depending on the period of history one examines, the justification for treating women as the weaker sex ranged from ignorant and misguided philosophical assumptions (Aristotle) to absurd religious interpretations that only served to empower men. For too long women had to endure sexual violence, harassment, condescension, exclusion, and the trauma that has been transmitted from one generation to the next. Only within the past 170 years has meaningful change redefined the public role of women. Through a series of successive feminist waves, women have succeeded in organizing around a shared goal of equality, realizing the right to vote, bringing awareness to the wage gap, moving up the corporate ladder, becoming politically involved in all levels of government, moving along a path of wealth accumulation, exposing toxic masculinity, and generally becoming a matriarchal force that will inspire future generations.

As I stated in the preface, I wrote this book to tell women they are on the threshold of powerful change. I have offered a cursory examination of how patriarchy evolved and spread through every crevice of our collective consciousness. I used a historical lens to help women not only understand, but also come to terms with the generational trauma that we inherited from a male-centered worldview. Despite the past struggles of women, and the ongoing struggles to achieve full equality, my intention in writing about women and wealth was not to create further conflict; rather my singular goal is to bring men and women together under the canopy of hope and reconciliation. In other words, the modest contribution I hope to make to the conversation about women in public life is that we also need a spiritual awakening to remind us of our common humanity and the kind of world we want to create for future generations. What we need today, more than any other time in recent memory, is a spiritual impulse to embrace the noble aspects of who we are and where we are going.

The narrative of endless accusations and assigning blame must give way to a future defined by a sensibility that embraces women as powerful matriarchal figures and men as partners in an ongoing affirmation of the feminine and the masculine. The institutions of patriarchy were not built in a day. In fact, who we are today is the result of centuries of hidden forces that elevated one gender at the expense of another. These historical, political, economic, philosophical, religious, and psychological forces shaped our attitudes, grievances, and narcissistic self-importance. Now we need a spiritual awakening to bring the feminine and the masculine into harmony. Women alone cannot bring down the institutions of patriarchy, and men cannot bring about enduring change without the leadership of women. In order for change to happen, we need an awakening, what I call a new way of being.

Let me explain what I mean. As a society we need a collective awakening experience that helps us expand our awareness of others. According to Steve Taylor, a psychologist and the author of *The Leap: The Psychology of Spiritual Awakening*, "awakening experiences are moments in which our awareness expands and intensifies. We transcend the worries that normally preoccupy us and feel a sense of elation or serenity. Our perceptions of the world around us become more vivid, and we feel a sense of connection to nature, other human beings or the whole universe in general."[1] What I would add to this description is that we need to have a spiritual impulse toward others, to embrace the better half of our humanity. In short, we need to learn a new way of being.

Men need to transcend their narrow view of a world defined by some misguided sense of masculine superiority. Women need to have the courage to transform their vulnerabilities into strengths. Change is upon us, and we must be prepared to embrace a world where women will play a central role in writing their own narrative.

There are many people who associate a spiritual awakening to a religious experience. I'm not using the term in this context; rather

I'm arguing that all of us, regardless of our religious background or beliefs, can experience a leap of faith toward humanity. Let's examine the psychological process of "waking up" and perceiving the world in a different way. This type of awakening "challenges and subverts your framework for understanding the nature of reality. During a stage of awakening, you shift your perspective on how you see the world. In doing so, you jettison an older, more limited framework for understanding the world and incorporate new concepts that you had previously ignored or rejected. A genuine awakening causes you to recognize that much of what you previously thought or understood was quite limited or partial."[2] In this respect, a spiritual awakening is the capacity to raise your consciousness by questioning the very prism through which you perceive the world.

The starting point of spiritual awakening is to accept the fundamental idea that the world is a socially constructed reality. What do I mean by that? I'm saying that the world is created by us, by our religious and moral beliefs, by our political and economic ideologies, and so on. If the world is created by us, then it can be changed by us. As I've stated earlier, it was largely men who created, defined, constructed, influenced, and enforced the prism through which we see the world. For centuries, women had little choice but to accept a world defined and maintained by men. For centuries, women were pushed aside, ignored, laughed at, looked upon with contempt, and generally excluded from the "important" business of creating a social order that placed men at the top of the hierarchy and women below.

All of this is on the verge of radical change.

Men need to reject their sense of privilege and entitlement. Men need to overcome their fear of change and perceived loss of power.

Men need to be awakened to the inevitable reality that change is coming and they must be part of this change. Women need to awaken to the fact they are now empowered to change the world. Women need to embrace all of their vulnerabilities and transform them into strengths. Women need to affirm their sense of power and collective voice to become the leaders of tomorrow. Both men and women need to accept the fundamental truth that enduring change can only come about when they both work together to create a future filled with the promise of hope, equity, justice, respect, and spiritual awareness.

It will now be women who will define their social position, assert their voice, write their own narrative, and reclaim their matriarchal sense of inclusive power. For centuries, patriarchy has survived on the premise that power must be exclusive to men. Women today are proving that power and leadership can be shared, inclusive, transparent, transformative, impactful, respectful, and mutually beneficial. The power structure of patriarchy is beginning to be replaced with a more nurturing and shared vision of a future defined by a fundamental respect for our humanity.

The sisterhood of women is more powerful than ever. The digital revolution is giving women a powerful set of platforms to locate and identify inequities and injustices in real time. The transparency of social media will expose sexual assault and harassment in the workplace, the wage gap and corporate bias, as well as the countless aggressions, both overt and subtle, that women experience every day. The sisterhood of women will no longer be an abstract cultural phenomenon; rather it is being transformed into a tangible cultural force. Sisterhood will rise and once again show the world the power and beauty of a partnership society, a society where women are respected and admired for their leadership, compassion, empathy, intuitive awareness, and maternal instinct to protect all of us—men and women.

I wrote this book to not only inspire and empower women but also invite men to learn about the traumas women have experienced as a result of patriarchy. Toxic masculinity is the dark side of patriarchy, where boys are socialized not to show emotions and where manhood is defined in relation to women. If women are weak, then men must be strong; if women are passive, then men must be aggressive; where women are emotional, then men never show emotions. Patriarchy spared no one and infused our perception of the world with false and distorted images of power and conquest. Once again, all of this is about to change. First, men are no longer going to be able to define their existential value in the world in contrast to women. Second, men need to confront their own trauma by challenging themselves to end the cycle of perceiving women as objects of conquest. In other words, men need to change their attitudes toward women by encouraging each other to change their behavior.

Part of what entrenched patriarchy in our collective imagination is that we had socialized boys and girls to play certain roles: Girls grew up internalizing being somehow less than men, and boys grew up to believe they were destined to dominate women. But as more and more women become leaders in public life—in the corporate world, the political sphere, the law, education, and so on—the socialization process will change for future generations. Boys will learn to experience and accept their emotions. Girls will learn they are no longer bound by outdated gender stereotypes and will become the leaders of tomorrow. As men overcome their toxic masculinity, women will continue to flourish in every conceivable area of public life.

There is a correlation between toxic masculinity and the vulnerabilities women have felt for generations. But as men's toxic behavior declines, women's confidence will rise. I'm not asking men here to surrender their masculinity; rather I'm asking them to transcend the old, tired definitions handed to them by a patriarchy that only seeks blind power and conquest. Society as a whole needs to stop perpetuating the toxic masculine stereotypes we see in action movies, video games, commercials, magazines, and other sources of entertainment where women are reduced to sexual objects. Toxic masculinity is also everywhere on social media, where young men hide behind the screen spewing hatred toward women. This cowardly behavior must, and will, come to an end. Social media companies like Facebook and Twitter are beginning to crack down on hate speech, but they need to do much, much more.

In *Redefining Financial Literacy*, I wrote about how the digital age is changing us in ways we are only beginning to understand. We live in an age of fleeting images and ephemeral ideas, an age in which information—and too often disinformation—has replaced substantive knowledge. In online groups that form around a given set of beliefs, the digital age has created dangerous echo chambers. These online groups both reinforce and amplify potentially dangerous beliefs about politics, race, and gender. Again, social media companies need to monitor misogynistic hate speech, which too often perpetuates the myth of masculine superiority. The problem is that social media gives people a degree of anonymity, which then encourages our worst impulses.

What we need instead is a moral framework that embraces our humanity. So far there has been a disconnect between our technological innovation and the spiritual awareness that binds us. However,

I believe the same social media platforms that have helped facilitate hatred and toxic masculinity can usher in a new era of social discourse where both men and women interact within a framework of mutual respect and collective unity. Although patriarchy emerged thousands of years ago with the introduction of alphabet-based language, thrived under Christianity, and survived the scientific and industrial revolutions, it will not survive the digital age.

Despite my reservations about the digital revolution, I do believe that it has fostered powerful, positive change. Social media platforms, despite their profound shortcomings, have been instrumental in shining a bright light on sexual harassment and assault, gender inequity, and the marginalized status of women. The 2017 Women's March was organized on Facebook. The #MeToo movement became a global cause as a result of Twitter.

My point is that as social media matures and becomes more responsible, patriarchy will be exposed for what it is—a false and oppressive doctrine that elevates one gender over another. I believe social media will create a kind of cultural transparency where the injustices against women will be projected and amplified for all to see. Corporations will be held accountable if they do not offer equal pay to women. Sexual harassment will be stamped out across industries as more women expose those in power who long believed they could get away with it.

The pursuit of the American Dream has for too long been the exclusive province of men. It's amazing to think that the dreams and aspirations of a nation were reserved for half the population. But this outdated cultural paradigm, too, will soon collapse under the weight of its own arrogance.

Today the cultural landscape is changing. Women are no longer at the mercy of men's whims. Women are today more educated than men and are rising in leadership positions in both corporate America and politics. Women are on the verge of dramatic and history-bending change. All the pieces are in place for women to assert and affirm their feminine power and courage. We are standing on the shoulders of the feminine giants who came before us. Our vulnerabilities are being transformed into enduring strengths. Our leadership, intuitive awareness, moral compass, spiritual sensibility, and inclusivity is reshaping the world—a world where men and women together embrace their shared humanity. Women will redefine the American Dream and give hope to everyone who wants to realize their own vision of prosperity and happiness.

Certainly, the future for women will be full of challenges, but also endless possibilities. I spent most of this book offering the reader facts and sources. Let me break away for a moment and offer my opinion about the future of women. For the first time in human history, women are on the verge of extraordinary advancements. In every conceivable field of human activity, women are embracing their destiny by climbing up the male-dominated hierarchy. In corporate America, women need not only knock on the doors of the executive suites but also push these doors wide open and demand fairness. Corporate boards, which are predominately made up of men, must change their stale culture of male domination and allow for diversity. In politics, women are winning seats at the local, state, and national level. You might even say that the proverbial glass ceiling has been shattered with the election of Kamala Harris as vice president of the United States.

One of the unintended consequences of the COVID-19 pandemic is that it led to innovation by women. The pandemic forced many women to establish an online business presence. Women are becoming digital entrepreneurs in greater numbers than ever before. Think about this for a moment: Women have largely been excluded from the first three waves of the industrial revolution. We are currently laying the foundation for the digital revolution, and women must be full participants in this fourth wave of change. I've said several times that the pay gap between men and women is unacceptable and that women can't wait for decades to achieve pay parity. Just as women created the #MeToo movement, women can now create #PayMeLikeAMan. This movement would hold accountable those companies who continue to pay women less than men.

Finally, women need to break free from the insidious myth that they are not good investors. If you are a woman who was raised to believe this myth, I urge you to toss it out the window. Research clearly shows that women are better investors, and that they are thoughtful, careful, patient, and seek the advice of a professional. If they are relying on a male financial advisor who speaks condescendingly to women or disrespects them, they can seek out a female advisor. One of the things I do at Cinergy Financial is to educate women not only about our financial products but also about different investment strategies, risk profile, time horizons, withdrawal rates, preparing for retirement, and a million other important financial details. Women are then free to ask questions without feeling intimidated.

It is this concept of education that is the driving force behind this book. For much of my career, I've made it my mission to improve the financial literacy of all my clients, particularly my female clients.

This is why the theme of *Redefining Financial Literacy* is the persistent problem of poor financial knowledge among Americans. As you've undoubtedly read, despite the three waves of feminine revolutions, women continue to fall behind their male counterparts when it comes to financial knowledge. This, as I've stated before, is the overarching obstacle that is preventing women from achieving full equality.

Women need to understand that they will soon become the dominant economic engine in this country. However, the transfer of wealth from what was once a male-dominated economy to a female-driven digital economy will come with risks. Will women have sufficient financial knowledge and awareness to not only maintain but also grow this wealth? Men have largely succeeded in creating generational wealth. The challenge for women is to improve their financial literacy. I've included actionable steps throughout the book that women can follow in order to improve their financial awareness. The time is now for women to take their rightful place as powerful economic agents in the world. Financial independence is a critical component of gender equality. It is my view that the fourth wave of feminine change is the financial revolution currently underway.

Let me close this book by circling back to spiritual awakening, which is where I started this chapter. I do not believe that our culture can survive very long without embracing the spiritual goodness of others. When we see each other as a means to an end or an obstacle to overcome, we lose something of our collective humanity.

A spiritual awakening is a moral awakening, a recognition of our value in the world. A spiritual awakening is an affirmation of our goodness. A spiritual awakening allows us to transcend our limitations by believing in something noble and virtuous. A spiritual awakening is a path for both men and women to walk hand in hand toward reconciliation and healing. A spiritual awakening is a reminder that we all have a moral compass to guide us.

To quote the English poet John Donne, no man is an island. I would also add that no woman is an island. Both men and women are bound together in a spiritual framework that allows us to acknowledge the misdeeds of the past while moving forward toward a greater sense of shared values, mutualism, inclusion, respect, and the awareness of an enlightened purpose in the world.

NOTES

PREFACE

1. Erin McCarthy, "Roosevelt's 'The Man in the Arena,'" mentalfloss.com, April 23, 2015. https://www.mentalfloss.com/article/63389/roosevelts-man-arena.
2. Ted Jenkin, "Here's Why Women's Money Decisions Will Shape the Future for the U.S.," cnbc.com, November 30, 2020. https://www.cnbc.com/2020/11/30/op-ed-heres-why-womens-money-decisions-will-shape-the-future-for-us.html.
3. Frank Ready, "Women Are Poised to Control a Massive Portion of US Wealth by 2030," benefitspro.com, August 3, 2020. https://www.benefitspro.com/2020/08/03/women-are-poised-to-control-a-massive-portion-of-us-wealth-by-2030/.
4. Cindy Couyoumjian, *Redefining Financial Literacy: Unlocking the Hidden Forces of Your Financial Future* (Austin, Texas: Greenleaf Book Group, 2021) p. 211.
5. Powercube, "Foucault: Power Is Everywhere," Powercube.net, Retrieved May 5, 2020. https://www.powercube.net/other-forms-of-power/foucault-power-is-everywhere/.
6. Powercube, "Foucault."
7. Suze Orman, "Women & Money: Are You Truly Financially Empowered?" suzeorman.com, September 6, 2018. https://www.suzeorman.com/blog/Women-Money-Are-You-Truly-Financially-Empowered.
8. Ozlem Denizmen, "Give Women Credit- Financial Empowerment Matters," World Economic Forum, January 25, 2014. https://www.weforum.org/agenda/2014/01/want-empower-women-give-credit/.
9. BrainyQuote, "Obstacles Quotes," brainyquote.com, Retrieved May 5, 2020. https://www.brainyquote.com/topics/obstacles-quotes.
10. Gregg Depersio, "What License Do Financial Advisors Need to Have?" Investopedia, July 1, 2020. https://www.investopedia.com/ask/answers/091815/do-financial-advisors-have-be-licensed.asp.
11. *Merriam-Webster*, "Dignity," merriam-webster.com, Retrieved December 11, 2020. https://www.merriam-webster.com/dictionary/dignity.

12. Internet Encyclopedia of Philosophy, "Human Dignity," iep.utm.edu, Retrieved December 11, 2020. https://iep.utm.edu/hum-dign/.

13. *New World Encyclopedia*, "Courage," newworldencyclopedia.org, Retrieved December 12, 2020. https://www.newworldencyclopedia.org/entry /Courage.

14. *New World Encyclopedia*, "Courage."

INTRODUCTION

1. John Detriche, "US Women Will Take Control of an Additional $20 trillion in Wealth This Decade," quartz.com, July 29, 2020. https:// qz.com/1885841/us-women-will-take-control-of-an-extra-19-trillion-in -wealth/.

2. Ben Renner, "Survey: Many Women Feel 'Trapped' in their Relationship Due to Financial Dependence," studyfinds.org, February 7, 2020. https://www .studyfinds.org/survey-many-women-feel-trapped-in-their-relationship-due -to-financial-dependence/.

3. Nancy Tengler, "Women: Now is the Time to Take Charge of Your Finances," hermoney.com, March 8, 2021. https:/ hermoney.com/invest /financialplanning/women-now-is-the-time-to-take-charge-of-your-finances/.

4. Angelita Williams and Jason Shevrin, "New Research: Female Investors Lag Behind Male Counterparts in Investment Knowledge and Confidence," finra.org, March 19, 2020. https://www.finra.org/media-center /newsreleases/2020/finra-foundation-news-newresearch-female -investors-lag-investment.

5. Maurie Backman, "A Summary of 20 Years of Research and Statistics on Women in Investing," fool.com, August 3, 2021. https://www.fool.com /research/women-ininvesting-research/.

6. Bethany Carner, "Women's Enrollment in MBAs Reaches Record High," businessbecause.com, November 12, 2021. https://www.businessbecause .com/news/mba-degree/7921/women-mba-enrollment-record-high.

7. Jim Dickson, "Women and Wealth: How Investment Managers Can Better Serve Women Clients," *Forbes*, June 23, 2020. https://www.forbes.com/sites /forbesfinancecouncil/2020/06/23/women-and-wealth-how-investment -managers-can-better-serve-women-clients/#1428c4e4361c.

8. Alisha Ebrahimi, "Female 500 CEOs Reach an All-Time High, but It's Still a Small Percentage," CNN Business, May 20, 2020. https://www.cnn .com/2020/05/20/us/fortune-500-women-ceos-trnd/index.html.

9. Aimee Picchi, "More Women Are Now Outearning Their Husbands—and Emotions Can Be Big," *USA Today*, March 3, 2020. https://www.usatoday.com/story/money/2020/03/03/gender-wage-gap-more-women-out-earning-husbands/4933666002/.

10. Picchi, "More Women Are Now Outearning Their Husbands."

11. Picchi, "More Women Are Now Outearning Their Husbands."

CHAPTER 1

1. University of Leeds, "Go with Your Gut—Intuition Is More than Just a Hunch, Says New Research," ScienceDaily, March 6, 2008. https://www.sciencedaily.com/releases/2008/03/080305144210.htm.

2. Colleen Oakley, "The Power of Female Intuition: Just What Is the 6th Sense That Sometimes Guides You? And What's the Best Way to Tune In?" WebMD, Retrieved July 14, 2020. https://www.webmd.com/balance/features/power-of-female-intuition#1.

3. Oakley, "The Power of Female Intuition."

4. Oakley, "The Power of Female Intuition."

5. Robert Johnson, "The 18 Smartest People in the World," *Business Insider*, April 6, 2011. https://www.businessinsider.com/the-smartest-people-in-the-world-2011-3.

6. Natasha Bertrand, "The 40 Smartest People of All Time," *Business Insider*, February 27, 2015. https://www.businessinsider.com/the-40-smartest-people-of-all-time-2015-2.

7. Judith Orloff, *Intuitive Healing: 5 Steps to Physical, Emotional, and Sexual Wellness* (New York: Harmony Books, 2001), p. xiv.

8. Grant Soosalu, Suzanne Henwood, et al., "Head Heart, and Gut in Decision Making: Development of a Multiple Brain Preference," journals.sagepub.com, March 18, 2019. https://journals.sagepub.com/doi/full/10.1177/2158244019837439.

9. Renee Morad, "Women's Intuition: It's a Real Thing. Ask a Neuroscientist," Ozy.com, September 16, 2017. https://www.ozy.com/news-and-politics/womens-intuition-its-a-real-thing-ask-a-neuroscientist/80595/.

10. Morad, "Women's Intuition."

11. Neel Burton, "The Psychology and Philosophy of Intuition," *Psychology Today*, October 26, 2018. https://www.psychologytoday.com/us/blog/hide-and-seek/201810/the-psychology-and-philosophy-intuition.

12. Burton, "The Psychology and Philosophy of Intuition."

13. *New World Encyclopedia*, "Intuition," Retrieved July 18, 2020. https://www .newworldencyclopedia.org/entry/Intuition.
14. Robert D. Richardson Jr., *Emerson: The Mind on Fire* (New York: Centennial Books, 1996), p. 147.
15. Jean-Francois Roy, "Emerson's Thought on Tuition and Intuition," Jeff's Literature Café, Retrieved July 18, 2020. https://sites.google.com/site /jeffsliteraturecafe/emerson-s-thought-on-tuition-and-intuition.
16. U.S. History, "Transcendentalism, An American Philosophy," ushistory.org, Retrieved July 19, 2020. https://www.ushistory.org/us/26f.asp.

CHAPTER 2

1. Daniel Leonard, "These Were Aristotle's Beliefs about Women," grunge.com, November 20, 2020. https://www.grunge.com/282893/these-were-aristotles -beliefs-about-women/.
2. Emily Swaim, "Freud's Perspective on Women," verywellmind.com, April 21, 2020. https://www.verywellmind.com/how-sigmund-freud-viewed -women-2795859.
3. Cynthia Miller, "Women Are Hard-Wired to Feel Inferior, Second-Rate, and Not Enough," medium.com, October 28, 2018. https://medium.com /influencercreation/women-are-hard-wired-to-feel-inferior-second-rate -and-not-enough-bde80192d606.
4. Jeremy Sutton, "What Is Intuition and Why Is It Important? 5 Examples," positivepsychology.com, November 16, 2020, https://positivepsychology .com/intuition/.
5. Sutton, "What Is Intuition."
6. Sutton, "What Is Intuition."
7. The University of Chicago Press, "Educating Intuition," press.uchicago.edu, Retrieved December 14, 2020. https://press.uchicago.edu/ucp/books/book /chicago/E/bo3624460.html.
8. W. I. B. Beveridge, *The Art of Scientific Investigation* (Scotts Valley, CA: CreateSpace Independent Publishing Platform, November 2, 2015), p. 73.
9. Beveridge, *The Art of Scientific Investigation*, p. 73.
10. Paul Sutter, "Relativity: The Thought Experiments Behind Einstein's Theory," space.com, June 18, 2018. https://www.space.com/40920-relativity-power -of-equivalence.html.
11. Leonard Shlain, "The Alphabet Versus the Goddess," alphabetgoddess.com, Retrieved August 19, 2021. https://www.alphabetvsgoddess.com/.

12. Anna Maria Pellizzari, "5 Steps to Empowering Yourself with Your Intuition," huffpost.com, April 17, 2017. https://www.huffpost.com/entry/5-steps-to -empowering-yourself-with-your-intuition_b_58f502e6e4b015669722517b.
13. Pellizzari, "5 Steps."
14. Dictionary.com, "Wise Up to the Difference Between 'Knowledge vs. Wisdom,'" dictionary.com, Retrieved May 3, 2021. https://www.dictionary .com/e/wisdom-vs-knowledge/.
15. Dictionary.com, "Wise up."

CHAPTER 3

1. Rosalind Miles, *Who Cooked the Last Supper: The Women's History of the World* (New York: Broadway Books, 2001), p. 1.
2. Louise Amoore, *The Global Resistance Reader* (London: Routledge, 2005), p. 19. Gramsci's quote from his Prison Notebooks was that the "starting-point of critical elaboration is the consciousness of what one really is, and is 'knowing thyself' as a product of the historical processes to date which has deposited in you an infinity of traces, without leaving an inventory."
3. Raneem Mokatrin, "Feminism 101: What Is Intergenerational Trauma?" femmagazine.com, July 18, 2018. https://femmagazine.com/feminism-101 -what-is-intergenerational-trauma/.
4. Mirel Zaman, "What Is Intergenerational Trauma? An Expert Explains," refinery29.com, June 1, 2020. https://www.refinery29.com/en -us/2020/06/9848448/what-is-intergenerational-trauma.
5. Martha Henriques, "Can the Legacy of Trauma Be Passed Down to the Generations?" bbc.com, March 26, 2019. https://www.bbc.com/future /article/20190326-what-is-epigenetics.
6. Allan G. Johnson, *The Gender Knot: Unraveling Our Patriarchal Legacy* (Philadelphia: Temple University Press, 2014), p. 5.
7. Philip Cohen, "America Is Still a Patriarchy," *The Atlantic*, November 19, 2012. https://www.theatlantic.com/sexes/archive/2012/11/america-is -still-a-patriarchy/265428/
8. Kiki Serantes, "Patriarchy Exists Because We Allow It To: We Must Resist the Propaganda That Divides and Separates Us in Boxes Too Small for Our Potential," Theodysseyonline.com, November 2, 2015. https://www .theodysseyonline.com/eat-cake-pervasive-patriarchy.
9. Meera Atkinson, "Patriarchy Perpetuates Trauma. It's Time to Face the Fact," *The Guardian*, April 29, 2018. https://www.theguardian.com

/commentisfree/2018/apr/30/patriarchy-perpetuates-trauma-its-time-to
-face-the-fact.

10. Michael Salter, "The Problem with a Fright against Toxic Masculinity,"
    theatlantic.com, February 27, 2019. https://www.theatlantic.com/health
    /archive/2019/02/toxic-masculinity-history/583411/.

11. Eliza Castile, "6 Ways the Patriarchy Hurts Men," bustle.com, November 19,
    2015. https://www.bustle.com/articles/124983-6-ways-the-patriarchy-is
    -harmful-to-men-because-feminism-isnt-just-for-women.

12. Ann Filemyr, "Healing the Patriarchal Wound," swc.edu, Retrieved March 16,
    2021. https://www.swc.edu/president-reflections/healing-the-patriarchal
    -wound-by-dr-ann-filemyr-president-southwestern-college-ecotherapy
    -certificate-director/.

13. *Merriam-Webster*, "Injury," merriam-webster.com, Retrieved December 31,
    2020. https://www.merriam-webster.com/dictionary/injury.

14. Jayne Leonard, "What Is Trauma? What to Know," medicalnewstoday.com,
    June 3, 2020. https://www.medicalnewstoday.com/articles/trauma.

15. The Cleveland Clinic, "Stress," my.clevelandclinic.org, Retrieved January 3,
    2021. https://my.clevelandclinic.org/health/articles/11874-stress.

16. The Cleveland Clinic, "Stress."

17. Andrew Limbong, "Microaggressions Are a Big Deal: How to Talk Them
    Out and When to Walk Away," npr.org, June 9, 2020. https://www.npr
    .org/2020/06/08/872371063/microaggressions-are-a-big-deal-how-to-talk
    -them-out-and-when-to-walk-away.

18. Limbong, "Microaggressions Are a Big Deal."

19. University of Washington Counseling Center, "Healthy Grieving: What
    Is Grief?" Washington.edu, Retrieved January 7, 2021. https://www
    .washington.edu/counseling/resources-for-students/healthy-grieving/.

20. Alleydog.com, "Awareness," allegydog.com, Retrieved January 7, 2021.
    https://www.alleydog.com/glossary/definition.php?term=Awareness.

21. Denise Fournier, "The Inescapable Importance of Acceptance," *Psychology
    Today*, November 27, 2017. https://www.psychologytoday.com/us
    /blog/mindfully-present-fully-alive/201711/the-inescapable-importance
    -acceptance.

22. Fournier, "The Inescapable Importance of Acceptance."

23. A Guide to Psychology and Its Practice, "Forgiveness," guidetopsychology
    .com, Retrieved January 9, 2021. http://www.guidetopsychology.com
    /forgive.htm.

24. Eileen Hunt Botting, "The Educated Woman, with Power Over Herself, Can
    Bring Down the Patriarchy for the Betterment of All Humanity," aeon.co,

July 25, 2018. https://aeon.co/classics/to-end-patriarchy-woman-must-first
-seize-power-over-herself.

25. Botting, "The Educated Woman."

26. Donna Hicks, "What Is the Real Meaning of Dignity," *Psychology Today*, April 10, 2013. https://www.psychologytoday.com/us/blog/dignity/201304/what-is-the-real-meaning-dignity-0.

27. Peggy Reeves Sanday, "Matriarchy as a Sociocultural Form: An Old Debate in New Light," web.sas.upenn.edu, Paper first presented July 1–7, 1998. https://web.sas.upenn.edu/psanday/articles/selected-articles/matriarchy-as-a-sociocultural-form-an-old-debate-in-a-new-light/.

28. Peggy Reeves Sanday, *Beyond the Second Sex: New Directions in the Anthropology of Gender* (Philadelphia: University of Pennsylvania Press, 1990), p. 3.

29. Philip Jameson, "Uncovering the Truth Behind Matriarchal Societies in the Ancient World," Ancient Origins, March 7, 2019. https://www.ancient-origins.net/history-ancient-traditions/ancient-cultures-matriarchal-society-0011588.

30. Jameson, "Uncovering the Truth."

31. Leonard Shlain, "The Alphabet Versus the Goddess," alphabetgoddess.com, Retrieved August 20, 2021. https://www.alphabetvsgoddess.com/timeline.html.

32. Shlain, "The Alphabet Versus the Goddess."

33. Dictionary.com, "Egalitarian," dictionary.com, Retrieved July 28, 2020. https://www.dictionary.com/browse/egalitarian.

34. Riane Eisler, *The Chalice and the Blade: Our History, Our Future* (San Francisco: HarperOne, 1988), p. xix.

35. Amanda Foreman, "The Ascent of Woman," bbc.co.uk, Retrieved July 31, 2020. https://www.bbc.co.uk/programmes/articles/1dRznJkKZ6DnG0fXMD2hxNP/catalhoyuk-an-example-of-true-gender-equality.

36. Foreman, "The Ascent of Woman."

37. Kevin Reilly, *Worlds of History Reader* (New York: St. Martin's, 2019), p. 16.

38. Carla Goldstein, "Patriarchy Is Contraindicated for Life," Eomega.org, 2018. https://www.eomega.org/article/patriarchy-is-contraindicated-for-life.

39. Elle Beau, "Patriarchy Really Is Only 6–9 Thousand Years Old," medium.com, April 29, 2021. https://medium.com/inside-of-elle-beau/patriarchy-really-is-only-6-9-thousand-years-old-6ee0fcdfd118.

40. Sandra Blakeslee, "Think Tank; Left Brain-Right Brain: The ABC's of Everything," *The New York Times*, September 11, 1999. https://www.nytimes.

com/1999/09/11/books/think-tank-left-brain-right-brain-the-abc-s-of
-everything.html.

41. E. E. Smith, "Are You Left- or Right-Brain Dominant?" *Psychology Today*,
    October 19, 2012. https://www.psychologytoday.com/us/blog/not-born
    -yesterday/201210/are-you-left-or-right-brain-dominant.

42. Leonard Shlain, *The Alphabet Versus the Goddess: The Conflict Between Word
    and Image* (London: Penguin Books, 1999), p. 1.

43. Elizabeth Reninger, "Gender and Taoism," learnreligions.com, June 25, 2019.
    https://www.learnreligions.com/gender-and-the-tao-3183069.

44. Maria Popova, "How the Invention of the Alphabet Usurped Female Power in
    Society and Sparked the Rise of Patriarchy in Human Culture," brainpickings
    .org, March 17, 2014. https://www.brainpickings.org/2014/03/17/shlain
    -alphabet-goddess/.

45. Popova, "How the Invention of the Alphabet."

CHAPTER 4

1. Gerda Lerner, *The Creation of Patriarchy* (Oxford: Oxford University Press,
   Reprint Edition, 1987), p. 5.

2. Dessa Meehan, "Containing the Kalon Kakon: The Portrayal of Women in
   Ancient Greek Mythology," *Armstrong Undergraduate Journal of History*,
   Retrieved September 12, 2020. https://www.armstrong.edu/history-journal
   /history-journal-containing-the-kalon-kakon-the-portrayal-of-women-in
   -ancien.

3. Meehan, "Containing the Kalon Kakon."

4. Hesiod, "The Works and Days," ancient-literature.com, April 24, 2020.
   https://www.ancient-literature.com/greece_hesiod_works.html. "The Works
   and Days" is a didactic poem written by the Greek poet Hesiod in 700 BCE.

5. Editors, "Socrates," *Stanford Encyclopedia of Philosophy*, Retrieved September
   16, 2020. https://plato.stanford.edu/entries/socrates/.

6. Editors, "Socrates (469–399 B.C.E.)," Internet Encyclopedia of Philosophy,
   Retrieved September 16, 2020. https://www.iep.utm.edu/socrates/.

7. Susan Moller Okin, "Philosopher Queens and Private Wives: Plato on
   Women and the Family," *Philosophy and Public Affairs* 6, no. 4. (1977):
   pp. 345–369.

8. Joshua J. Mark, "Aristotle," Ancient History Encyclopedia, Retrieved
   September 17, 2020. https://www.ancient.eu/aristotle/.

9. Mark, "Aristotle."

10. Andrea Borghini, "Plato and Aristotle on Women: Selected Quotes,"
    ThoughtCo, June 22, 2019. https://www.thoughtco.com/about-us.

11. Karen J. Torjensen, *When Women Were Priests: Women's Leadership in the Early Church and the Scandal of their Subordination in the Rise of Christianity* (San Francisco: Harper, 1950), p. 4.

12. Joshua J. Mark, "Ten Would-Be Famous Women of Early Christianity," worldhistory.org, June 26, 2019. https://www.worldhistory.org/article/1409 /ten-should-be-famous-women-of-early-christianity/.

13. Torjensen, *When Women Were Priests*.

14. Torjensen, When Women Were Priests.

15. "Genesis 2:18," biblegateway.com, 2020. https://www.biblegateway.com /passage/?search=Genesis+2%3A18&version=NIV.

16. Philip Pullella, "Pope: Church Should Admit History of Abuse of Women, Male Domination," reutors.com, April 2, 2019. https://www.reuters.com /article/us-pope-synod-letter/pope-church-should-admit-history-of-abuse -of-women-male-domination-idUSKCN1RE0UV.

17. Phillip Pullella, "Pope: Church Should Admit History of Abuse of Women."

18. Colleen Dulle, "Women Are Rising to New Heights at the Vatican. Could they Change the Church Forever?" americanmagazine.org, September 16, 2021. https://www.americamagazine.org/faith/2021/09/16/vatican-top -women-change-smerilli-becquart-scaraffia-241413.

19. Elizabeth Gould Davis, *The First Sex* (New York: Penguin Books, 1972), p. 252.

20. Davis, *The First Sex*, p. 254, quoting from a moral tale of medieval times as written by Georffrey de la Tour de Landry in 1371.

21. Terry Davidson, *Conjugal Crime* (New York: Dutton First Edition, 1978), p. 99.

22. "Under the Rule of Thumb: Battered Women and the Administration of Justice," Report of the United States Commission on Civil Rights, 1982, p. 2. https://www.nlm.nih.gov/exhibition/confrontingviolence/assets /transcripts/OB12012_200_dpi.pdf.

23. "Under the Rule of Thumb."

24. "The Abuse of Women—A Worldwide Issue—American Traditions," Library Index, 2020. https://www.libraryindex.com/pages/2031/Abuse-Women -Worldwide-Issue-AMERICAN-TRADITIONS.html.

25. "The Abuse of Women."

26. Reva B. Siegel, "The Rule of Love: Wife Beating As Prerogative and Privacy," Yale Law School Legal Scholarship Repository, 2020. https:// digitalcommons.law.yale.edu/cgi/viewcontent.cgi?article=7700&context=ylj.

27. The Abuse of Women—A Worldwide Issue—American Traditions," Library Index, 2020. https://www.libraryindex.com/pages/2031/Abuse-Women -Worldwide-Issue-AMERICAN-TRADITIONS.html.

28. Joan Zorza, "The Criminal Law of Misdemeanor Domestic Violence, 1970–1990," Jstor.org, 1992. https://www.jstor.org/stable/1143824?seq=1.

29. "Mathew 5:14." Bible Hub, 2020. https://biblehub.com/matthew/5-14.htm.

30. Daniel T. Rodgers, *As a City on a Hill: The Story of America's Most Famous Lay Sermon* (Princeton, NJ: Princeton University Press, 2018).

31. Holly Hartman, "Gender in Colonial America: Women and Witches," Western Oregon University Digital Commons, 2009. https://digitalcommons.wou.edu/cgi/viewcontent.cgi?article=1109&context=his.

32. Mary Beth Norton, "The Constitutional Status of Women in 1787," *Law & Inequality: A Journal of Theory and Practice* 6, no. 1 (June 1988). https://scholarship.law.umn.edu/cgi/viewcontent .cgi?article=1558&context=lawineq.

33. Norton, "The Constitutional Status of Women."

CHAPTER 5

1. National Park Service, "The Declaration of Sentiments," nps.gov, Retrieved January 31, 2022. https://www.nps.gov/articles/declaration-of-sentiments .htm.

2. National Park Service, "The First Women's Right Convention," nps.gov, 2020. https://www.nps.gov/wori/learn/historyculture/the-first-womens-rights -convention.htm.

3. Louise Benner, "Women in the 1920s in North Carolina," NCepedia, 2004. https://www.ncpedia.org/history/20th-Century/1920s-women.

4. FDR Presidential Library, "Frances Perkins," fdrlibrary.org, 2016. https://www.fdrlibrary.org/iw/perkins.

5. Frances Perkins Center, "Her Life: The Woman Behind the New Deal," francesperkinscenter.org, 2020. https://francesperkinscenter.org/life-new/.

6. Frances Perkins Center, "Her Life: The Woman Behind the New Deal."

7. Frances Perkins Center, "Her Life: The Woman Behind the New Deal."

8. Frances Perkins Center, "Her Life: The Woman Behind the New Deal."

9. Kirstin Downey, *The Woman Behind the New Deal: The Life of Frances Perkins, FDR's Secretary of Labor and His Moral Conscience* (New York: Nan A. Talese Publishing, 2009), p. 2.

10. Gordon Berg, "Labor Hall of Fame: Frances Perkins and the Flowering of Economic and Social Policies," US Bureau of Labor Statisitics, Retrieved January 26, 2022, https://www.bls.gov/opub/mlr/1989/06/art5full.pdf.

11. Editors, "Great Depression," History.com, 2020. https://www.history.com /topics/great-depression/great-depression-history.

12. Editors, "Great Depression."

13. Frances Perkins Center, "Her Life: The Woman Behind the New Deal."
14. Frances Perkins Center, "Her Life: The Woman Behind the New Deal."

CHAPTER 6

1. The National WWII Museum, "Gender on the Home Front," nationalww2museum.org, 2020. https://www.nationalww2museum.org/war/articles/gender-home-front.
2. Margaret Henderson, "Betty Friedan 1921–2006," *Australian Feminist Studies* 22, no. 53 (2007): 163–166.
3. Henderson, "Betty Friedan 1921–2006."
4. John F. Kennedy Presidential Library and Museum, "A Growing Women's Movement and the Equal Pay Act of 1963," jfklibrary.org, Retrieved November 25, 2020. https://www.jfklibrary.org/sites/default/files/2020-07/New%20Frontiers%20Summer%202020.pdf.
5. Bonnie J. Dow, "What Can We Learn from TV Coverage of Feminism in 1970?" Women's Media Center, September 22, 2015. https://www.womensmediacenter.com/news-features/what-can-we-learn-from-tv-coverage-of-feminism-in-1970.
6. Kim Moore, "On the Shoulders of Giants," flippengroup.com, Retrieved March 17, 2021. https://flippengroup.com/on-the-shoulders-of-giants/.
7. Yasmin Omar, "Why Ruth Bader Ginsburg Is Our Feminist Hero," harpersbazaar.com, September 19, 2020. https://www.harpersbazaar.com/uk/culture/entertainment/a25722034/why-ruth-bader-ginsburg-is-our-feminist-hero/.
8. Neil A. Lewis, "Rejected as a Clerk, Chosen as a Justice—Ruth Bader Ginsburg," *The New York Times*, June 15, 1993. https://www.nytimes.com/1993/06/15/us/rejected-as-a-clerk-chosen-as-a-justice-ruth-bader-ginsburg.html.
9. Herma Hill Kay, "Ruth Bader Ginsburg. Professor of Law," *Columbia Law Review* 104, no. 2 (2004): 2–20. https://web.archive.org/web/20160322055103/http://scholarship.law.berkeley.edu/cgi/viewcontent.cgi?article=1019&context=facpubs.
10. Jill Lepore, "Ruth Bader Ginsburg, the Great Equalizer," *The New Yorker*, September 18, 2020. https://www.newyorker.com/news/postscript/ruth-bader-ginsburg-supreme-court-the-great-equalizer-obituary.
11. Lepore, "Ruth Bader Ginsburg."
12. Editorial Staff, "A Civil Rights Giant: Ruth Bader Ginsburg Stood her Ground in Seeking Justice for Others," nny360.com, September 22, 2020.

https://www.nny360.com/opinion/editorials/editorial-a-civil-rights
-giant-ruth-bader-ginsburg-stood-her-ground-in-seeking-justice-for/article
_b8d3bd35-0973-58be-a3a1-02fb37ed00f5.html.

13. John Miller, "Derr's Work Advanced Gender Equality," spokesman.com, June
11, 2013. https://www.spokesman.com/stories/2013/jun/11/derrs-work
-advanced-gender-equality/.

14. Jonathan Vanian, "5 Key Supreme Court Cases That Highlight Ruth Bader
Ginsburg's Legacy," fortune.com, September 18, 2020. https://fortune
.com/2020/09/18/ruth-bader-ginsburg-legacy-supreme-court-cases/.

15. Vanian, "5 Key Supreme Court Cases."

CHAPTER 7

1. Constance Grady, "The Waves of Feminism, and Why People Keep
Fighting Over Them, Explained," vox.com, July 20, 2018. https://www.vox
.com/2018/3/20/16955588/feminism-waves-explained-first-second-third
-fourth.

2. TeachRock, "Handout 1, Rebecca Walker, 'I Am the Third Wave,'" teachrock
.org, Retrieved September 17, 2020. https://teachrock.org/wp-content
/uploads/Handout-1-Rebecca-Walker-"I-Am-the-Third-Wave".pdf?x96081.

3. Sarah Pruitt, "How Anita Hill's Testimony Made America Cringe—And
Change," history.com, April 2, 2019. https://www.history.com/news/anita
-hill-confirmation-hearings-impact.

4. *Encyclopædia Britannica*, "The Cosby Show," britannica.com, August 18,
2020. https://www.britannica.com/topic/The-Cosby-Show.

5. Callum Borchers and Jamie Bologna, "America's Dad? The Rise and
Fall of Bill Cosby," wbur.org, April 24, 2019. https://www.wbur.org
/radioboston/2019/04/24/americas-dad-cosby.

6. Borchers and Bologna, "America's Dad?"

7. Gene Maddaus, "Bill Cosby's Downfall the Result of Small Decisions and Big
Culture Shift," *Variety*, September 25, 2018. https://variety.com/2018/biz
/news/bill-cosby-downfall-everything-leading-up-to-it-1202955615/.

8. Lucia Graves, "Hannibal Buress: How a Comedian Reignited the Bill Cosby
Allegations," *The Guardian*, April 26, 2018. https://www.theguardian.com
/world/2018/apr/26/hannibal-buress-how-a-comedian-reignited-the-bill
-cosby-allegations.

9. Gabriel Sherman, "The Revenge of Roger's Angels: How Fox News Women
Took Down the Most Powerful, and Predatory, Man in Media," *New York*

Magazine, September 2, 2016. https://nymag.com/intelligencer/2016/09
/how-fox-news-women-took-down-roger-ailes.html.

10. David Usborne, "The Peacock Patriarchy," esquire.com, August 5, 2018.
https://www.esquire.com/news-politics/a22627827/matt-lauer-nbc-me
-too/.

11. Lloyd Grove, "Ann Curry Claims NBC Had Pervasive Culture of Verbal
Sexual Harassment," thedailybeast.com, January 17, 2018. https://www
.thedailybeast.com/ann-curry-claims-nbc-had-pervasive-culture-of-verbal
-sexual-harassment.

12. Colin Dwyer, "Harvey Weinstein Sentenced to 23 Years in Prison for
Rape and Sexual Abuse," npr.org, March 11, 2020. https://www.npr.org
/2020/03/11/814051801/harvey-weinstein-sentenced-to-23-years-in-prison.

13. Terina Allen, "Harvey Weinstein's Career Downfall," *Forbes*, February
24, 2020. https://www.forbes.com/sites/terinaallen/2020/02/24
/harvey-weinstein-found-guilty-his-career-downfall-and-5-careers-that
-he-ruined/#7f5bcd9b7eb2.

14. Allen, "Harvey Weinstein's Career Downfall."

15. Audrey Carlsen, Maya Salam, et al., "#MeToo Brought Down 200 Powerful
Men. Nearly Half of their Replacements Are Women," *The New York Times*,
October 29, 2018. https://www.nytimes.com/interactive/2018/10/23/us
/metoo-replacements.html.

16. Carlsen, Salam, et al., "#MeToo Brought Down 200 Powerful Men."

17. Jeff Berman, "Number of CFPs Grew 3% in 2020," thinkadvisor.com,
January 12, 2021. https://www.thinkadvisor.com/2021/01/12/number
-of-female-cfps-grew-3-in-2020/?slreturn=20220011174928.

18. Darla Mercado, "Here's the Ken Fisher Audio That Inflamed Executives
at a Financial Conference," cnbc.com, October 11, 2019. https://www.
cnbc.com/2019/10/11/ken-fisher-inflames-financial-advisors-with-sexist-
comments.html.

19. Sabrina Willmer and Gwen Everett, "Fisher Apologizes for Remarks, Is
Barred from Tiburon Events," bloomberg.com, October 10, 2019. https://
www.bloomberg.com/news/articles/2019-10-10/ken-fisher-apologizes-for
-offensive-remarks-two-days-later.

20. Mercado, "Ken Fisher Audio."

21. Darla Mercado, "Ken Fisher's Remarks About Women Show the Financial
Advice Industry Has a Long Way to Go," cnbc.com, October 20, 2019.
https://www.cnbc.com/2019/10/30/ken-fishers-sexist-remarks-a-reminder
-that-advice-industry-is-slow-to-change.html.

22. Willmer and Everett, "Fisher Apologizes for Remarks."

23. Mercado, "Ken Fisher's Remarks."
24. Mercado, "Ken Fisher's Remarks."

CHAPTER 8

1. Patti Fagan, "Ladies, We Must Embrace Our Power," pattifagancoaching.com, June 24, 2019. https://pattifagancoaching.com/ladies-we-must-embrace-our -power/.
2. US Bank, "Women and Wealth: Insights Study," usbank.com, July 2020. https://www.usbank.com/dam/documents/pdf/wealth-management /perspectives/women-and-wealth-insights-study_07-2020.pdf.
3. Allianz, "The Allianz Women, Money, and Power Study," agewave.com, Retrieved December 6, 2020. https://agewave.com/what-we-do/landmark -research-and-consulting/research-studies/the-allianz-women-money-and -power-study/.
4. Lindsay Tigar, "5 Psychological Benefits of Financial Freedom," hermoney.com, January 17, 2020. https://www.hermoney.com/connect /confessionals/5-psychological-benefits-of-financial-freedom/.
5. Aimee Picchi, "More Women Are Now Outearning Their Husbands—and Emotions Can Be Big," *USA Today*, March 3, 2020. https://www.usatoday .com/story/money/2020/03/03/gender-wage-gap-more-women-out -earning- husbands/4933666002/.
6. E. Napoletano, "How the Gender Income Gap Impacts Women's Retirement," *Forbes*, May 19, 2020. https://www.forbes.com/advisor /retirement/retirement-gender-income-gap/.
7. Napoletano, "The Gender Income Gap."
8. Laurel Road, "Survey: Lacking Personal Finance Education Contributes to Fiscal Woes Later in Life; Millennials Seek Recourse," laurelroad.com, March 11, 2019. https://www.laurelroad.com/press/survey-lacking-personal -finance-education-contributes-to-fiscal-woes-later-in-life-millennials-seek -recourse/.
9. Road, "Survey: Lacking Personal Finance Education."
10. Caroline Castrillon, "Why We Need to Close the Financial Literacy Gap for Women," *Forbes*, November 3, 2019. https://www.forbes.com/sites /carolinecastrillon/2019/11/03/why-we-need-to-close-the-financial-literacy -gap-for-women/#d9277e7ce546.
11. Danielle Orange-Scott, "Financial Literacy Should Be Taught to Kids—Not Adults," educationdive.com, January 2, 2020. https://www.educationdive .com/news/financial-literacy-should-be-taught-to-kids-not-adults/569092/.

12. Eric Rosenbaum, "How Each US State Is Shaping the Personal Finance IQ of Its Students," cnbc.com, February 5, 2020. https://www.cnbc .com/2020/02/05/how-each-us-state-is-shaping-the-personal-finance-iq-of -students.html.

13. Suze Orman, "Why Every Woman Needs to Stop Relying on Men for Money Advice," suzeorman.com, September 27, 2018. https://www.suzeorman .com/blog/Why-Every-Woman-Needs-to-Stop-Relying-on-Men-for-Money -Advice.

14. Center for American Women and Politics, "Women in the U.S. Congress 2021," cawp.rutgers.edu, Retrieved August 23, 2021. https://cawp.rutgers .edu/women-us-congress-2021.

15. Alec Dent, "Do 40 Percent of Americans Have Less Than $400 in the Bank?" *The Dispatch*, April 8, 2020. https://factcheck.thedispatch.com/p/do-40 -percent-of-americans-have-less.

16. Fulfilled Finances Editors, "10 Steps to Financial Freedom for Women," fulfilledfinaces.com, March 12, 2021. https://fulfilledfinances.com/10-steps -to-financial-freedom/.

17. AllBusiness Editors, "Top 10 Reasons to Invest Your Money," allbusiness.com, Retrieved July 22, 2021. https://www.allbusiness.com/top-10-reasons-to -invest-money-93916-1.html.

18. Julia Kagan, "These Five Steps Will Help You Toward a Safe, Secure, and Fun Retirement," Investopedia, June 15, 2021. https://www.investopedia.com /articles/retirement/11/5-steps-to-retirement-plan.asp.

19. AARP, "How Much Longer Will Social Security Be Around?" aarp.org, September 22, 2020. https://www.aarp.org/retirement/social-security /questions-answers/how-much-longer-will-social-security-be-around.html.

20. Julia Kagan, "What Is Estate Planning?" Investopedia, April 30, 2021. https://www.investopedia.com/terms/e/estateplanning.asp.

21. Lisa Smith, "What Is a Will and Why Do I Need One Now?" Investopedia, April 25, 2021. https://www.investopedia.com/articles/pf/08/what-is-a-will .asp.

22. Julia Kagan, "Trust," Investopedia, October 19, 2020. https://www .investopedia.com/terms/t/trust.asp.

23. Laurel Wamsley, "American Life Expectancy Dropped by a Full Year in 1st Half of 2020," npr.org. https://www.npr.org/2021/02/18/968791431 /american-life-expectancy-dropped-by-a-full-year-in-the-first-half-of-2020.

24. Coryanne Hicks, "Q&A: Women and Real Estate Planning," *U.S. News & World Report*, March 3, 2021. https://money.usnews.com/financial-advisors /articles/q-a-women-and-estate-planning.

CHAPTER 9

1. Will Kenton, "Financial Literacy," Investopedia, April 19, 2020. https://www.investopedia.com/terms/f/financial-literacy.asp.
2. Rebecca Lake, "Women and the Great Wealth Transfer," Investopedia, December 2, 2020. https://www.investopedia.com/financial-advisor/women-and-great-wealth-transfer/.
3. Lake, "Women and the Great Wealth Transfer."
4. Lake, "Women and the Great Wealth Transfer."
5. Nathan Bomey, "'It's Really Over': Corporate Pensions Head for Extinction as Nature of Retirement Plans Changes," *USA Today,* December 10, 2019. https://www.usatoday.com/story/money/2019/12/10/corporate-pensions-defined-benefit-mercer-report/2618501001/.
6. Jackie Freyman, "Looking at the Past to Create a Map to the Future," *Forbes,* April 27, 2020. https://www.forbes.com/sites/forbescommunicationscouncil/2020/04/27/looking-at-the-past-to-create-a-map-to-the-future/#7a3b37f865ce.
7. Karen Demasters, "Women Hold Majority of Personal Wealth, But Still Minorities in Advisory Field," *Financial Advisor Magazine,* March 25, 2020. https://www.fa-mag.com/news/women-need-to-lead-in-finances--consultant-says-54850.html.
8. Digital History, "Overview of the Gilded Age," digitalhistory.com, Retrieved September 16, 2019. https://www.digitalhistory.uh.edu/era.cfm?eraid=9.
9. Alan Axelrod, *The Gilded Age: 1876–1912: Overture to the American Century* (New York: Sterling, 2017), pp. 2–3.
10. Marysville University, "America's Gilded Age: Robber Barons and Captains of Industry," marysville.edu, Retrieved October 4, 2019. https://online.maryville.edu/business-degrees/americas-gilded-age/.
11. Marysville University, "America's Gilded Age: Robber Barons and Captains of Industry."
12. *Encyclopædia Britannica,* "Transcendentalism," britannica.com, Retrieved January 16, 2021. https://www.britannica.com/event/Transcendentalism-American-movement.
13. Rick Hampson, "America's Second Gilded Age: More Class Envy than Class Conflict," *USA Today,* May 17, 2018. https://www.usatoday.com/story/news/2018/05/17/americas-gilded-ages-then-and-now-and-how-they-differ/615185002/.
14. Hampson, "America's Second Gilded Age."
15. Hampson, "America's Second Gilded Age."

16. Karl Evers-Hillstrom, "Majority of Lawmakers in 116th Congress Are Millionaires," opensecrets.org, April 23, 2020. https://www.opensecrets.org /news/2020/04/majority-of-lawmakers-millionaires/.

17. Sibile Marcellus, "Wage Inequality Gets Worse: Bottom 90% Stuck in $30,000 Range as Top .1% Take Home Way More than $1 Million on Average," Yahoo Finance, December 3, 2020. https://finance.yahoo.com /news/wage-inequality-gets-worse-bottom-90-stuck-in-30000-range-as-top -01-take-home-way-more-than-1-million-on-average-200646118.html.

18. Virginia Tech Daily, "Election 2020: Virginia Tech Expert Says More Women in Representative Government Means Less Corruption," vtnews.vt.edu, February 18, 2020. https://vtnews.vt.edu/articles/2020/02/science-women _coruption_government_election.html.

19. Virginia Tech, "Study Finds Less Corruption in Countries Where More Women Are in Government," ScienceDaily, June 15, 2018. https://www .sciencedaily.com/releases/2018/06/180615094850.htm.

20. Oxford Languages, "Greed," Google.com, Retrieved January 18, 2021. https://www.google.com/?client=safari.

21. Lindsay Dodgson, "Women Are More Generous than Men Because of How Their Brains Work, According to Science," businessinsider.com, March 8, 2018. https://www.businessinsider.com/new-research-shows-women-are -more-generous-than-men-2017-10.

22. Dodgson, "Women Are More Generous than Men."

23. Statista, "Percentage of the U.S. Population Who Have Completed Four Years of College or More from 1940 to 2020, by Gender," statista.com, Retrieved July 26, 2021. https://www.statista.com/statistics/184272/educational -attainment-of-college-diploma-or-higher-by-gender/.

24. Janelle Jones, "5 Facts about the State of the Gender Pay Gap," U.S. Department of Labor Blog, March 19, 2021. https://blog.dol .gov/2021/03/19/5-facts-about-the-state-of-the-gender-pay-gap.

25. Sarah Coury, Jess Huang, et al., "Women in the Workplace 2020," McKinsey & Company, September 30, 2020. https://www.mckinsey.com/featured -insights/diversity-and-inclusion/women-in-the-workplace.

26. Coury, Huang, et al., "Women in the Workplace 2020."

27. Abigail Ng, "COVID Widened the Gender Gap—It Will Now Take 135 Years to Close That Divide, WEF Says," cnbc.com, April 1, 2021. https:// www.cnbc.com/2021/04/01/wef-covid-worsened-the-gender-gap-it-will -take-135-years-to-close.html.

28. Jocelyn Frye, "10 Essential Actions to Promote Equal Pay," Center for American Progress, March 24, 2021. https://www.americanprogress.org /issues/women/reports/2021/03/24/497478/10-essential-actions-promote -equal-pay/.

29. Congressional Research Service, "Federal Workforce Statistics Sources: OPM and OMB," fas.org, June 24, 2021. https://fas.org/sgp/crs/misc/R43590.pdf.

30. Frye, "10 Essential Actions to Promote Equal Pay."

31. Megan O'Donnell, Ugonma Nwankwo, et al., "Closing Gender Pay Gaps," Center for Global Development, September 16, 2020. https://www.cgdev .org/publication/closing-gender-pay-gaps.

32. O'Donnell, Nwankwo, et al., "Closing Gender Pay Gaps."

33. Julie Marks, "What Caused the Stock Market Crash of 1929?" history.com, April 13, 2018. https://www.history.com/news/what-caused-the-stock -market-crash-of-1929.

34. Kimberly Amadeo, "President Herbert Hoover's Economic Policies," The Balance, January 31, 2020. https://www.thebalance.com/president-hoovers -economic-policies-4583019.

35. Kimberly Amadeo, "The Great Depression, What Happened, What Caused It, How It Ended," The Balance, updated May 27, 2020. https://www .thebalance.com/the-great-depression-of-1929-3306033.

36. Kimberly Amadeo, "Glass-Steagall Act of 1933, Its Purpose and Repeal," The Balance, April 14, 2020. https://www.thebalance.com/glass-steagall-act -definition-purpose-and-repeal-3305850.

37. David Wessel, Louise Sheiner, et al., "Gender and Racial Diversity of Federal Government Economics," brookings.edu, September 2019. https://www .brookings.edu/wp-content/uploads/2019/09/Diversity-report_updated-3 .pdf.

38. Binyamin Appelbaum, "Blame Economists for the Mess We're In," The New York Times, August 24, 2019.

39. Appelbaum, "Blame Economists for the Mess We're In."

40. Appelbaum, "Blame Economists for the Mess We're In."

41. Appelbaum, "Blame Economists for the Mess We're In."

42. Jim Chappelow, "Laissez-Faire," Investopedia, July 25, 2019. https://www .investopedia.com/terms/l/laissezfaire.asp.

43. Rick Paulas, "The Case Against Milton Friedman's Capitalism," Pacific Standard, March 16, 2018. https://psmag.com/economics/the-case-against -milton-friedmans-capitalism.

44. Moyers & Company, "The Powell Memo: A Call-to-Arms for Corporations," billmoyers.com, September 14, 2012. https://billmoyers.com/content/the -powell-memo-a-call-to-arms-for-corporations/.

45. ACLU, "ACLU Opposes Nomination of Judge Alito," web.archive.org, Retrieved March 20, 2021. https://web.archive.org/web/20070406173742 /http://www.aclu.org/scotus/alito/.

46. Sandeep Vaheesan, "How Robert Bork Fathered the New Gilded Age," premarket.com, September 5, 2019. https://promarket.org/2019/09/05 /how-robert-bork-fathered-the-new-gilded-age/.

47. Vaheesan, "How Robert Bork Fathered the New Gilded Age."

48. Julia Kagan, "Trust," Investopedia, October 19, 2020. https://www .investopedia.com/terms/t/trust.asp.

49. *Encyclopædia Britannica*, "Standard Oil: American Corporation," britannica .com, Retrieved March 22, 2021. https://www.britannica.com/topic /Standard-Oil.

50. Joe Hagan, "The Hive Interview: Can We Undo the GOP's Decimation of America?" *Vanity Fair*, August 10, 2020. https://www.vanityfair.com /news/2020/08/the-hive-interview-can-we-undo-the-gops-decimation-of -america.

51. Mark W. Johnson, "Do the U.S.'s Big Four Tech Companies Have a Vision for the Future?" *Harvard Business Review*, July 24, 2020. https://hbr .org/2020/07/do-the-u-s-s-big-four-tech-companies-have-a-vision-for-the -future.

CHAPTER 10

1. James Chen, "Risk," Investopedia, October 6, 2020. https://www .investopedia.com/terms/r/risk.asp.

2. Chen, "Risk."

3. James Chen, "Political Risk," Investopedia, March 25, 2020. https://www .investopedia.com/terms/p/politicalrisk.asp.

4. Chen, "Political Risk."

5. Greg Wiliensky, "Rising Political Risk Fuels Uncertainty," janushenderson .com, September 24, 2020. https://www.janushenderson.com/en-sg /investor/article/rising-political-risk-fuels-uncertainty-sg/.

6. Wiliensky, "Rising Political Risk Fuels Uncertainty."

7. Wiliensky, "Rising Political Risk Fuels Uncertainty."

8. Kim Parker and Richard Fry, "More than Half of U.S. Households Have Some Investment in the Stock Market," pewresearch.org, March 25, 2020. https://www.pewresearch.org/fact-tank/2020/03/25/more-than-half-of-u-s -households-have-some-investment-in-the-stock-market/.

9. Mark Kolakowski, "Why Morgan Stanley Says the 60/40 Portfolio Is Doomed," Investopedia, November 16, 2019. https://www.investopedia.com/why-morgan-stanley-says-the-60-40-portfolio-is-doomed-4775352.

10. Statista, "Projected Annual Inflation Rate in the United States from 2010 to 2021," statista.com, January 20, 2021. https://www.statista.com/statistics/244983/projected-inflation-rate-in-the-united-states/.

11. Market Business News, "What Is Economic Risk? Definition and Example," marketbusinessnews.com, Retrieved March 27, 2021. https://marketbusinessnews.com/financial-glossary/economic-risk/.

12. Sarah Li Cain, "Economic Risk," investinganswers.com, March 22, 2021. https://investinganswers.com/dictionary/e/economic-risk.

13. Cain, "Economic Risk."

14. Masterclass Staff, "How Globalization Works: Pros and Cons of Globalization," masterclass.com, November 8, 2020. https://www.masterclass.com/articles/how-globalization-works-pros-and-cons-of-globalization#3-examples-of-globalization.

15. Masterclass Staff, "How Globalization Works."

16. Masterclass Staff, "How Globalization Works."

17. John Bromels, "What Are Stock Market Corrections?" The Motley Fool, November 16, 2020. https://www.fool.com/investing/how-to-invest/stocks/stock-market-corrections/.

18. Jack Holmes, "Boeing Wants a Bailout after Years of Bad Corporate Governance—and Without Giving Taxpayers Anything in Return," esquire.com, April 29, 2020. https://www.esquire.com/news-politics/a32314911/boeing-60-billion-bailout-coronavirus-737-max-equity-stake/.

19. Holmes, "Boeing Wants a Bailout."

20. Holmes, "Boeing Wants a Bailout."

21. Allan Sloan, "Boeing's Crisis Is Largely of Its Own Making," The Washington Post, March 26, 2020. https://www.washingtonpost.com/business/2020/03/26/boeing-crisis-own-making/.

22. Sloan, "Boeing's Crisis Is Largely of Its Own Making."

23. Matt Phillips, "The Stock Buyback Binge May Be Over," The New York Times, March 24, 2020. https://www.nytimes.com/2020/03/24/business/coronavirus-stock-buybacks.html.

24. Phillips, "The Stock Buyback Binge."

25. Allison Schrager, "The 60-40 Split Between Stocks and Bonds Was Once Solid Financial Advice—But No Longer," Yahoo Finance, November 29, 2019. https://finance.yahoo.com/news/60-40-split-between-stocks-120057862.html.

26. Russell Investment Blog, "Is the Stock-Bond Correlation Positive or Negative?" russellinvestments.com, October 26, 2021. https://russellinvestments.com/us/blog/is-the-stock-bond-correlation-positive-or-negative.

27. Paul Grambsch and Adam Proger, "In the Wake of COVID-19, Is It Time to Revisit Investment Norms?" wvsae.org, Retrieved April 5, 2021. https://wvsae.org/in-the-wake-of-covid-19-is-it-time-to-revisit-investment-norms/.

28. Chris Seabury, "The Cost of Free Markets," Investopedia, February 8, 2020. https://www.investopedia.com/articles/economics/08/free-market-regulation.asp.

29. Seabury, "The Cost of Free Markets."

30. Will Kenton, "The Glass-Steagall Act," Investopedia, March 31, 2021. https://www.investopedia.com/terms/g/glass_steagall_act.asp.

31. Harriet Edleson, "Almost Half of Americans Fear Running out of Money in Retirement," AARP, May 21, 2019. https://www.aarp.org/retirement/planning-for-retirement/info-2019/retirees-fear-losing-money.html.

32. Associated Press, "U.S. Life Expectancy Rises for the First Time in 4 Years—But Just a Little," *Los Angeles Times*, January 29, 2020. https://www.latimes.com/science/story/2020-01-29/us-life-expectancy-rises.

33. Lauren Medina, Shannon Sabo, et al., "Living Longer: Historical and Projected Life Expectancy in the United States, 1960 to 2060," census.gov, February 2020. https://www.census.gov/content/dam/Census/library/publications/2020/demo/p25-1145.pdf.

34. Nicola Pizzolato, *The Making and Unmaking of Fordism* (London: Palgrave Macmillan, 2013), p. 19. https://link.springer.com/chapter/10.1057/9781137311702_2.

35. Digital Fordism, "Digital Fordism," yorku.ca, Retrieved March 3, 2021. http://www.yorku.ca/anderson/Intro%20Urban%20Studies/Unit2/fordism.htm.

36. Kendra Cherry, "The Dunning-Kruger Effect," verywellmind.com, June 14, 2019. https://www.verywellmind.com/an-overview-of-the-dunning-kruger-effect-4160740.

37. Cherry, "The Dunning-Kruger Effect."

38. Cherry, "The Dunning-Kruger Effect."

39. Mark DeCambre and Andrew Keshner, "Is GameStop's Surge Market Manipulation by a Mob of Reddit Users, a Savvy Group of Investors—Or Both?" MarketWatch, January 31, 2021. https://www.marketwatch.com/story/is-gamestop-stock-being-manipulated-by-social-media-users-or-is-it-free-speech-legal-experts-weigh-in-11611636278.

40. DeCambre and Keshner, "Is GameStop's Surge Market Manipulation."
41. American Association of University Women, "The Myth of the Male Math Brain," aauw.org, Retrieved July 28, 2021. https://www.aauw.org/resources /article/the-myth-of-the-male-math-brain/.
42. Sarah D. Sparks, "In Math, Teachers' Unconscious Biases May be More Subtle than You Think," *Education Week*, December 13, 2019. https://www.edweek .org/leadership/in-math-teachers-unconscious-biases-may-be-more-subtle -than-you-think/2019/12.
43. American Association of University Women, "The Myth of the Male Math Brain."
44. American Association of University Women, "The Myth of the Male Math Brain."
45. James McWhinney, "A Simple Overview of Quantitative Analysis," Investopedia, October 6, 2020. https://www.investopedia.com/articles /investing/041114/simple-overview-quantitative-analysis.asp.
46. McWhinney, "A Simple Overview of Quantitative Analysis."
47. Emily Guy Birken and Benjamin Curry, "Why Women Are Better Investors," *Forbes*, March 30, 2021. https://www.forbes.com/advisor/investing/woman -better-investors/.
48. Birken and Curry, "Why Women Are Better Investors."
49. Maurie Backman, "A Summary of 20 Years of Research and Statistics on Women in Investing," The Motley Fool, March 4, 2021. https://www.fool .com/research/women-in-investing-research/.
50. Backman, "A Summary of 20 Years of Research."

CHAPTER 11

1. Leslie Kramer, "How the Great Inflation of the 1970s Happened," Investopedia, October 1, 2020. https://www.investopedia.com/articles /economics/09/1970s-great-inflation.asp.
2. Josh Zeitz, "How Americans Lost Faith in Government," *The Washington Post*, January 30, 2018. https://www.washingtonpost.com/news/made-by -history/wp/2018/01/30/how-americans-lost-faith-in-government/.
3. Kurt Anderson, *Evil Geniuses: The Unmaking of America* (New York: Random House, 2020), p. xxi.
4. Anderson, *Evil Geniuses*, p. xxi.
5. Alan Schwartz, "Why Milton Friedman Was Right and Wrong," *Financial Review*, September 13, 2020. https://www.afr.com/policy/economy

/business-real-social-responsibility-is-to-be-a-rule-taker-not-a-maker
-20200913-p55v3x.

6. Schwartz, "Why Milton Friedman Was Right and Wrong."

7. Mathias Hein Jessen, "The Corporate State," Transnational Institute, January 30, 2020. https://www.tni.org/en/publication/the-corporate-state.

8. Jessen, "The Corporate State."

9. Norman Jay Ornstein and William Arthur Galston, "American Democracy & the Common Good," American Academy of Arts & Sciences, Spring 2013. https://www.amacad.org/daedalus/american-democracy-common-good.

10. Mark Kolakowski, "At $2.08 Trillion, Apple Is Bigger Than These Things," Investopedia, March 17, 2021. https://www.investopedia.com/news/apple
-now-bigger-these-5-things/.

11. American Economic Liberties Project, "Confronting America's Concentration Crisis: A Ledger of Harms and Frameworks for Advancing Economic Liberty for All," economicliberties.us, August 6, 2020. https://
www.economicliberties.us/our-work/confronting-americas-concentration
-crisis-a-ledger-of-harms-and-framework-for-advancing-economic-liberty
-for-all/.

12. American Economic Liberties Project, "Confronting America's Concentration Crisis."

13. Renu Zaretsky, "Corporate Taxes: Are They Fair? Who Really Pays Them, and Why?" taxpolicycenter.org, March 4, 2020. https://www.taxpolicycenter
.org/taxvox/corporate-taxes-are-they-fair-who-really-pays-them-and-when.

14. Mathew Gardner and Steve Wamhoff, "55 Corporations Paid $0 in Federal Taxes on 2020 Profits," itep.org, April 2, 2021. https://itep.org/55-profitable
-corporations-zero-corporate-tax/

15. Mathew Johnson, "How Fortune 500 Companies Avoid Paying Income Taxes," Investopedia, January 28, 2021. https://www.investopedia.com/news
/how-fortune-500-companies-avoid-paying-income-tax/.

16. Reem Heakal, "What Is a Corporate Credit Rating?" Investopedia, August 8, 2020. https://www.investopedia.com/articles/03/102203.asp.

17. Nicolas Vega, "Here's How Much Debt Americans Have at Every Age," cnbc.com, October 13, 2021. https://www.cnbc.com/2021/10/13/how
-much-debt-each-generation-has-in-the-us.html.

18. Frank Holmes, "These U.S. Companies Have the Highest Debt-to-Equity Ratios Right Now," usfunds.com, April 1, 2020. https://www.usfunds.com
/investor-library/frank-talk-a-ceo-blog-by-frank-holmes/these-u-s-companies
-have-the-highest-debt-to-equity-ratios-right-now/#.YKYwImgvO3A.

19. William Lazonick, Mustafa Erdem Sakinc, et al., "Why Stock Buybacks Are Dangerous for the Economy," *Harvard Business Review*, January 7, 2020. https://hbr.org/2020/01/why-stock-buybacks-are-dangerous-for-the-economy.

20. Lazonick, Sakinc, et al., "Why Stock Buybacks Are Dangerous."

21. Ganesh Sitaraman, "The Collapse of Neoliberalism," *The New Republic*, December 23, 2019. https://newrepublic.com/article/155970/collapse-neoliberalism.

22. Sitaraman, "The Collapse of Neoliberalism."

23. World Benchmarking Alliance, "It's a Man's World: Men Still Dominate the Most Influential Companies in the World," World Benchmarking Alliance, September 30, 2020. https://www.worldbenchmarkingalliance.org/news/its-a-mans-world-men-still-dominate-the-most-influential-companies-in-the-world/.

24. Richie Zweigenhaft, "Fortune 500 CEOs, 2000–2020: Still Male, Still White," The Society Pages, October 28, 2020. https://thesocietypages.org/specials/fortune-500-ceos-2000-2020-still-male-still-white/.

25. Mary Mazzoni, "Women CEOs Are Breaking Records in the Fortune 500," triplepundit.com, June 7, 2021. https://www.triplepundit.com/story/2021/women-ceos-fortune-500/723736.

26. Kellogg Insight, "Companies Are Adding More Women to Their Boards. What's Driving the Change?" Kellogg Insight, May 3, 2021. https://insight.kellogg.northwestern.edu/article/women-company-boards.

27. Kellogg Insight, "Companies Are Adding More Women to Their Boards."

CHAPTER 12

1. Chris B. Murphy, "Nominal Rate of Return," Investopedia, July 21, 2020. https://www.investopedia.com/terms/n/nominal-rate-of-return.asp.

2. Rebecca Lake, "The 60/40 Portfolio Is Dead for Retirement Planning," *U.S. News*, April 23, 2019. https://money.usnews.com/investing/investing-101/articles/why-the-60-40-portfolio-is-dead-for-retirement-planning.

3. Lake, "The 60/40 Portfolio Is Dead."

4. Glenn Curtis, "Six Biggest Bond Risks," Investopedia, December 19, 2017. https://www.investopedia.com/articles/bonds/08/bond-risks.asp.

5. Cliff Stanton, "Charting a New Course with Alts," thinkadvisor.com, October 30, 2017. https://www.thinkadvisor.com/2017/10/30/charting-a-new-course-with-alts/.

6. Lisa Smith, "Modern Portfolio Theory vs. Behavioral Finance," Investopedia, August 17, 2019. https://www.investopedia.com/articles/investing/041213 /modern-portfolio-theory-vs-behavioral-finance.asp.

7. Brett Arends, "Your Financial Advisor's 'Sleep Easy' Portfolio May Be a Lot Riskier than You Think," MarketWatch, December 13, 2018. https:// www.marketwatch.com/story/your-portfolio-may-be-riskier-than-you -think-2018-10-11.

8. Sigrid Forberg, "The 60/40 Rule of Investing Is Dead, Experts Say—It's Time to Get More Creative," yahoo.com, June 13, 2021. https://www.yahoo.com /now/60-40-rule-investing-dead-180000135.html.

9. Michael Rosen, "Op-Ed: Traditional 60/40 Portfolio Has Actually Reached Its Expiration Date," cnbc.com, September 2, 2021. https://www.cnbc .com/2021/09/02/traditional-60-40-portfolio-has-actually-reached-its -expiration-date.html.

10. Rosen, "Op-Ed: Traditional 60/40 Portfolio Has Actually Reached Its Expiration Date."

11. Rob Isbitts, "Why the 60/40 Portfolios Are in a Slump," *Forbes,* June 25, 2019. https://www.forbes.com/sites/robisbitts2/2019/06/25/why-6040 -portfolios-are-in-a-slump/#7491dc14aa0b.

12. Isbitts, "Why the 60/40 Portfolios Are in a Slump."

13. Lake, "The 60/40 Portfolio Is Dead for Retirement Planning."

14. Julia Kagan, "Four Percent Rule," Investopedia, May 1, 2020. https://www .investopedia.com/terms/f/four-percent-rule.asp.

15. Jane Wollman Rusoff, "Wade Pfau: Pandemic Tears up 4% Rule," thinkadvisor.com, April 14, 2020. https://www.thinkadvisor .com/2020/04/14/wade-pfau-virus-crisis-has-slashed-4-rule-nearly-in-half/.

16. Rusoff, "Wade Pfau: Pandemic Tears up 4% Rule."

17. Investopedia Staff, "Quantitative Easing," Investopedia, January 3, 2021. https://www.investopedia.com/terms/q/quantitative-easing.asp.

18. Investopedia Staff, "Quantitative Easing."

19. Brent Schrotenboer, "US Is 'Printing' Money to Help Save the Economy from the COVID-19 Crisis, but Some Wonder How Far It Can Go," *USA Today,* May 12, 2020. https://www.usatoday.com/in-depth/money/2020/05/12 /coronavirushow-u-s-printing-dollars-save-economy-during-crisis -fed/3038117001/.

20. Sunny Oh, "10-Year Treasury Yield Plunged to Its Lowest in 234 Years, Says Deutsche Bank," MarketWatch, August 1, 2020. https://www.marketwatch .com/story/10-year-treasury-yield-plunged-to-its-lowest-in-234-years-says -deutsche-bank-11596214464.

21. United States Department of the Treasury, "Daily Treasury Yield Curve Rates," treasury.gov, Retrieved January 31, 2021. https://www.treasury .gov/resource-center/data-chart-center/interest-rates/pages/TextView .aspx?data=yieldYear&year=2005.

22. Howard Gold, "We Haven't Seen Interest Rates This Low Since Before Hammurabi, so What Bonds Should You Buy?" MarketWatch, July 18, 2019. https://www.marketwatch.com/story/we-havent-seen-interest-rates-this-low -since-before-hammurabi-so-what-bonds-should-you-buy-2019-07-18.

23. Gold, "We Haven't Seen Interest Rates This Low."

24. Lisa Mahapatra, "8 Brilliant Lessons from the Investor That Taught Warren Buffett Everything He Knows," businessinsider.com, February 6, 2013. https://www.businessinsider.com/eight-lessons-from-benjamin -graham-2013-2.

25. David Kaufman, "Revisiting Benjamin Graham, the Father of Alternative Investing," financialpost.com, April 26, 2013. https://financialpost.com /investing/benjamin-graham-revisited.

26. Lex Zaharoff, "What Is an Alternative Investment?" HTG Investment Advisors, October 12, 2017. https://www.htgadvisors.com/what-is-an -alternative-investment/.

27. David F. Swensen, *Pioneering Portfolio Management: An Unconventional Approach to Institutional Investment, Fully Revised and Updated* (New York: Free Press, 2009), p. 1.

28. Geraldine Fabrikant, "Keep It Simple, Says Yale's Top Investor," *The New York Times*, February 17, 2008. https://www.nytimes.com/2008/02/17 /business/17swensen.html.

29. Maurie Backman, "A Summary of 20 Years of Research and Statistics on Women in Investing," The Motley Fool, August 3, 2021. https://www.fool .com/research/women-in-investing-research/.

30. Backman, "A Summary of 20 Years of Research."

31. Larry Swedroe, "Overconfidence—Investor's Worst Enemy," evidenceinvestor .com, November 22, 2019. https://www.evidenceinvestor.com /overconfidence-investors-worst-enemy/.

32. Adam Hayes, "Irrational Exuberance," Investopedia, August 4, 2021. https:// www.investopedia.com/terms/i/irrationalexuberance.asp.

33. Behavioural Strategy Group, "The Upside of Irrationality—Overconfidence Bias," behaviouralstrategygroup.com, March 31, 2021. https:// behaviouralstrategygroup.com/2021/03/31/the-upside-of-irrationality -overconfidence-bias/.

34. Judy Paradi and Paulette Fillion, "Why Women Leave Their Financial Advisors and How to Prevent It," strategymarketing.ca, Retrieved August 6, 2021. https://www.strategymarketing.ca/wp-content/uploads/Why-women-leave-their-financial-advisors-and-how-to-prevent-it.pdf.

CHAPTER 13

1. Steve Taylor, "The After-Effects of Awakening," *Psychology Today*, February 23, 2018. https://www.psychologytoday.com/us/blog/out-the-darkness/201802/the-after-effects-awakening.
2. Patrick Paul Garlinger, "What Does It Mean to 'Awaken'?" medium.com, January 1, 2019. https://medium.com/@divineppg/what-does-it-mean-to-awaken-f8224082b48d.

INDEX

ABOUT THE AUTHOR

CINDY COUYOUMJIAN is the author of *Redefining Financial Literacy*. She is the founder of Cinergy Financial with over 36 years of experience in the financial industry. Cindy was nominated in 2021 for the Women in Asset Management Award and was among the top nominees in two categories—Role Model Award and the Lifetime Achievement Award. Cindy holds numerous securities registrations including her FINRA Series 63, 6, 65, 7, 22, 24, and 26. In addition, Cindy also holds the California Insurance License (License # 0719038).

Cindy is the architect behind the REALM investment portfolio, which is an innovative multi-asset-class portfolio that is both flexible and customizable to each individual investor. Beyond the numerous financial services Cindy offers, she is also an educator and motivational speaker. When she is not meeting with clients, you may find her giving her monthly lectures and seminars on such groundbreaking topics as the Google Mind, the Gilded Age, and the Moral Imperative of Financial Literacy.

Cindy is currently working on her next book, which will explore our retirement system. If you are interested in attending one of

Cindy's lectures or have a question or comment, please email her at cindy@cinergyfinancial.com.

Cindy Couyoumjian is a registered representative offering securities and advisory services through Independent Financial Group LLC (IFG), a registered investment adviser. Member FINRA/SIPC. Cinergy Financial, Greenleaf Book Group Press, R. F. Georgy, and IFG are unaffiliated.